ARCTIC OCEAN
172–173
Europe-Asia Boundary
ASIA
102–125
EUROPE
84–101
PACIFIC OCEAN
166–167
AFRICA
126–143
INDIAN OCEAN
170–171
AUSTRALIA, NEW ZEALAND & OCEANIA
144–155
AUSTRALIA
PHYSICAL WORLD 18–19
POLITICAL WORLD 34–35
WORLD OCEANS 162–173
ANTARCTICA
156–161

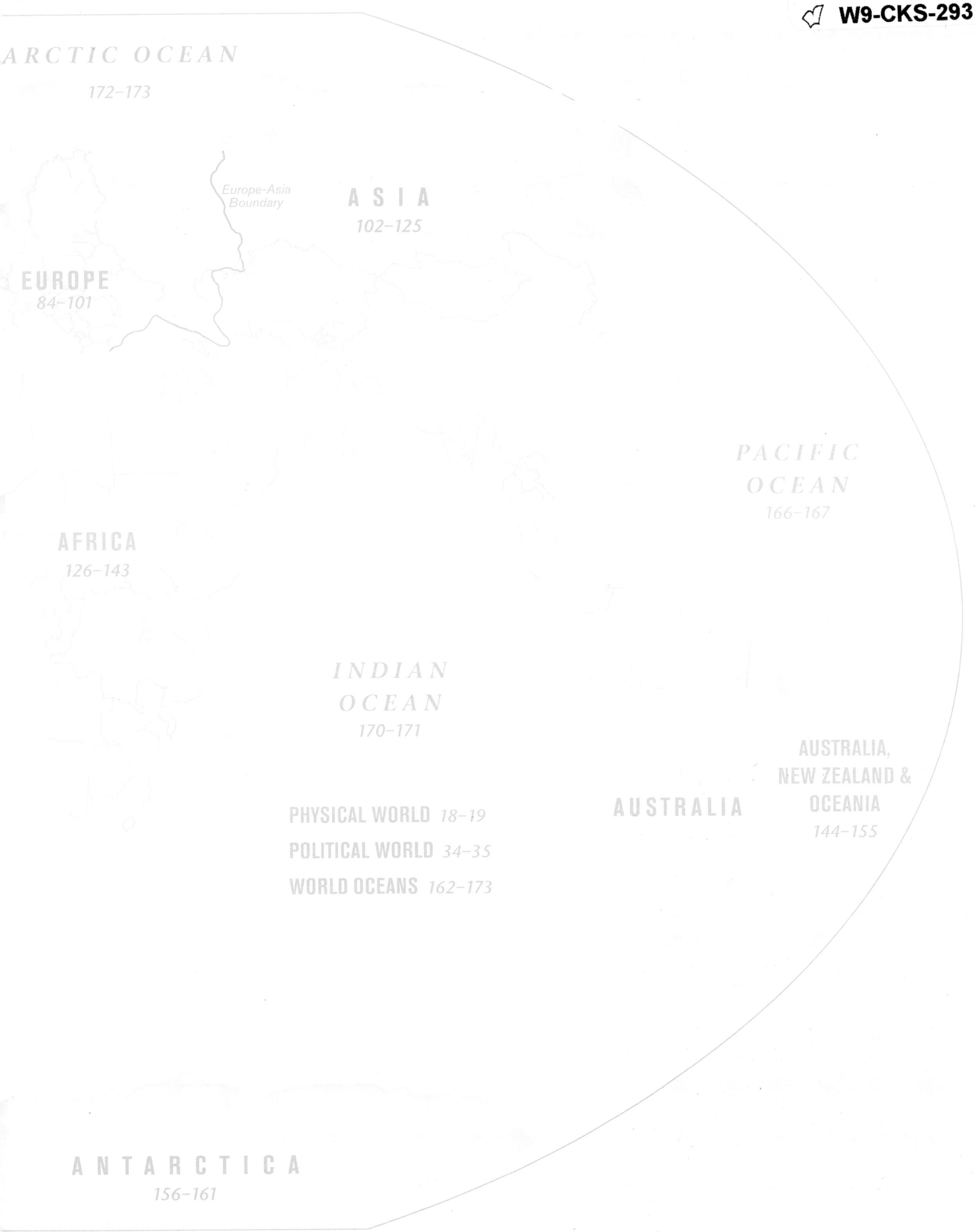

YOU ARE HERE

NATIONAL GEOGRAPHIC
KiDS

WORLD ATLAS

FIFTH EDITION

NATIONAL GEOGRAPHIC
WASHINGTON, D.C.

TABLE OF CONTENTS

North America: Mexican boy, page 58

South America:
Llama, page 75

Europe: Colosseum, pages 90–91

Title page (left to right): spider monkey, Costa Rica; Lower Yellowstone Falls, Wyoming,
U.S.A; Cuna craftswoman, Panama; Montreal skyline, Quebec, Canada; Siberian tiger;
Guggenheim Museum, Bilbao, Spain; young girl, Gambia; fall foliage, U.S.A.

Antarctica: Penguins, page 158

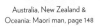

Australia, New Zealand & Oceania: Maori man, page 148

Africa: Mother and child, page 131

Asia: Panda, page 106

GETTING
STARTED

How to Use This Atlas

This atlas is a window for exploring the world. To learn about maps, use the first section, Understanding Maps. Basic facts about Earth as a planet are presented in the section called Planet Earth. Maps in the Physical World section focus on different aspects of nature and the environment. The Political World section contains world maps about how humans live on the planet. In the pages that follow, the maps, photographs, and essays are arranged by continent and region. You can find details about specific countries in the Flags & Facts section beginning on page 174.

"YOU ARE HERE"
Locator globes help you see where one area is in relation to others. On regional pages (as shown here), the area covered by the main map is yellow on the globe, and its continent is green. On pages with continent maps, the locator globe shows the whole continent in yellow. The surrounding land is gray.

STATS & FACTS
At the left-hand edge of each continent opener and regional page is a bar that includes basic information about the subject. This feature is a great first stop if you're writing a report.

CHARTS & GRAPHS
Each region includes a chart or graph that shows information visually.

80 NORTHEASTERN SOUTH AMERICA

THE CONTINENT
SOUTH AMERICA

THE BASICS
STATS
Largest country
Brazil
3,287,594 sq mi
(8,514,877 sq km)
Smallest country
Suriname
63,251 sq mi (163,820 sq km)
Most populous country
Brazil 207,353,000
Least populous country
Suriname 592,000
Predominant languages
Portuguese, English, Dutch, Hindi
Predominant religions
Christianity, Hinduism, Islam
Highest GDP per capita
Brazil $15,200
Lowest GDP per capita
Guyana $7,900
Highest life expectancy
Brazil 74 years
Lowest life expectancy
Guyana 68 years

GEO WHIZ
Guyana's roughly 300 species of catfish are hunted for the international aquarium trade.

Brazil's Pantanal is the world's largest freshwater wetland.

Paramaribo, Suriname's capital, is a melting pot of Dutch, Hindu, Chinese, East Indian, and Javanese cultures. Dutch is the only official language.

Northeastern South America

○ GOAL! Maracanã Stadium in Rio de Janeiro is packed with enthusiastic soccer fans. Brazil has a long history of producing world-class soccer teams, winning the coveted World Cup five times as of 2017.

Brazil dominates the region as well as the continent in size and population. It is the world's fifth largest country in area, and it is home to half of South America's 419 million people. São Paulo and Rio de Janeiro are among the world's largest cities, and the country's vast agricultural lands make it a top global exporter of coffee, soybeans, beef, orange juice, and sugar. The vast Amazon rain forest, once a dense wilderness of unmatched biodiversity, is now threatened by farmers, loggers, and miners. Lands colonized by the British, Dutch, and French make up sparsely settled Guyana and Suriname as well as French Guiana, a French overseas department. Formerly known as the Guianas, these lands are populated by people of African, South Asian, and European heritage.

VAST WATERSHED

The United States and South America are shown at the same scale.

Amazon Basin

SOUTH AMERICA

The Amazon River basin includes 2.4 million square miles (6.1 million sq km). It would cover much of the contiguous, or lower 48, U.S. states.

◑ NATIONAL RHYTHM. Samba, often called Brazil's national music, combines the music traditions of the country's populations—Amerindian, Portuguese, and African. Here a samba band practices on Rio de Janeiro's Ipanema Beach.

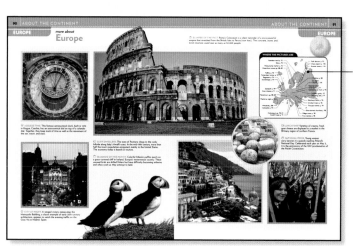

90 | ABOUT THE CONTINENT   ABOUT THE CONTINENT | **91**

EUROPE   more about
                Europe   EUROPE

WHERE ARE THE PICTURES?
If you want to know where a picture in a regional section of this atlas was taken, look for the map in the photo essay. Find the label that describes the picture you're curious about, and follow the line to its location.

Maps use symbols to represent political and physical features. At right is the key to the symbols used in this atlas. If you are wondering what you're looking at on a map, check here.

INDEX AND GRID

Look through the index for the place-name you want. Next to it is a page number in bold, a letter, and another number. Go to the page. Draw imaginary lines from the letter along the side of the map and the number along the top. Your place will be close to where the lines meet.

Boulia, Australia **153** C6
Bourke, Australia **153** E7
Boyoma Falls, Dem. Rep. of the Congo **141** E5
Brahmaputra (river), Asia **121** C7
Braila, Romania **99** B7
Brasília, Brazil **81** E5

COLOR BARS

Every section of this atlas has its own color. Look for the color on the Table of Contents pages and across the top of every page in the atlas. Within that color bar, you'll see the name of the section and the title for each topic or map. These color bars are a handy way to find the section you want.

NORTHEASTERN SOUTH AMERICA | 81

THE CONTINENT
SOUTH AMERICA

① THE SIX-BANDED ARMADILLO, found throughout the dry grassland areas of the region, lives on plants and insects. Unlike others of its species, it remains active during the day.

Map Key
⊛ Country capital
•● City or town
⋯⋯ Boundary
⋯⋯ Claimed boundary

Azimuthal Equidistant Projection

① BAUXITE TO ALUMINUM. By exploiting rich deposits of bauxite, the ore from which aluminum is made, and inexpensive hydropower, Suriname produces aluminum ingots, such as these headed for global markets.

North America

South America

Europe

Asia

Africa

Australia, New Zealand & Oceania

Antarctica

BAR SCALE

To find out how far on Earth's surface it is from one place on a map to another, use the scale. A bar scale appears on every map. It shows how distance on paper relates to distance in the real world.

MAP KEY

•●● City or town	791 ft / 241 m + Mountain peak with elevation above sea level	＋‖ Waterfall	Dry salt lake
⊛ Country capital		⊐ Dam	Glacier
⊙ Other capital*	-282 ft. / -86 m • Low point with elevation below sea level	⊥⊥⊥ Canal	Swamp
◆ Small country		▲▲▲ Ice shelf	Sand
∴ Ruin	⋯⋯ Defined boundary	Reef	Tundra
▪ Point of interest	⋯ ⋯ Disputed or undefined boundary	Lake	Lava
★ Pole	⋯⋯ Claimed boundary	Intermittent lake	Below sea level
*This includes capitals for states, provinces, territories, dependencies, and other political entities.	～ River		

UNDERSTANDING
MAPS

Exploring Your World

Earth is a big place. Even from space you can't see it all at one time. But with a map you can see the whole world or just a part of it. Thanks to the Internet, you can download programs that allow you to experience Earth from space, pick a place you want to explore, and zoom closer and closer until you are "standing" right there! These screenshots (right) take you from Chicago to space at the click of a mouse. You can even find a satellite view of your neighborhood (box below).

Compare the computer-enhanced satellite images with the maps on the opposite page. You will see how the same places can be shown in very different ways.

FIND YOUR HOUSE

This SkylineGlobe image shows the offices of National Geographic in Washington, D.C. To see where you live, go to showmystreet.com, one of several websites that allow you to view satellite imagery of the world.

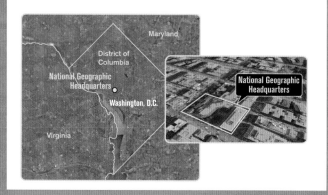

COMPUTER ENHANCED
VIEWS OF ...

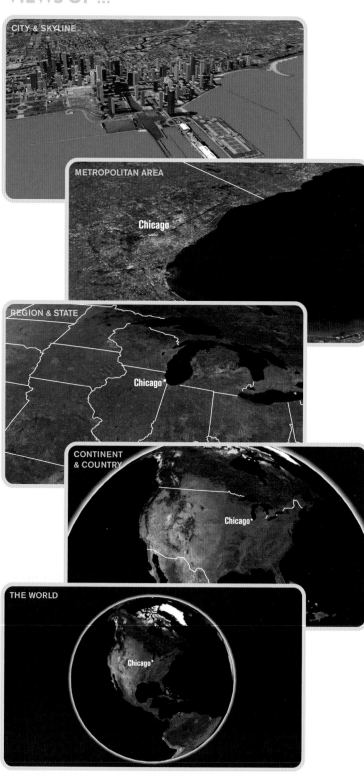

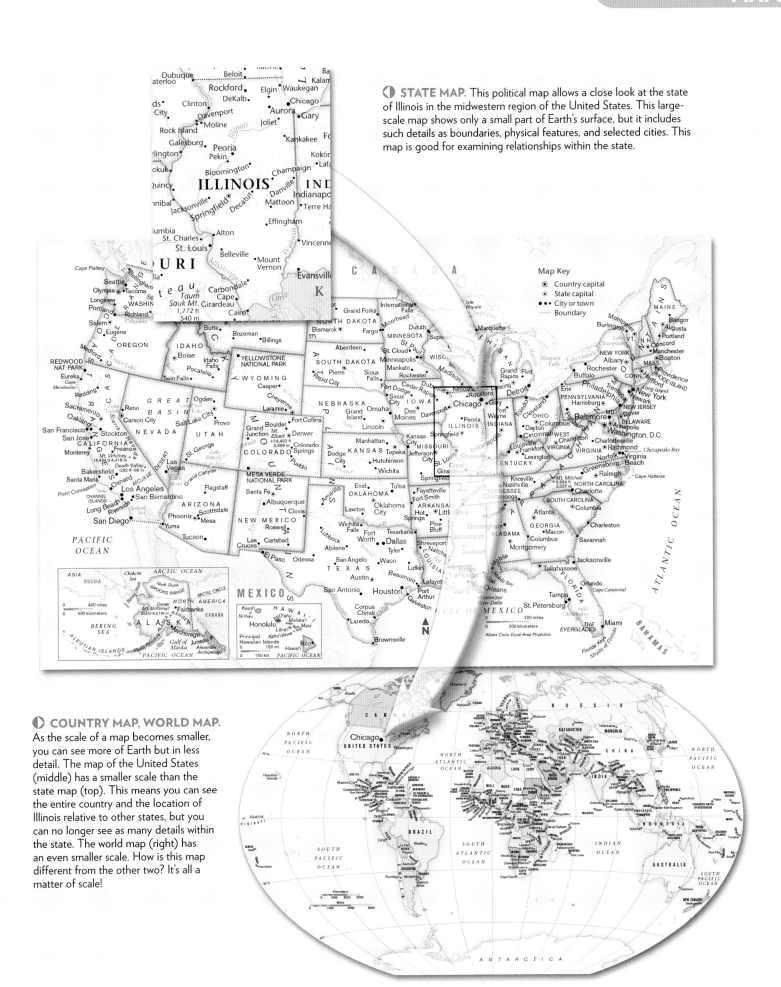

STATE MAP. This political map allows a close look at the state of Illinois in the midwestern region of the United States. This large-scale map shows only a small part of Earth's surface, but it includes such details as boundaries, physical features, and selected cities. This map is good for examining relationships within the state.

COUNTRY MAP, WORLD MAP. As the scale of a map becomes smaller, you can see more of Earth but in less detail. The map of the United States (middle) has a smaller scale than the state map (top). This means you can see the entire country and the location of Illinois relative to other states, but you can no longer see as many details within the state. The world map (right) has an even smaller scale. How is this map different from the other two? It's all a matter of scale!

Map Key
- ⊛ Country capital
- ⊙ State capital
- •••• City or town
- ⋯⋯⋯ Boundary

Kinds of Maps

Maps are special tools that tell a story about Earth. Some maps show physical features, such as mountains or vegetation. Other maps illustrate different human features on Earth—political boundaries, urban centers, and economic systems.

Maps are not perfect. A globe is a scale model of Earth with accurate relative sizes and locations. Because maps are flat, they involve distortions of size, shape, and direction. Also, cartographers—people who create maps—make choices about what information to include. Because of this, it is important to study many different types of maps to learn the complete story of Earth.

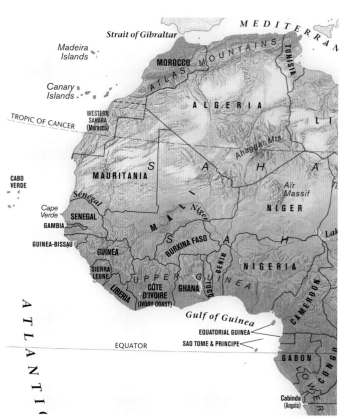

PHYSICAL MAPS. Earth's natural features—landforms, water bodies, and vegetation—are shown on physical maps. The map above uses color and shading to illustrate mountains, lakes, rivers, and deserts in western Africa. Country names and borders are added for reference, but they are not natural features.

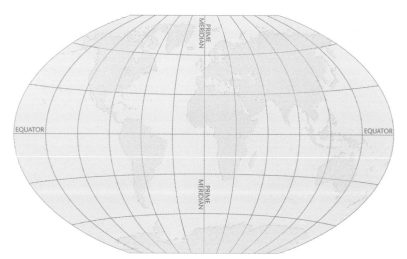

MAP PROJECTIONS. To create a map, cartographers transfer an image of the round Earth onto a flat surface, a process called projection. Some types of projection include cylindrical, conic, azimuthal, and interrupted. Each has certain advantages, but all have some distortions. The world maps in the thematic section of this atlas are a projection called Winkel Tripel (above), a compromise projection that moderates size and shape distortions. As you use this atlas, look for different map projections on the regional maps, identified below the scale bar.

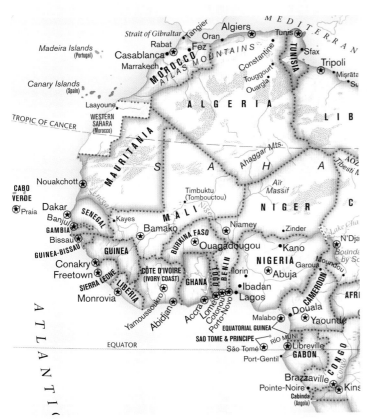

🌐 **POLITICAL MAPS.** These maps represent human characteristics of the landscape, such as boundaries, cities, and other place-names. Natural features are added only for reference. On the map above, capital cities are represented with a star inside a circle, while other cities are located with black dots.

🌐 **THEMATIC MAPS.** Patterns related to a particular topic, or theme, such as population distribution, appear on these maps. The map above displays a region's climate zones, which range from tropical wet (bright green) to tropical wet and dry (light green) to semiarid (dark yellow) to arid (light yellow).

Long ago, cartographers worked with pen and ink, carefully handcrafting maps based on explorers' observations and diaries. Today, mapmaking is a high-tech business. Cartographers use Earth data stored in "layers" in a geographic information system (GIS) and special computer programs to create maps that can be easily updated as new information becomes available. These cartographers are making changes to a map in another National Geographic Kids atlas.

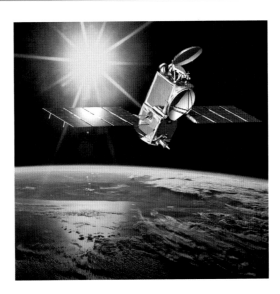

Satellites in orbit around Earth act as eyes in the sky, recording data about the planet's land and ocean areas. The data is converted to numbers that are transmitted back to computers that are specially programmed to interpret the data. They record it in a form that cartographers can use to create maps.

How to Read a Map

Every map has a story to tell, but first you have to know how to read the map.

Maps are useful for finding places because every place on Earth has a special address called its absolute location. Imaginary lines, called latitude and longitude, create a grid that makes finding places easy because every spot on Earth has a unique latitude and longitude. In addition, special tools, making use of the Global Positioning System (GPS), communicate with orbiting satellites to determine absolute location.

Maps are also useful for determining distance and direction. The map scale shows the relationship between distance on the map and actual distance on Earth. Since north is not always at the top of every map, a compass rose or arrow is used to indicate direction.

Maps represent other information by using a language of symbols. To find out what each symbol means, you must use the map key. Think of this key as your secret decoder, identifying information represented by each symbol on the map.

◗ **LATITUDE AND LONGITUDE.** Lines of latitude run west to east parallel to the Equator. They measure distance in degrees from 0° latitude (Equator) to 90°N (North Pole) or to 90°S (South Pole). Lines of longitude run north to south and measure distance in degrees east or west from 0° longitude (prime meridian) to 180° longitude. The prime meridian runs through Greenwich, England.

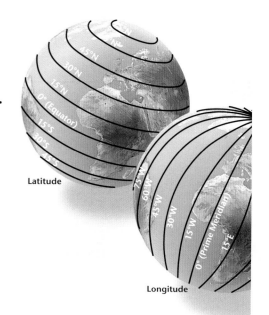

Latitude

Longitude

◗ **ABSOLUTE LOCATION.** The imaginary grid composed of lines of latitude and longitude helps us locate places on a map. Suppose you are playing a game of global scavenger hunt. The prize is hidden at absolute location 30°S, 60°W. On the map at right, look south of the Equator to find the line of latitude labeled 30°S and west of 0° longitude to find the line of longitude labeled 60°W. Trace these lines with your fingers until they meet (arrow at right). The prize must be located in central Argentina.

SCALE & DIRECTION

The scale on a map can be shown as a fraction, as words, or as a line or bar. It relates distance on the map to distance in the real world. Sometimes the type of map projection is named below the scale. Maps may include an arrow or compass rose to indicate north on the map. Maps in this atlas are oriented north, so they do not use a north indicator.

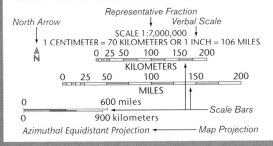

Representative Fraction

North Arrow   Verbal Scale
SCALE 1:7,000,000
1 CENTIMETER = 70 KILOMETERS OR 1 INCH = 106 MILES
0   25 50   100   150   200
KILOMETERS
0   25   50   100   150   200
MILES
0   600 miles
                                        — Scale Bars
0   900 kilometers
Azimuthal Equidistant Projection ◄——— Map Projection

SYMBOLS

Points, lines, and areas are the three main types of map symbols. Points, which can be either dots or small icons, represent the location or the number of things, such as cities or landmarks. Lines are used to show boundaries, roads, or rivers and can vary in color or thickness. Area symbols use patterns or color to show regions, such as a sandy area or a neighborhood.

POINT
A point symbol, a black dot, indicates a city, such as Omdurman.

LINE
Sudan's country boundary appears as a line symbol: a dotted line with a colored edge.

AREA
Sandy places, such as parts of the Libyan Desert, are shown by a tan, speckled area.

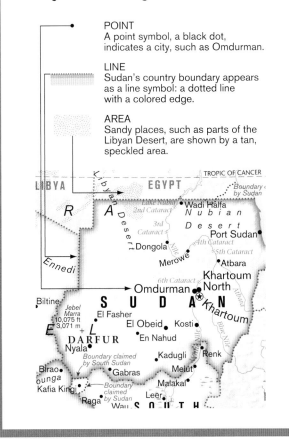

◖ APPLYING WHAT YOU'VE LEARNED. Now that you know how to read a map, can you find Sapporo in the eastern Asian country of Japan? The index for this atlas says Sapporo is on page 115 B10. Go to page 115, place one finger on the B at the side of the map and another finger on the 10 at the top. Now trace straight across from the B and down from the 10. Sapporo is near where your fingers meet!

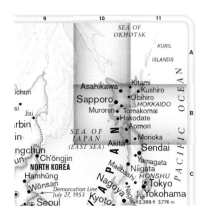

Earth in Space

Earth is part of a cosmic family called the solar system. It is one of the planets that revolves around a giant solar nuclear reactor that we call the sun.

The extreme heat and pressure on the sun cause atoms of hydrogen to combine in a process called fusion, producing new atoms of helium and releasing tremendous amounts of energy. This energy makes life on Earth possible.

Time on Earth is defined by our relationship to the sun. It takes Earth, following a path called an orbit, approximately 365 days—one year—to make one full revolution around the sun. As Earth makes its way around the sun, it also turns on its axis, an imaginary line that passes between the North and South Poles. This motion, called rotation, occurs once every 24 hours and results in day and night.

◑ **TIME ZONES.**
Long ago, when people lived in relative isolation, they measured time by the position of the sun. That meant that noon in one place was not the same as noon in a place 100 miles (160 km) to the west. Later, with the development of long-distance railroads, people needed to coordinate time. In 1884, a system of 24 standard time zones was adopted. Each time zone reflects the fact that Earth rotates west to east 15 degrees each hour. Time is counted from the prime meridian (0° longitude).

Callisto

Titan

Jupiter

Saturn

Uranus

Neptune

Triton

Charon

Haumea

Pluto

Makemake

Eris

Note: Art shows relative sizes of the sun and planets, but distances are not to scale.

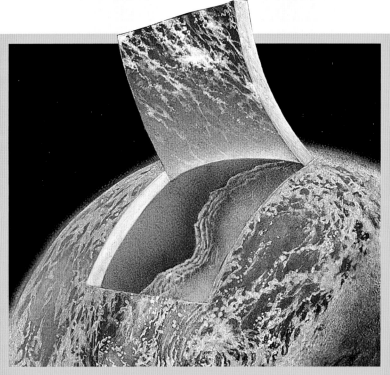

⊜ **SOLAR SYSTEM.** The sun and its family of planets are located near the outer edge of the Milky Way, a giant spiral galaxy. Earth is the third planet from the sun and one of the four "terrestrial" planets. These planets—Mercury, Venus, Earth, and Mars—are made up of solid rocky material. Beyond these inner planets are the four gas giants—Jupiter, Saturn, Uranus, and Neptune. Recently, astronomers—scientists who study space—have named a new category called "dwarf" planets that includes Pluto, Ceres, Eris, Haumea, and Makemake. More of these dwarf planets may soon be identified. Many planets, including Earth, have one or more moons orbiting them. The art above names a few: Io, Callisto, Titan, Triton, and Charon.

◗ **ENVELOPE OF AIR.** Earth is enclosed within a thick layer of air called the atmosphere. Made up of a mixture of nitrogen, oxygen, and other gases, the atmosphere provides us with the life-giving air that we breathe. It also protects us from dangerous radiation from the sun. Weather systems move through the atmosphere, redistributing heat and moisture and creating Earth's climates.

Earth in Motion

If we could step into a time machine and travel 500 million years into the past, we probably would not recognize Earth. Back then, most of the landmasses we call continents were joined together in a single giant landmass called Pangaea (below). So how did the continents break away from Pangaea and move to their current positions? The answer lies in a process called plate tectonics. These maps and diagrams tell the story.

A LOOK WITHIN. Earth's crust is a thin shell of solid rock that covers the partially molten rock of the mantle (upper and lower). Currents of heat rising and falling within the mantle break the crust into large pieces called plates. As plates creep across Earth's surface, they reshape its features. Major plates appear on the map at right. Earthquakes and volcanoes are most frequent where plates collide or grind past each other.

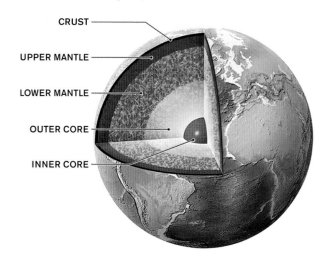

CRUST
UPPER MANTLE
LOWER MANTLE
OUTER CORE
INNER CORE

CONTINENTS ON THE MOVE

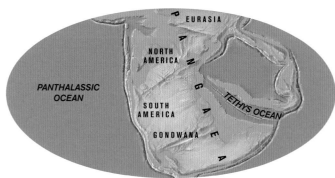

1 PANGAEA. About 240 million years ago, Earth's landmasses were joined together in one supercontinent—Pangaea—that extended from pole to pole.

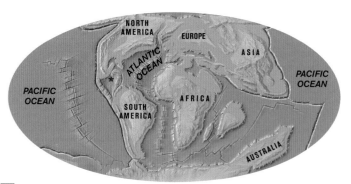

3 EXTINCTION. About 65 million years ago, an asteroid smashed into Earth (red * on map), possibly leading to the extinction of half of all species, including the dinosaurs—one of several major extinctions.

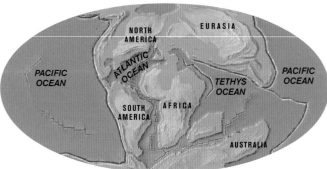

2 BREAKUP. By 94 million years ago, Pangaea had broken into what would become today's continents. Dinosaurs roamed Earth during this period of warmer climates.

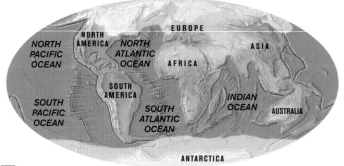

4 ICE AGE. By 18,000 years ago, the continents had drifted close to their present positions, but most far northern and far southern lands were buried beneath huge glaciers.

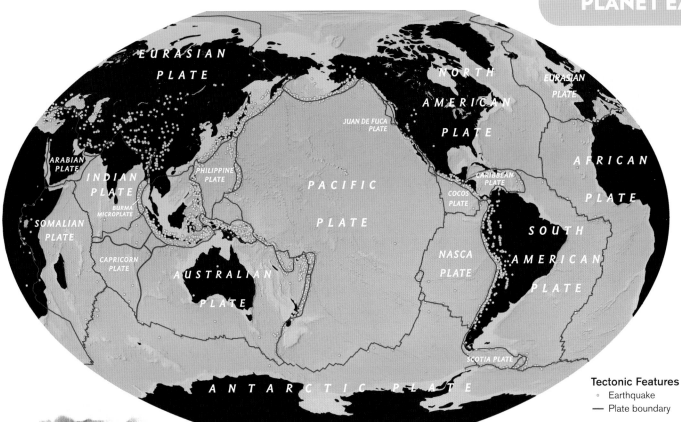

Tectonic Features
- Earthquake
— Plate boundary

Earth Shapers

Earth's features are constantly undergoing change—being built up, destroyed, or just rearranged. Plates are in constant, very slow motion. Some plates collide, others pull apart, and still others slowly grind past each other. As the plates move, mountains are uplifted, volcanoes erupt, and new land is created.

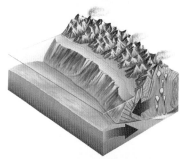

VOLCANOES form when molten rock, called magma, rises to Earth's surface. Some volcanoes occur as one plate pushes beneath another plate. Other volcanoes result when a plate passes over a column of magma, called a hot spot, rising from the mantle.

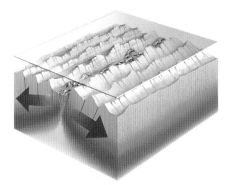

SPREADING results when oceanic plates move apart. The ocean floor cracks, magma rises, and new crust is created. The Mid-Atlantic Ridge spreads a few centimeters—about an inch—a year, pushing Europe and North America farther apart.

FAULTING happens when two plates grind past each other, creating large cracks along the edges of the plates. A famous fault is the San Andreas, in California, U.S.A., where the Pacific and North American plates meet, causing damaging earthquakes.

SUBDUCTION occurs when an oceanic plate dives under a continental plate. This often results in volcanoes and earthquakes, as well as mountain building.

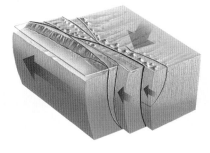

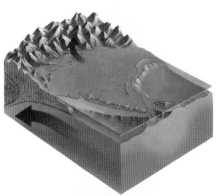

COLLISION of two continental plates causes plate edges to break and fold, creating mountains, Earth's highest landforms. The Himalaya are the result of the Indian plate colliding with the Eurasian plate, an ongoing process that began 50 million years ago.

The Physical World

Earth is dominated by large landmasses called continents—seven in all—and by an interconnected global ocean that is divided into four parts by the continents. More than 70 percent of Earth's surface is covered by oceans. Land areas cover the remaining 30 percent.

Different landforms give variety to the surface of the continents. The Rockies and Andes mark the western edge of North and South America, and the Himalaya tower above southern Asia. The Plateau of Tibet forms the rugged core of Asia, while the Northern European Plain extends from the North Sea to the Ural Mountains. Much of Africa is a plateau, and dry plains cover large areas of Australia. In Antarctica, mountains rise more than 16,000 feet (4,897 m) beneath massive ice sheets.

Mountains and trenches make the ocean floors as varied as the surface of any continent (see page 164). The Mid-Atlantic Ridge runs the length of the Atlantic Ocean. In the western Pacific Ocean, trenches drop to depths greater than 36,000 feet (10,984 m).

◗ **LAND AND WATER.** This world physical map shows Earth's seven continents—North America, South America, Europe, Africa, Asia, Australia, and Antarctica—as well as the four oceans: Pacific, Atlantic, Indian, and Arctic. Some people regard the area from Antarctica to 60°S, where the oceans merge, as a fifth ocean called the Southern Ocean.

ARCTIC OCEAN

Islands
Ellesmere I.
Oodaaq I.
Franz Josef Land
North Land
New Siberian Islands
East Siberian Sea
Laptev Sea
Baffin Bay
Baffin Island
GREENLAND
Greenland Sea
Svalbard
Novaya Zemlya
Kara Sea
Barents Sea
Iceland
Norwegian Sea
Central Siberian Plateau
Bering Sea
Kamchatka Peninsula
Labrador Sea
Labrador
Scandinavia
West Siberian Plain
S I B E R I A
Angara
Lena
Sea of Okhotsk
Aleutian Islands
British Isles
North Sea
Northern European Plain
Ob
A S I A
Ural
Yenisey
Lake Baikal
Amur
Sakhalin
Kuril Islands
Hokkaido
Ireland
Great Britain
Baltic Sea
Volga
Ural Mountains
Irtysh
The Steppes
Ob
Altay Mountains
JAPAN
EUROPE
El'brus 18,510 ft 5,642 m
Caucasus Mts.
Aral Sea
Tian Shan
Gobi
Sea of Japan (East Sea)
Korea
Honshu
Alps
Danube
Caspian Sea
Taklimakan Desert
Yellow
North China Plain
Nampo Islands
Iberian Peninsula
Corsica
Black Sea
Kunlun Mountains
NORTH PACIFIC OCEAN
NORTH ATLANTIC OCEAN
Madeira Is.
Sardinia
Sicily
Crete
Plateau of Tibet
Brahmaputra
Yangtze
East China Sea
Kyushu
Azores
Atlas Mountains
Mediterranean Sea
Cyprus
Zagros Mountains
H I M A L A Y A
Ryukyu Is.
Taiwan
Canary Is.
Dead Sea -1,401 ft -427 m
Persian Gulf
Mt. Everest 29,035 ft 8,850 m
Indus
Ganges
Libyan Desert
Arabian Peninsula
INDIA
Hainan
Luzon
Philippine Sea
Mariana Islands
SAHARA
Nile
Red Sea
Arabian Sea
Deccan Plateau
Bay of Bengal
Mekong
South China Sea
Philippine Islands
Cape Verde Islands
Niger
SAHEL
Ethiopian Highlands
Andaman Islands
Andaman Sea
Indochina Peninsula
Caroline Islands
MICRONESIA
Upper Guinea
AFRICA
Gulf of Aden
Somali Peninsula
Nicobar Is.
Malay Peninsula
Marshall Islands
Bioko
White Nile
Blue Nile
Sri Lanka
Gilbert Is.
Gulf of Guinea
Congo
Lake Victoria
Maldive Islands
São Tomé
Congo Basin
Kilimanjaro 19,340 ft 5,895 m
Sumatra
Borneo
Greater Sunda Islands
Celebes
Moluccas
New Guinea
Bismarck Archipelago
MELANESIA
Lower Guinea
Lake Tanganyika
INDONESIA
Solomon Is.
Tocantins
São Francisco
ilian lands
CA
Seychelles
Comoros Is.
Madagascar
INDIAN OCEAN
Java
Lesser Sunda Is.
Arafura Sea
Coral Sea
SOUTH ATLANTIC OCEAN
Zambezi
Namib Desert
Kalahari Desert
Mascarene Is.
Réunion
Mauritius
Rodrigues
Vanuatu
Fiji Is.
New Caledonia
Drakensberg
Western Plateau
AUSTRALIA
Lake Eyre -49 ft -15 m
Central Lowlands
GREAT DIVIDING RANGE
Darling
SOUTH PACIFIC OCEAN
Cape of Good Hope
Murray
Great Australian Bight
Mt. Kosciuszko 7,310 ft 2,228 m
North I.
Prince Edward Islands
Crozet Islands
Kerguelen Islands
Tasmania
Tasman Sea
NEW ZEALAND
Falkland Islands
South Georgia
Scotia Sea
South Sandwich Islands
South I.
Auckland Islands
South Shetland Islands
South Orkney Islands
Antarctic Peninsula
Land
WEDDELL SEA
Ronne Ice Shelf
South Magnetic Pole
Vinson Massif 16,067 ft 4,897 m
Queen Maud Land
EAST ANTARCTICA
TRANSANTARCTIC MTS.
Victoria Land
Ross Ice Shelf
Ross Sea
ARCTIC MOUNTAINS
A N T A R C T I C A

90° 60° 30°W 0° 30°E 60° 90° 120° 150° 180°

The Land

A closer look at Earth's surface reveals many varied forms and features that make each place unique. This drawing of an imaginary landscape captures 41 natural and human-made features and shows how they relate to each other. For example, a large moving "river" of ice (called a glacier) descends from a high mountain range, and a harbor, built by people, creates safe anchorage for ships.

Such features can be found all over the world because the same forces are at work around the globe. Volcanoes and movement of the plates of Earth's crust are constantly creating and building up new landforms, while external forces such as wind, water, and ice continuously wear down surface features.

Earth is dynamic—constantly changing, never the same.

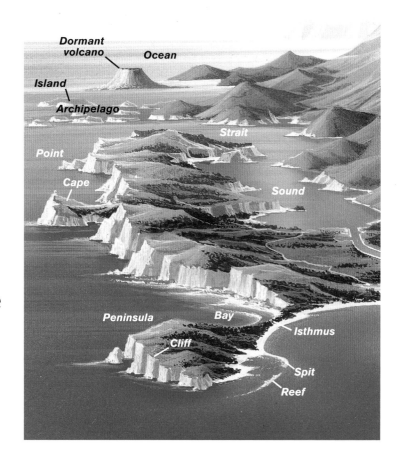

Dormant volcano · Ocean · Island · Archipelago · Strait · Point · Cape · Sound · Peninsula · Bay · Isthmus · Cliff · Spit · Reef

RIVER

As a river moves through flatlands, it twists and turns. Above, the Rio Los Amigos winds through a rain forest in Peru.

CANYON

Steep-sided valleys called canyons are created mainly by running water. Buckskin Gulch (above) is the deepest slot canyon in the American Southwest.

DESERT

Deserts are a land feature created by climate, specifically by a lack of water. Above, a camel caravan crosses the Sahara, in northern Africa.

OASIS

Occasionally, water rises from deep below a desert, creating an oasis—a fertile area that supports trees and sometimes crops—such as this one in Africa.

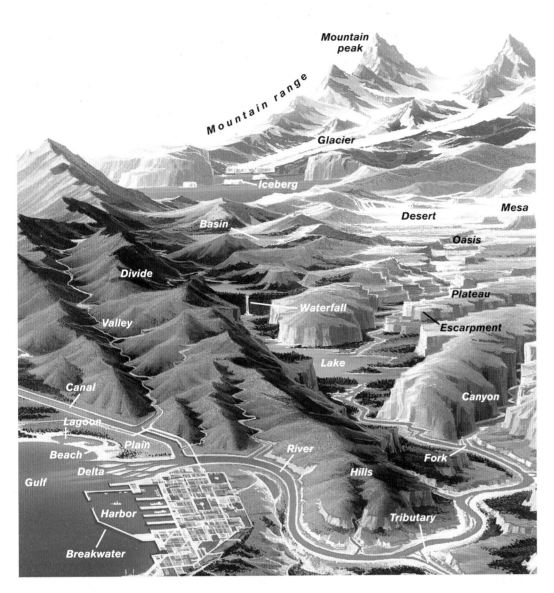

Mountain peak

Mountain range

Glacier

Iceberg

Basin

Desert

Mesa

Oasis

Divide

Plateau

Waterfall

Escarpment

Valley

Lake

Canal

Canyon

Lagoon

Plain

Beach

River

Fork

Delta

Hills

Gulf

Harbor

Tributary

Breakwater

A NAME FOR EVERY FEATURE.

Land has a vocabulary all its own, each name identifying a specific feature of the landscape. A cape, for example, is a broad chunk of land extending out into the sea. It is not pointed, however, because then it would be a point. Nor does it have a narrow neck. A sizable cape or point with a narrow neck is a peninsula. The narrow neck is an isthmus. Such specific identifiers have proven useful over the centuries. In the early days of exploration, even the simplest maps showed peninsulas, bays, and straits. Sailors used these landmarks to reach safe harbor or to avoid disastrous encounters.

◖ **EXPLORING THE LANDSCAPE.**
How many of these landscape features have you seen on your travels or in the area where you live?

MOUNTAIN

Mountains are Earth's tallest landforms, and Mount Everest in Asia (above) rises highest of all at 29,035 feet (8,850 m) above sea level.

GLACIER

Glaciers, such as Hubbard in Alaska, U.S.A. (above), move slowly from mountains to the sea. Climate change may be causing them to melt.

VALLEY

Valleys, cut by running water or moving ice, may be broad and flat or narrow and steep, such as the Indus River Valley in Ladakh, India (above).

WATERFALL

Waterfalls form when a river reaches an abrupt change in elevation. Above, South America's Kaieteur Falls, in Guyana, drops 800 feet (244 m).

World Climate

Weather is the condition of the atmosphere—temperature, precipitation, humidity, wind—at a given place at a given time. Climate, however, is the average weather for a particular place over a long period of time. Climate is not a random occurrence. It is a pattern that is controlled by factors such as latitude, elevation, prevailing winds, temperature of ocean currents, and location on land relative to water. Climate is generally constant, but many people are concerned that the activity of humans may be causing a change in the patterns of climate.

THE BASICS

According to the National Oceanic and Atmospheric Administration (NOAA), 2016 ranks first as the hottest year on record, and future years may be even hotter. The 2016 global annual temperature for combined land and ocean surfaces was 1.78° F (.99° C) warmer than the mid-20th-century average.

Ice cores taken from Antarctica and Greenland allow scientists to gain detailed information about the history of Earth's climate and its atmosphere—especially the presence of green-house gases—dating back thousands of years.

According to climatologists—people who study climate—Earth experienced what is called the Little Ice Age, which lasted from the 17th century to the late 19th century. During that time, temperatures were cold enough to cause glaciers to advance.

⬤ **CLIMATE GRAPHS.** Temperature and precipitation data provide a snapshot of the climate at a particular place. This information can be shown in a special type of graph called a climate graph (below). Average monthly temperatures (scale on the left side of the graphs) are represented by the lines at the tops of the colored areas, while average monthly precipitation totals (scale on the right side of the graphs) are reflected in the bars. For example, the graph for Belém, Brazil, shows a constant warm temperature of about 80°F (27°C) with abundant rainfall year-round. In contrast, the graph for Fairbanks, Alaska, shows a cool, variable temperature with only limited precipitation.

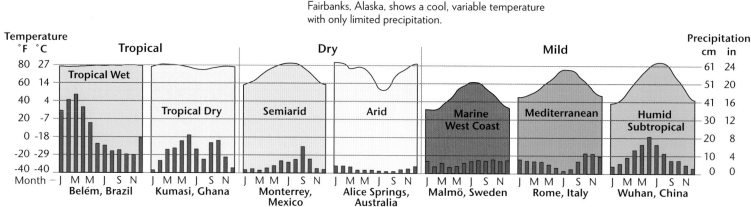

Temperature °F °C — Tropical — Dry — Mild — Precipitation cm in

Tropical Wet — Tropical Dry — Semiarid — Arid — Marine West Coast — Mediterranean — Humid Subtropical

Belém, Brazil · Kumasi, Ghana · Monterrey, Mexico · Alice Springs, Australia · Malmö, Sweden · Rome, Italy · Wuhan, China

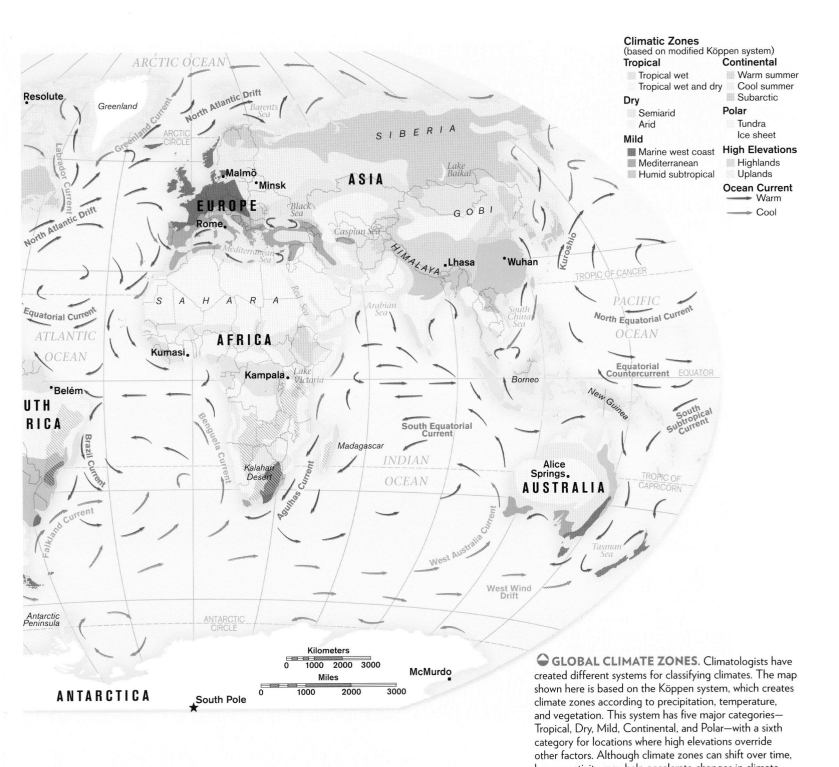

Climatic Zones
(based on modified Köppen system)

Tropical
- Tropical wet
- Tropical wet and dry

Dry
- Semiarid
- Arid

Mild
- Marine west coast
- Mediterranean
- Humid subtropical

Continental
- Warm summer
- Cool summer
- Subarctic

Polar
- Tundra
- Ice sheet

High Elevations
- Highlands
- Uplands

Ocean Current
- → Warm
- → Cool

GLOBAL CLIMATE ZONES. Climatologists have created different systems for classifying climates. The map shown here is based on the Köppen system, which creates climate zones according to precipitation, temperature, and vegetation. This system has five major categories— Tropical, Dry, Mild, Continental, and Polar—with a sixth category for locations where high elevations override other factors. Although climate zones can shift over time, human activity may help accelerate changes in climate.

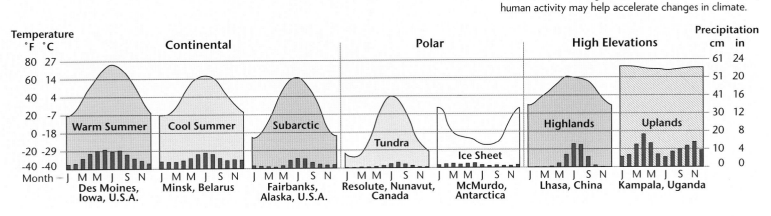

	Continental			Polar		High Elevations	
	Warm Summer	Cool Summer	Subarctic	Tundra	Ice Sheet	Highlands	Uplands
	Des Moines, Iowa, U.S.A.	Minsk, Belarus	Fairbanks, Alaska, U.S.A.	Resolute, Nunavut, Canada	McMurdo, Antarctica	Lhasa, China	Kampala, Uganda

Temperature °F °C: 80 27, 60 14, 40 4, 20 -7, 0 -18, -20 -29, -40 -40

Precipitation cm in: 61 24, 51 20, 41 16, 30 12, 20 8, 10 4, 0 0

Month — J M M J S N

Factors Influencing Climate

Earth's climate is a bit like a big jigsaw puzzle. To understand it, you need to fit all the pieces together, because climate is influenced by a number of different, but interrelated factors. These include latitude, topography (shape of the land), elevation above sea level, wind systems, ocean currents, and distance from large bodies of water. Climate has always affected the way we live, but can humans affect climate? Pollution from industries and motor vehicles may be changing Earth's climate.

◗ TOPOGRAPHY. Mountain ranges are natural barriers to the movement of air. In North America, prevailing westerly winds carry air full of moisture from the Pacific Ocean to the West Coast. As air rises over the Coast Ranges, light precipitation falls. Farther inland, the much taller Sierra Nevada range triggers heavy precipitation as air rises higher. On the leeward side of the Sierra Nevada, sinking air warms, water evaporates, and dry "rain shadow" conditions prevail. As winds continue across the interior plateau, the air remains dry because there is no significant source of moisture.

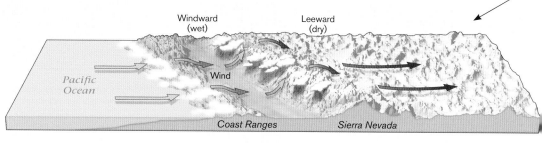

Windward (wet)   Leeward (dry)

Pacific Ocean   Wind

Coast Ranges   Sierra Nevada

Cool   Warm   Temperature changes as air moves over mountains

◒ ELEVATION. In general, climate conditions become cooler as elevation increases. Since cooler air holds less moisture, less precipitation falls. As temperature and moisture conditions change, vegetation also changes. In the mountain diagram (below), a dense mixed forest grows near the base of the mountain on the windward side. As elevation increases and temperatures decline, the mixed forest changes to all evergreen, followed by alpine meadows, until finally the mountain's rocky peaks are covered by snow and ice. As air moves down the leeward slope of the mountain, it warms and evaporates moisture, causing the leeward side to be drier and have less vegetation.

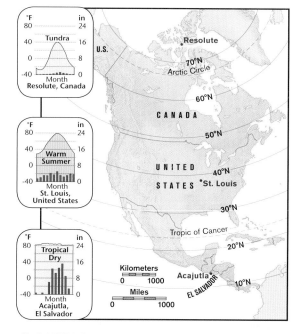

°F / in
80 / 24
40 / 16 — Tundra
0 / 8
-40 / 0
Month
Resolute, Canada

U.S.   Resolute
70°N Arctic Circle
60°N
CANADA
50°N
UNITED
STATES   St. Louis   40°N
30°N
Tropic of Cancer
20°N

Kilometers
0   1000
Miles
0   1000

Acajutla
EL SALVADOR   10°N

°F / in
80 / 24
40 / 16 — Warm Summer
0 / 8
-40 / 0
Month
St. Louis, United States

°F / in
80 / 24 — Tropical Dry
40 / 16
0 / 8
-40 / 0
Month
Acajutla, El Salvador

◒ LATITUDE. Energy from the sun drives global climates. Latitude—distance north or south of the Equator—affects the amount of solar energy received. Places near the Equator (Acajutla, El Salvador, above) have warm temperatures year-round. As distance from the Equator increases (St. Louis, U.S.A., and Resolute, Canada, above), average temperatures decline, and cold winters become more pronounced.

WINDWARD

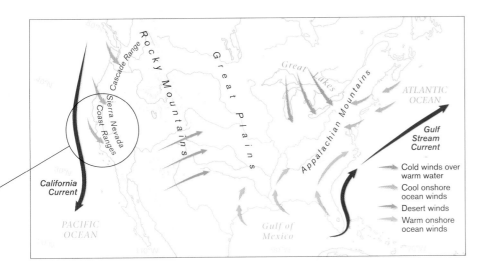

⬤ **DIGGING OUT.** Arctic winds roar across Canada, picking up moisture from the Great Lakes (purple arrows on map, left). As the moist air crosses over the frozen land, temperatures fall and heavy precipitation—called lake effect snow—occurs, burying cars and roads as shown here in Oswego, New York, U.S.A.

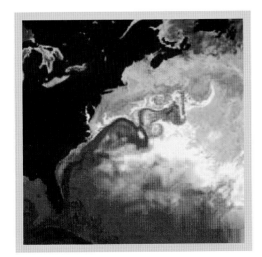

⬤ **WARM CURRENT.**
The Gulf Stream, a warm ocean current averaging 50–93 miles (80–150 km) wide, sweeps up the East Coast of North America (red arrow on map above). One branch continues across the North Atlantic Ocean and above the Arctic Circle (map, page 23). In the color-enhanced satellite image (left), the Gulf Stream looks like a dark red river moving up the coast. This "river" of warm water influences climate along its path, bringing moisture and mild temperatures to the East Coast of the United States and causing ice-free ports above the Arctic Circle in Europe.

CLIMATE CHANGE

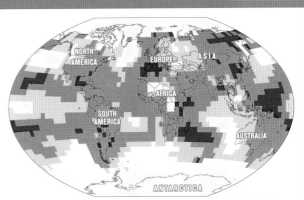

Land & Ocean Temperature Averages (January–July 2017)

No data   Cooler than average   Near average   Warmer than average   Much warmer than average   Record warmest

Earth's climate history is a story of change, with warm periods followed by periods of bitter cold. The early part of the 21st century has seen some of the warmest temperatures ever recorded (map, above). Scientists are concerned that this warming trend may be related to human activity and may pose many risks to people, including rising sea levels. As average temperatures rise, glaciers melt and ocean waters expand, causing sea levels to rise and flood coastal areas, indicated by the red areas in Florida (below, right).

Current

2100

World Vegetation

Natural vegetation—plants that would grow under ideal conditions at a particular place—depends on several factors. The quality and type of soil and climate are key. In fact, vegetation often reflects patterns of climate. (Compare the vegetation map at right with the world climate map on pages 22–23.) Forests thrive in places with ample precipitation; grasses are found where there is less precipitation or only seasonal rainfall; and xerophytes—plants able to survive lengthy periods with little or no water—are found in arid areas that receive very little annual precipitation.

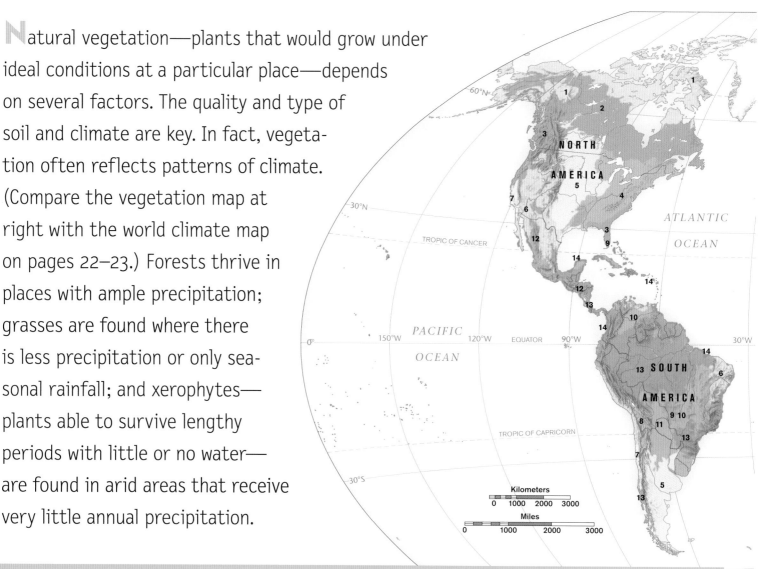

TUNDRA

With only two to three months of above-freezing temperatures, tundra plants are mostly dwarf shrubs, short grasses, mosses, and lichens (above). Much of Canada's Yukon has tundra vegetation, which turns red as winter approaches.

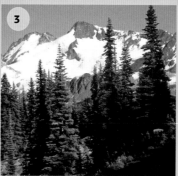

TEMPERATE CONIFEROUS

Needleleaf trees with cones to protect their seeds from bitter winters grow in cold climates with short summers, such as occur in British Columbia, Canada (above). These trees are important in lumber and papermaking industries.

TEMPERATE BROADLEAF

Broadleaf trees that grow in mid-latitude areas with mild temperatures, such as in Shenandoah National Park in Virginia, U.S.A. (above), are deciduous, meaning they lose their leaves in winter. Many of these forests have been cleared for cropland.

TEMPERATE GRASSLAND

Grasslands, such as this tall-grass prairie in south-western Missouri, U.S.A., are found in areas where precipitation is too low to support forests. Many temperate grasslands have been converted to cropland for grain production.

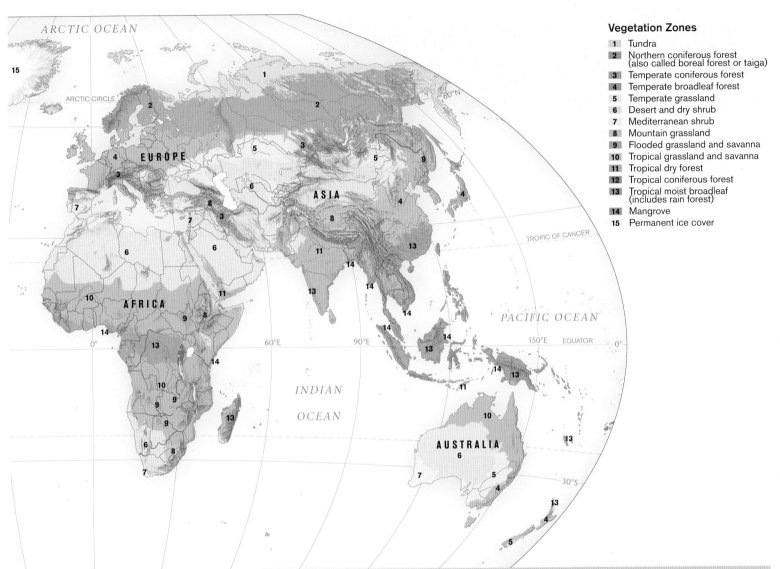

ARCTIC OCEAN

ARCTIC CIRCLE

EUROPE

ASIA

AFRICA

AUSTRALIA

PACIFIC OCEAN

INDIAN

OCEAN

TROPIC OF CANCER

EQUATOR

60°N

0°

60°E

90°E

150°E

30°S

Vegetation Zones

1 Tundra
2 Northern coniferous forest (also called boreal forest or taiga)
3 Temperate coniferous forest
4 Temperate broadleaf forest
5 Temperate grassland
6 Desert and dry shrub
7 Mediterranean shrub
8 Mountain grassland
9 Flooded grassland and savanna
10 Tropical grassland and savanna
11 Tropical dry forest
12 Tropical coniferous forest
13 Tropical moist broadleaf (includes rain forest)
14 Mangrove
15 Permanent ice cover

DESERT AND DRY SHRUB

Deserts, areas that receive less than 10 inches (25 cm) of rainfall a year, have vegetation that is specially adapted to survive under dry conditions, such as these dry shrubs and cacti growing in the Sonoran Desert in Arizona, U.S.A.

TROPICAL GRASSLAND

Tall grasses and scattered trees that can survive a hot, dry season dominate low latitude grasslands, also called savannas. Africa's grasslands are home to game animals, such as this male lion crossing the savanna in Botswana.

RAIN FOREST

A waterfall tumbles over a cliff in the Costa Rican rain forest. Rain forest trees can grow to as much as 200 feet (61 m) above the forest floor. The overlapping branches of the tallest trees keep sunlight from reaching the forest floor.

CROPLAND

People remove natural vegetation in many places to create fields to grow crops to feed both people and animals. Here, a farmer in the Catskill Mountains of New York, U.S.A., cultivates land that was likely once a temperate forest.

Environmental Hot Spots

People are putting more and more pressure on the environment by dumping pollutants into the air and water and by removing natural vegetation to extract mineral resources or to create cropland for farming. In more developed countries, industries create waste and pollution; farmers use fertilizers and pesticides that run off into water supplies; and motor vehicles release exhaust fumes into the air. In less developed countries, forests are cut down for fuel or to clear land for farming; grasslands are turned into deserts as farmers and herders overuse the land; and expanding urban areas face problems of water quality and sanitation.

HUMAN FOOTPRINT. This map uses population density, land use, transportation, and energy production and use to identify environmental hot spots—areas of Earth where human impact is greatest.

NORTH AMERICA

New York

Los Angeles

Mexico City

SOUTH AMERICA

Lima

Environmental Stresses
- Megacity with more than 10 million people
- Deforestation
- Desertification
- Major air pollution
- Major human impact to the oceans

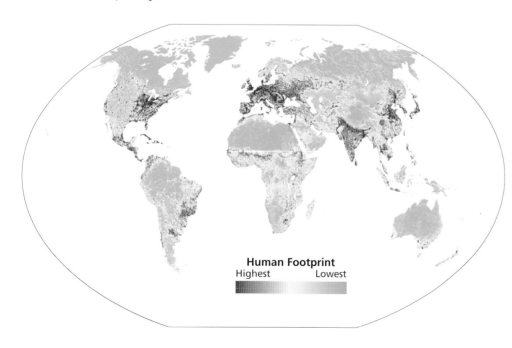

Human Footprint
Highest   Lowest

AIR POLLUTION

Poor air quality is a serious environmental problem. Industrial plants are a major source of pollution. Smoke, which contains particles that combine with moisture in the air to create acid rain, is released from a factory in Poland (above).

EUROPE
London
Paris
Moscow

ASIA

Istanbul

Beijing Tianjin Tokyo
Osaka

Chongqing Shanghai

Cairo

Delhi Dhaka Guangzhou Shenzhen
Karachi

Kolkata
(Calcutta)

AFRICA

Mumbai
(Bombay)

Chennai
(Madras)

Manila

Bengaluru
(Bangalore)

Lagos

Kinshasa

Jakarta

Rio de Janeiro
São Paulo

AUSTRALIA

Buenos Aires

Kilometers
0   1000   2000   3000

Miles
0   1000   2000   3000

DEFORESTATION

Loss of forest cover, such as on this hillside in Malaysia, contributes to a buildup of carbon dioxide in the atmosphere, as well as to a loss of biodiversity—variety of species—common problems in the tropics.

DESERTIFICATION

Villagers in Mauritania (above) shovel sand away from their schoolhouse. In semiarid areas, which receive limited and often unreliable rainfall, land that is overgrazed or overcultivated can become desertlike.

OCEAN POLLUTION

Plastic trash, ranging from bottles and bags to microscopic bits, is a serious threat to sea birds and other marine life. Scientists estimate eight million tons (7.3 million t) of plastic, including this trash off Dakar, Senegal, end up in the oceans every year.

Endangered Species

Earth's environment is made up of a complex system of life-forms ranging from microscopic organisms to giant blue whales. Throughout Earth's history, species such as the dinosaurs have become extinct. Scientists have concluded that in recent years many species are becoming endangered at an increasing rate as humans spread into natural areas for agricultural and urban use and contribute to climate change by using fossil fuels. Loss of species could mean less food, fewer medical discoveries to fight disease, and loss of plants and animals that enrich our lives each day.

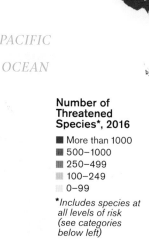

NORTH AMERICA

PACIFIC OCEAN

Number of Threatened Species*, 2016

■ More than 1000
■ 500–1000
■ 250–499
■ 100–249
■ 0–99

**Includes species at all levels of risk (see categories below left)*

SPECIES AT RISK

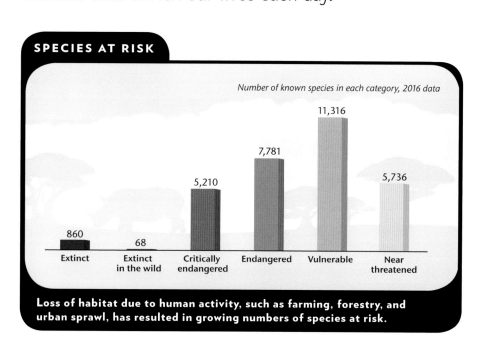

Number of known species in each category, 2016 data

				11,316	
			7,781		
		5,210			5,736
860	68				
Extinct	Extinct in the wild	Critically endangered	Endangered	Vulnerable	Near threatened

Loss of habitat due to human activity, such as farming, forestry, and urban sprawl, has resulted in growing numbers of species at risk.

Extinct*	Extinct in the wild	Critically endangered	Endangered	Vulnerable	Near threatened
no reasonable doubt that the last example of the species has died	best available evidence indicates the species is extinct in its natural habitat, surviving only in captivity	best available evidence indicates the species faces extremely high risk of extinction in the wild	best available evidence indicates the species faces very high risk of extinction in the wild	best available evidence indicates the species faces high risk of becoming endangered in the wild	best available evidence indicates the species is not yet vulnerable, but is likely to be without ongoing conservation action

**Categories and definitions are based on IUCN Red List.*

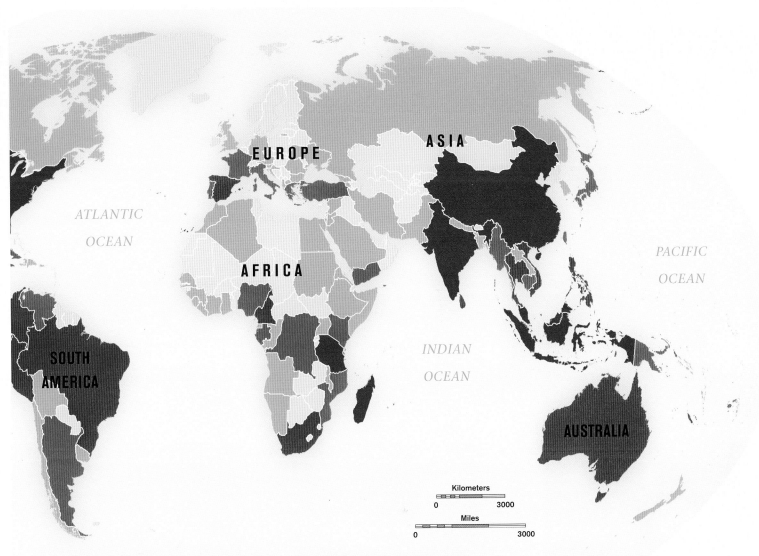

EUROPE

ASIA

ATLANTIC
OCEAN

PACIFIC
OCEAN

AFRICA

SOUTH
AMERICA

INDIAN
OCEAN

AUSTRALIA

Kilometers

0   3000

Miles

0   3000

ANTARCTICA

CRITICALLY ENDANGERED

Human activity poses the greatest threat to Earth's rich variety of species. Climate change and loss of habitat put many species at great risk. Experts estimate that species are facing extinction at a greater rate than at any other time in human history. The species shown here were declared critically endangered as of 2016.

Diademed Sifaka

Eastern Gorilla

Chinese Pangolin

Swift Parrot

Canterbury Knobbled Weevil

Geometric Tortoise

Torrey Pine

Gentiana kurroo

Natural Disasters

Every world region has its share of natural disasters. The Ring of Fire—grinding tectonic plate boundaries that follow the coasts of the Pacific Ocean—shakes with volcanic eruptions and earthquakes (page 17). Coastal areas can be swept away by quake-caused tsunamis. The U.S. heartland endures blizzards in winter and dangerous tornadoes that can strike in spring, summer, or fall. Tropical cyclones batter many coastal areas with ripping winds, torrents of rain, and huge storm surges along their deadly paths.

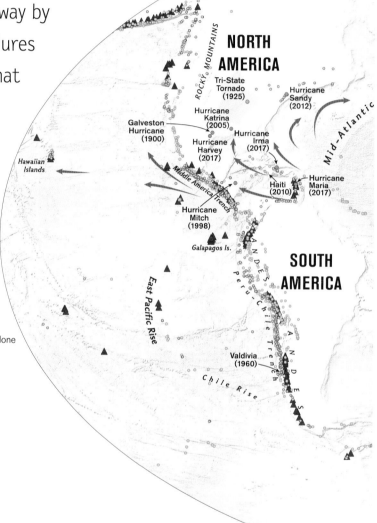

Natural Disasters
(1900–2017)

← Typical storm track of hurricane, typhoon, or cyclone

"Tornado Alley" (highest concentration of tornadoes worldwide)

○ Earthquake greater than 6.5 magnitude

○ Tsunami quake epicenter

◉ Notable tornado

◉ Notable hurricane, typhoon, or cyclone

▲ Notable volcanic eruption

⬤ **TORNADO.** A funnel cloud roars across open country near Campo, Colorado, U.S.A. More of these storms occur in "Tornado Alley" (see map) than anywhere else on Earth.

◖ **RAGING HURRICANE.** In early September 2017, Hurricane Irma roared through the Caribbean and southeastern United States. With peak sustained winds of 185 miles an hour (298 km/h), the storm destroyed almost every structure on the small island of Barbuda (right) in the Lesser Antilles.

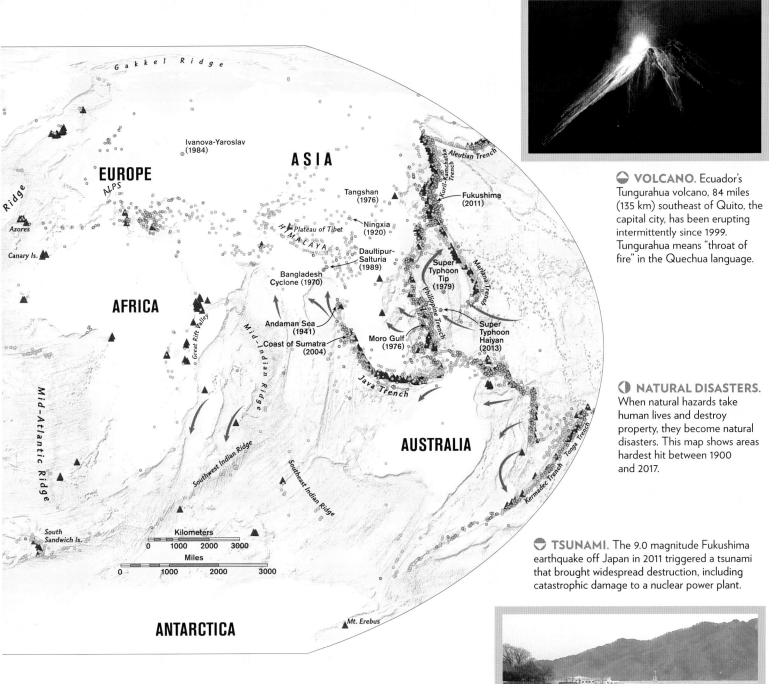

Gakkel Ridge

EUROPE

ALPS

ASIA

Ivanova-Yaroslav
(1984)

Aleutian Trench

Kuril-Kamchatka Trench

Tangshan
(1976)

Fukushima
(2011)

Ridge

Ningxia
(1920)

Azores

Plateau of Tibet

HIMALAYA

Canary Is.

Daultipur-
Salturia
(1989)

Mariana Trench

Super
Typhoon
Tip
(1979)

AFRICA

Bangladesh
Cyclone (1970)

Philippine Trench

Andaman Sea
(1941)

Great Rift Valley

Coast of Sumatra
(2004)

Moro Gulf
(1976)

Super
Typhoon
Haiyan
(2013)

Mid-Indian Ridge

Java Trench

AUSTRALIA

Mid-Atlantic Ridge

Southwest Indian Ridge

Southeast Indian Ridge

Tonga Trench

Kermadec Trench

South
Sandwich Is.

Kilometers

0   1000   2000   3000

Miles

0   1000   2000   3000

ANTARCTICA

Mt. Erebus

◑ MEASURING QUAKES.
Scientists, like this one, use an
instrument called a seismograph
to measure and record the
strength of tremors caused by
shifts in Earth's crust.

🌋 **VOLCANO.** Ecuador's
Tungurahua volcano, 84 miles
(135 km) southeast of Quito, the
capital city, has been erupting
intermittently since 1999.
Tungurahua means "throat of
fire" in the Quechua language.

◑ NATURAL DISASTERS.
When natural hazards take
human lives and destroy
property, they become natural
disasters. This map shows areas
hardest hit between 1900
and 2017.

🌊 **TSUNAMI.** The 9.0 magnitude Fukushima
earthquake off Japan in 2011 triggered a tsunami
that brought widespread destruction, including
catastrophic damage to a nuclear power plant.

The Political World

Earth's land area is mainly made up of seven giant continents that people have divided into smaller political units called countries—with two exceptions. Australia is a continent with a single country, and Antarctica is set aside for scientific research. But the other five continents include almost 200 independent countries. This political map shows boundaries—imaginary lines agreed to by treaties—that separate countries. Some boundaries are very stable and have been recognized for many years. Other boundaries are relatively new and are still disputed. Countries come in all shapes and sizes. Russia and Canada are giants. Other countries, such as Luxembourg in western Europe, are small. Some countries are long and skinny—look at Chile in South America! Still other countries, such as Indonesia and Japan in Asia, are made up of groups of islands.

◗ **COUNTRIES AND CAPITALS.** The world political map looks a bit like a patchwork quilt. Each country's boundary is outlined in one color. Some countries also include territory beyond the main land area. For example, the United States is shaded bright green, but so are Alaska and Hawai'i, which are also U.S. states. Most countries have one city—called the capital—that is the center of political decision-making. For example, Beijing is the capital of China. But a few countries have more than one capital, such as La Paz and Sucre in Bolivia. The capital of each country is marked with a star inside a circle.

POLITICAL WORLD

World Population

How big is a billion? It's hard to imagine. But Earth's population is 7.4 billion and rising, with more than a billion living in both China and India. And more than 60 million people are added to the world each year. Most population growth occurs in the less developed countries of Asia, Africa, and Latin America, while some countries in Europe are hardly increasing at all. Population changes can create challenges for countries. Fast-growing countries with young populations need food, housing, and schools. Countries with low growth rates and older populations need workers to sustain their economies.

MOST POPULOUS COUNTRIES

(2017 estimates)	
1. China	1,379,303,000
2. India	1,281,936,000
3. United States	326,626,000
4. Indonesia	260,581,000
5. Brazil	207,353,000

MOST CROWDED COUNTRIES

Population Density (People per sq mi/sq km; 2017 estimates)	
1. Monaco	30,645.0 / 15,322.5
2. Singapore	21,891.9 / 8,449.0
3. Bahrain	4,815.5 / 1,856.5
4. Maldives	3,414.9 / 1,317.8
5. Malta	3,412.6 / 1,317.5

◗ DENSITY. Demographers, people who study population, use density to measure how concentrated population is, but density is just an average. For example, the population density of Egypt is more than 250 people per square mile (97 people per sq km). This incorrectly assumes that the population is evenly spread throughout the country. Actually, most people live along the Nile River. Likewise, Earth's population is not evenly spread across the land. Some places are almost empty, others are very crowded.

◗ CITY DWELLERS. More than half the world's people have shifted from rural areas to urban centers, with some countries adding more than 100 million to their urban populations between 1950 and 2015 (map, right). In more developed countries, about 75 percent of the population is urban, compared with just 46 percent in less developed countries. But the fastest growing urban areas are in less developed countries, where thousands flock to cities, such as Dhaka, Bangladesh (photo, far right), in search of a better life. In 2016, there were 31 cities with populations of 10 million or more.

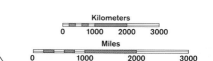

NORTH AMERICA

Los Angeles

Mexico City

PACIFIC OCEAN

Kilometers
0 1000 2000 3000

Miles
0 1000 2000 3000

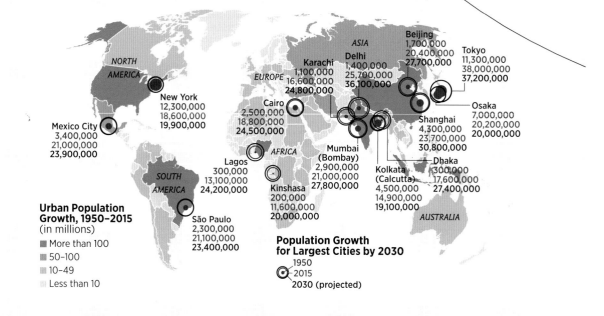

NORTH AMERICA

EUROPE

ASIA

AFRICA

SOUTH AMERICA

AUSTRALIA

New York
12,300,000
18,600,000
19,900,000

Mexico City
3,400,000
21,000,000
23,900,000

Cairo
2,500,000
18,800,000
24,500,000

Lagos
300,000
13,100,000
24,200,000

São Paulo
2,300,000
21,100,000
23,400,000

Karachi
1,100,000
16,600,000
24,800,000

Delhi
1,400,000
25,700,000
36,100,000

Beijing
1,700,000
20,400,000
27,700,000

Tokyo
11,300,000
38,000,000
37,200,000

Osaka
7,000,000
20,200,000
20,000,000

Shanghai
4,300,000
23,700,000
30,800,000

Mumbai (Bombay)
2,900,000
21,000,000
27,800,000

Kolkata (Calcutta)
4,500,000
14,900,000
19,100,000

Kinshasa
200,000
11,600,000
20,000,000

Dhaka
300,000
17,600,000
27,400,000

Urban Population Growth, 1950–2015 (in millions)
- ■ More than 100
- ■ 50–100
- ■ 10–49
- ■ Less than 10

Population Growth for Largest Cities by 2030
- 1950
- 2015
- 2030 (projected)

C.E. 1   50   100   150   200   250   300   350   400   450   500   550   600   650   700   750   800   850
Year

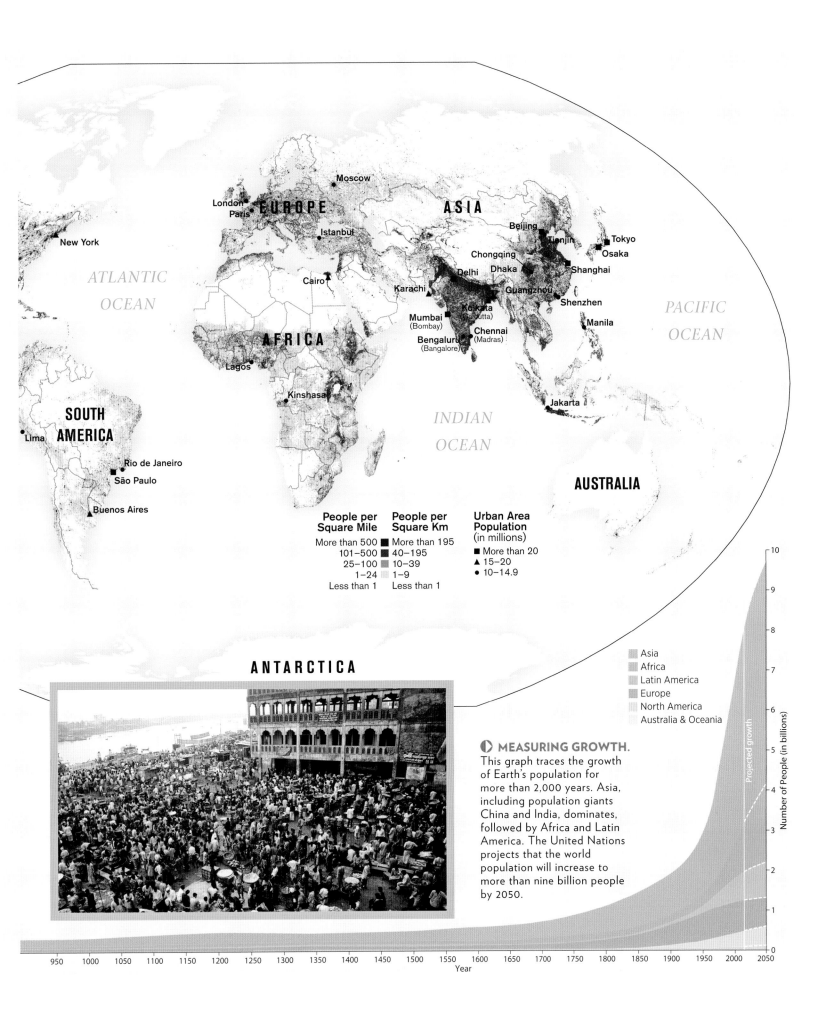

People per Square Mile
- More than 500
- 101–500
- 25–100
- 1–24
- Less than 1

People per Square Km
- More than 195
- 40–195
- 10–39
- 1–9
- Less than 1

Urban Area Population (in millions)
- More than 20
- 15–20
- 10–14.9

Asia
Africa
Latin America
Europe
North America
Australia & Oceania

Projected growth

Number of People (in billions)

MEASURING GROWTH. This graph traces the growth of Earth's population for more than 2,000 years. Asia, including population giants China and India, dominates, followed by Africa and Latin America. The United Nations projects that the world population will increase to more than nine billion people by 2050.

POLITICAL WORLD

Population Trends

Population growth rates are slowing, total fertility rates are declining, and populations are aging. Nevertheless, world population will continue to increase for many years to come because the base population is so large. More than 60 million people are added, on average, to the world's population each year, 90 percent of whom are born in less developed countries where poverty is greatest.

In more affluent countries, life expectancy is higher and populations are aging. By 2050, almost one-quarter of the world's population will be 60 years of age or older.

POPULATION GROWTH RATE (%)	
Lowest (2017 estimates)	
1. Lebanon	-1.1
2. Latvia	-1.08
3. Lithuania	-1.08
4. Moldova	-1.05
5. Bulgaria	-0.61

POPULATION GROWTH RATE (%)	
Highest (2017 estimates)	
1. South Sudan	3.83
2. Angola	3.52
3. Malawi	3.31
4. Burundi	3.25
5. Uganda	3.2

◖ **POPULATION GROWTH.**
This map shows projected population change (%) from 2015 to 2050. Russia, China, Japan, and much of Europe face a decline in population due to low birth rates and women waiting longer to have children. Countries in Africa can expect to see an opposite trend as fertility rates remain high.

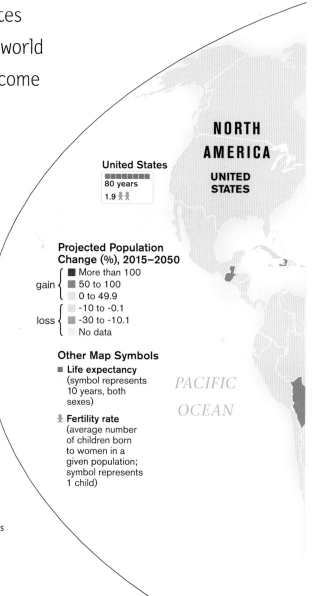

NORTH AMERICA

United States
80 years
1.9

UNITED STATES

Projected Population Change (%), 2015–2050

gain {
- More than 100
- 50 to 100
- 0 to 49.9

loss {
- -10 to -0.1
- -30 to -10.1
- No data

Other Map Symbols
- **Life expectancy** (symbol represents 10 years, both sexes)
- **Fertility rate** (average number of children born to women in a given population; symbol represents 1 child)

PACIFIC OCEAN

POPULATION PYRAMIDS

A population pyramid compares population by age and sex and can be used to predict future trends. Countries, such as Nigeria, with high birth rates and high percentages of young people have a pyramid-shaped graph, which suggests continued growth. Countries with low birth rates, such as Italy, have narrow bases with bulges in the higher age brackets, indicating an aging population.

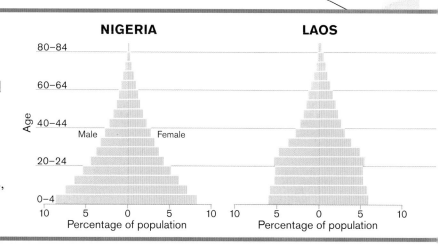

NIGERIA

LAOS

Age

Male   Female

Percentage of population   Percentage of population

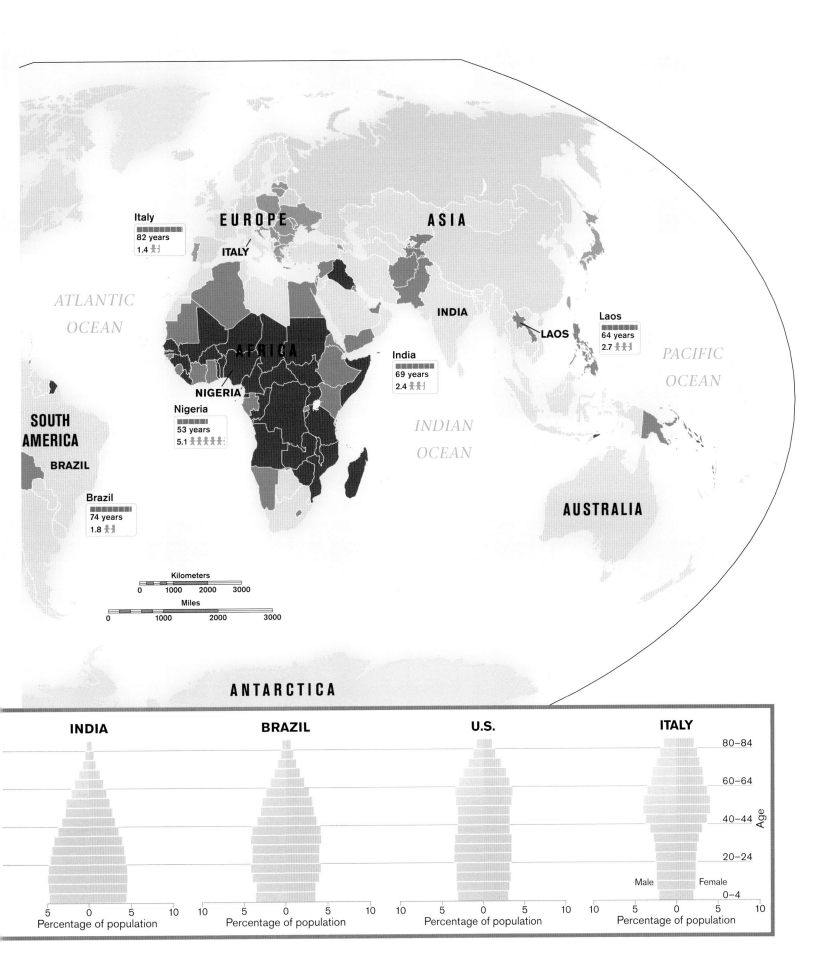

Italy
82 years
1.4

EUROPE

ITALY

ASIA

ATLANTIC
OCEAN

INDIA

Laos
64 years
2.7

LAOS

AFRICA

India
69 years
2.4

PACIFIC
OCEAN

NIGERIA

INDIAN
OCEAN

SOUTH
AMERICA

Nigeria
53 years
5.1

BRAZIL

Brazil
74 years
1.8

AUSTRALIA

Kilometers
0   1000   2000   3000

Miles
0   1000   2000   3000

ANTARCTICA

INDIA

BRAZIL

U.S.

ITALY

80–84

60–64

40–44

Age

20–24

Male   Female

0–4

5   0   5   10
Percentage of population

10   5   0   5   10
Percentage of population

10   5   0   5   10
Percentage of population

10   5   0   5   10
Percentage of population

World Languages & Literacy

Earth's 7.4 billion people live in 195 independent countries, but they speak more than 5,000 languages. Experts believe that humans may once have spoken as many as 10,000 languages. Some countries, such as Germany, have one official language. Other countries, such as Zimbabwe, have many official languages.

Literacy is the ability to read and write in one's native language. High literacy rates are associated with more developed countries. But literacy is also a gender issue, since women in less developed countries often lack access to education.

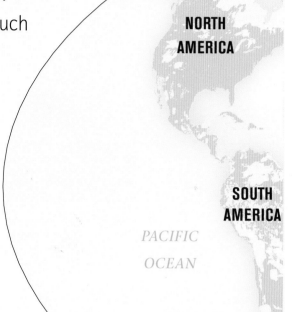

NORTH AMERICA

SOUTH AMERICA

PACIFIC OCEAN

LEADING LANGUAGES

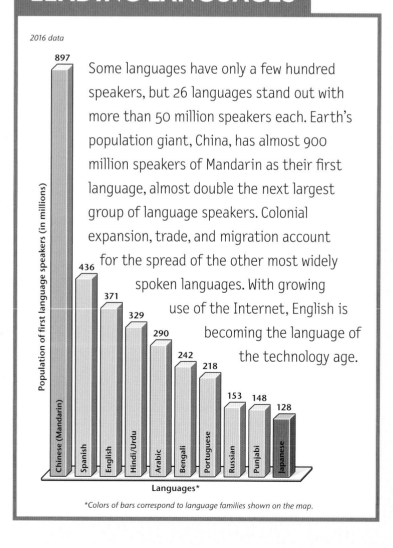

2016 data

Some languages have only a few hundred speakers, but 26 languages stand out with more than 50 million speakers each. Earth's population giant, China, has almost 900 million speakers of Mandarin as their first language, almost double the next largest group of language speakers. Colonial expansion, trade, and migration account for the spread of the other most widely spoken languages. With growing use of the Internet, English is becoming the language of the technology age.

Population of first language speakers (in millions)

897 — Chinese (Mandarin)
436 — Spanish
371 — English
329 — Hindi/Urdu
290 — Arabic
242 — Bengali
218 — Portuguese
153 — Russian
148 — Punjabi
128 — Japanese

Languages*

Colors of bars correspond to language families shown on the map.

⬆ **EDUCATION AND LITERACY.** These Nenet boys in Siberia spend hours learning the national language—Russian—but this may result in the loss of their native language. Literacy can lead to good jobs in the future for these boys and improved economic success for their country.

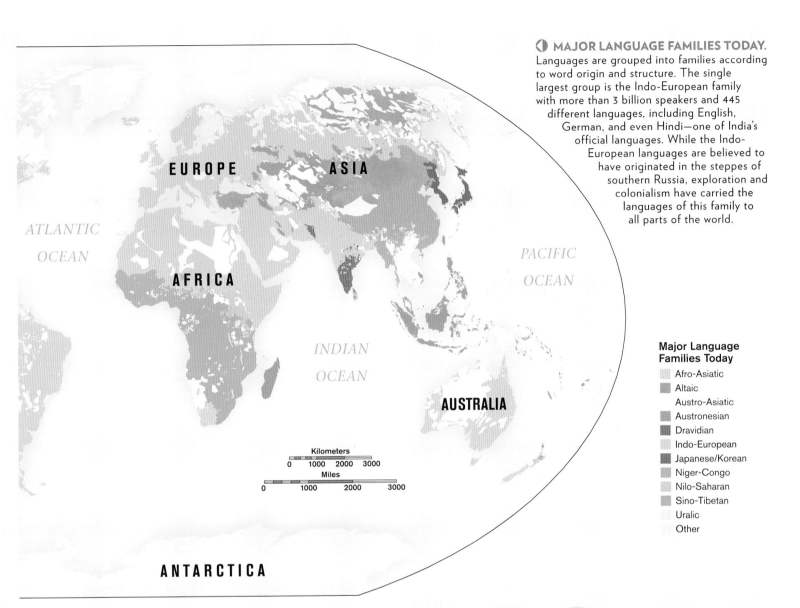

◑ MAJOR LANGUAGE FAMILIES TODAY.
Languages are grouped into families according to word origin and structure. The single largest group is the Indo-European family with more than 3 billion speakers and 445 different languages, including English, German, and even Hindi—one of India's official languages. While the Indo-European languages are believed to have originated in the steppes of southern Russia, exploration and colonialism have carried the languages of this family to all parts of the world.

EUROPE   ASIA

ATLANTIC
OCEAN

AFRICA

PACIFIC
OCEAN

INDIAN
OCEAN

AUSTRALIA

Kilometers
0   1000   2000   3000
Miles
0   1000   2000   3000

**Major Language
Families Today**

Afro-Asiatic
Altaic
Austro-Asiatic
Austronesian
Dravidian
Indo-European
Japanese/Korean
Niger-Congo
Nilo-Saharan
Sino-Tibetan
Uralic
Other

ANTARCTICA

◐ ONE LANGUAGE, TWO FORMS. Some languages, including Chinese, use characters instead of letters. The Golden Arches provide a clue to the meaning of the characters on the restaurant sign. Many signs, such as the one in the foreground, also show words in pinyin, a spelling system that uses the Western alphabet.

◒ UNIVERSAL LANGUAGE. The widespread use of technology—for example, the electronic games that hold the attention of these children in France—has crossed the language barrier. Computers, the Internet, and electronic communication devices use a universal language that knows no national borders.

World Religions

Rooted in people's attempts to explain the unknown, religion takes many forms. Some belief systems, such as Christianity, Islam, and Judaism, are monotheistic, meaning that followers believe in just one supreme being. Others, like Hinduism, Shintoism, and most indigenous belief systems, are polytheistic, meaning that followers believe in many gods.

All of the major religions have their origins in Asia, but they have spread around the world. Christianity, with the largest number of followers, has three main divisions—Roman Catholic, Eastern Orthodox, and Protestant. Islam, with almost one-fourth of all believers, has two main divisions—Sunni and Shia. Together, Hinduism and Buddhism account for more than another one-fifth of believers. Judaism, dating back some 4,000 years, is the oldest of all the major monotheistic religions.

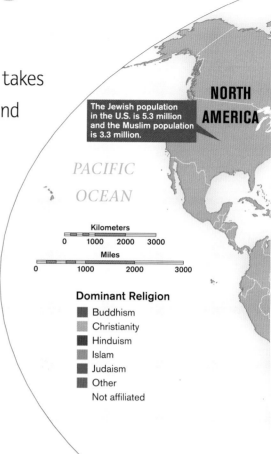

NORTH AMERICA

The Jewish population in the U.S. is 5.3 million and the Muslim population is 3.3 million.

PACIFIC OCEAN

Kilometers
0   1000   2000   3000

Miles
0   1000   2000   3000

Dominant Religion
- Buddhism
- Christianity
- Hinduism
- Islam
- Judaism
- Other
- Not affiliated

BUDDHISM

Founded about 2,500 years ago in northern India by a Hindu prince named Gautama Buddha, Buddhism spread throughout eastern and southeastern Asia. Buddhist temples house statues, such as the Mihintale Buddha (above) in Sri Lanka.

CHRISTIANITY

Based on the teachings of Jesus Christ, born some 2,000 years ago in the area of modern-day Israel, Christianity has spread worldwide and actively seeks converts. Followers in Switzerland (above) participate in a procession with lanterns and crosses.

HINDUISM

Dating back more than 4,000 years, Hinduism is practiced mainly in India. Hindus follow sacred texts known as the Vedas and believe in reincarnation. During the festival of Diwali, Hindus light candles (above) to symbolize the victory of good over evil.

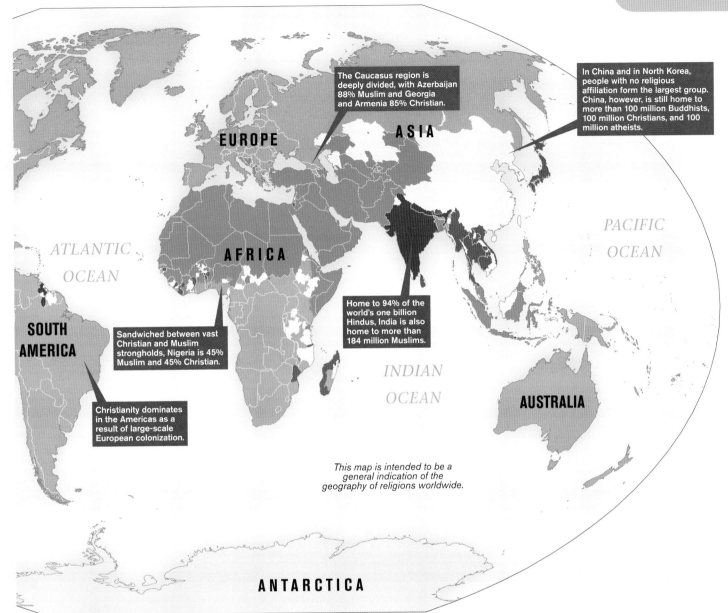

The Caucasus region is deeply divided, with Azerbaijan 88% Muslim and Georgia and Armenia 85% Christian.

In China and in North Korea, people with no religious affiliation form the largest group. China, however, is still home to more than 100 million Buddhists, 100 million Christians, and 100 million atheists.

EUROPE

ASIA

PACIFIC OCEAN

ATLANTIC OCEAN

AFRICA

Home to 94% of the world's one billion Hindus, India is also home to more than 184 million Muslims.

SOUTH AMERICA

Sandwiched between vast Christian and Muslim strongholds, Nigeria is 45% Muslim and 45% Christian.

INDIAN OCEAN

AUSTRALIA

Christianity dominates in the Americas as a result of large-scale European colonization.

This map is intended to be a general indication of the geography of religions worldwide.

ANTARCTICA

ISLAM

Muslims believe that the Koran, Islam's sacred book, records the words of Allah (God) as revealed to the Prophet Muhammad around 610 C.E. Believers (above) circle the Kabah in the Haram Mosque in Mecca, Saudi Arabia, the spiritual center of the faith.

JUDAISM

The traditions, laws, and beliefs of Judaism date back some 4,000 years to Abraham, its founder, and to the Torah, the first five books of the Old Testament. Followers pray before the Western Wall (above), which stands below Islam's Dome of the Rock in Jerusalem, Israel.

RELIGIOUS FOLLOWERS

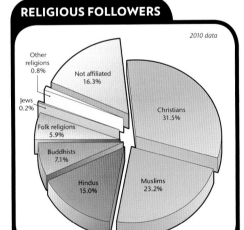

2010 data

- Other religions 0.8%
- Not affiliated 16.3%
- Jews 0.2%
- Christians 31.5%
- Folk religions 5.9%
- Buddhists 7.1%
- Hindus 15.0%
- Muslims 23.2%

Most people identify with a major religion. Some are nonreligious.

World Economies

A country's economy can be divided into three parts, or sectors—primary, which includes agriculture, forestry, fishing, and mining; secondary, which includes industry and manufacturing; and tertiary, which includes services ranging from retail sales to mail delivery, to teaching or jobs in medicine. Sometimes a fourth sector, called quaternary, is added. This includes information technology, research, and knowledge creation. The map shows that the economies of the United States, western Europe, and Japan are dominated by service sector jobs. These countries rely heavily on the use of technology and enjoy a high gross domestic product (GDP) per capita—the value of goods and services produced each year, averaged per person in each country. The overall quality of life in these countries is good. In contrast, many people in Africa and Asia still depend on the primary sector, which generates a low GDP per capita.

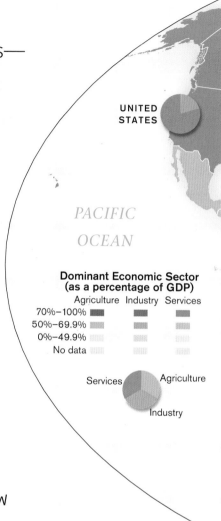

UNITED STATES

PACIFIC OCEAN

Dominant Economic Sector
(as a percentage of GDP)

	Agriculture	Industry	Services
70%–100%			
50%–69.9%			
0%–49.9%			
No data			

Services   Agriculture

Industry

🌐 **INFORMATION.** Computers and other technologies have opened employment opportunities dealing with information and knowledge creation. These college students in the United Kingdom learn skills in an information technology lab that will prepare them for 21st-century jobs.

🌐 **INDUSTRY.** A man assembles a hybrid Prius car on an automated assembly line in a Toyota factory in Japan. The manufacture of cars is an important industrial activity and a key part of the global economy.

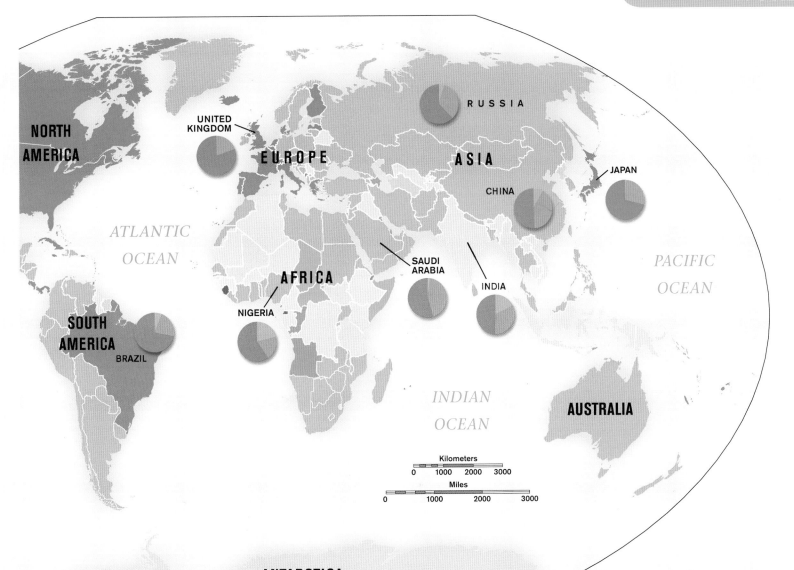

NORTH AMERICA

UNITED KINGDOM

EUROPE

RUSSIA

ASIA

JAPAN

CHINA

ATLANTIC OCEAN

PACIFIC OCEAN

SAUDI ARABIA

AFRICA

NIGERIA

INDIA

SOUTH AMERICA

BRAZIL

INDIAN OCEAN

AUSTRALIA

Kilometers
0 1000 2000 3000

Miles
0 1000 2000 3000

ANTARCTICA

AGRICULTURE. People in less developed countries, such as these women in Mozambique, often grow a variety of crops just to support their families. This practice is called subsistence agriculture. In more developed countries, farmers use machines to produce large quantities of commercial crops.

SERVICES. People employed in the service sector, such as these national forest firefighters in Washington State, U.S.A., use their skills and training to provide services rather than products. Teachers, lawyers, and store clerks, among others, are also part of the service sector.

World Trade

World trade has expanded rapidly since the end of World War II in 1945. In fact, trade has grown faster than world production. Some countries, such as the United States, China, and Germany, have complex economies that involve trading many different products as well as commercial services, such as financial and information management. But many less developed countries rely on only a few products—sometimes even just one product—to generate trade income (map, right).

Wealthy countries often protect their economies by negotiating agreements and imposing taxes that limit trade in products from other countries. The World Trade Organization works to reduce such trade barriers so that all countries can compete in the global economy.

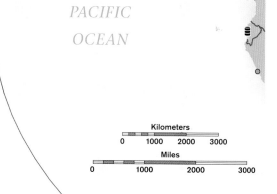

NORTH AMERICA

PACIFIC OCEAN

Kilometers
0   1000   2000   3000

Miles
0   1000   2000   3000

TOP MERCHANDISE EXPORTERS	
(2015 data, billion U.S. dollars)	
1. China	$2,275
2. United States	$1,505
3. Germany	$1,329
4. Japan	$625
5. Netherlands	$567

TOP MERCHANDISE IMPORTERS	
(2015 data, billion U.S. dollars)	
1. United States	$2,308
2. China	$1,682
3. Germany	$1,050
4. Japan	$648
5. United Kingdom	$626

TOP COMMERCIAL SERVICE EXPORTERS	
(2015 data, billion U.S. dollars)	
1. United States	$690
2. United Kingdom	$345
3. China	$285
4. Germany	$247
5. France	$240

TOP COMMERCIAL SERVICE IMPORTERS	
(2015 data, billion U.S. dollars)	
1. United States	$469
2. China	$466
3. Germany	$289
4. France	$228
5. United Kingdom	$208

◑ **TRADE.** The map (right) shows the richest and poorest economies around the world. The wealth of economies can be measured in terms of gross national income (GNI) per person—income derived from all economic activity.

◑ **GLOBAL EXCHANGE.** The world economy depends on container ports where ships deliver goods for sale or redistribution. Some ports, called transshipment ports, move containers from one form of transportation (such as a ship) to another (such as a truck) so that goods can be delivered to a final destination.

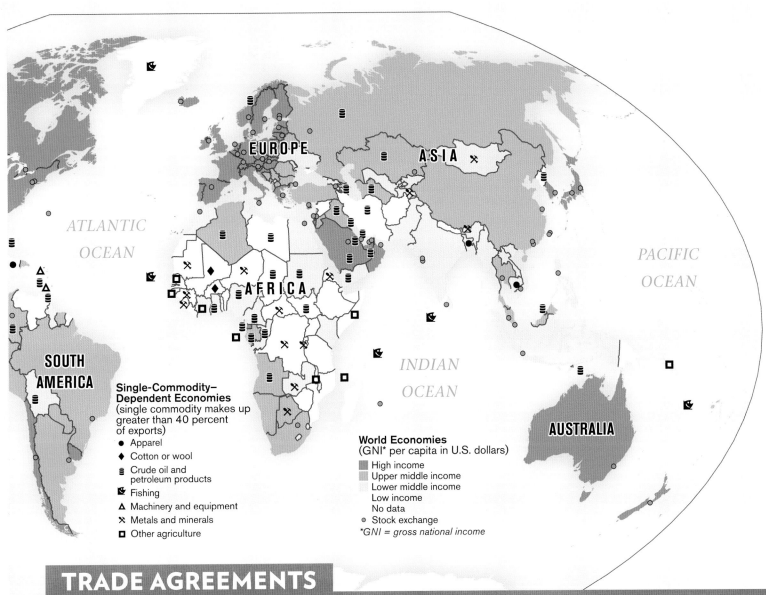

Single-Commodity–Dependent Economies
(single commodity makes up greater than 40 percent of exports)

- ● Apparel
- ◆ Cotton or wool
- ⬢ Crude oil and petroleum products
- 🐟 Fishing
- △ Machinery and equipment
- ✗ Metals and minerals
- ▢ Other agriculture

World Economies
(GNI* per capita in U.S. dollars)

- High income
- Upper middle income
- Lower middle income
- Low income
- No data
- ○ Stock exchange

*GNI = gross national income

TRADE AGREEMENTS

Trade within regions is increasing. Neighboring countries agree to offer each other trade benefits that can improve the economy of the whole region. Such agreements allow products, workers, and money to move more easily among the partners. But these agreements may also prevent trade with other countries that may be able to provide products at a lower cost.

Major Regional Trade Agreements

- **APEC:** Asia-Pacific Economic Cooperation
- **ASEAN:** Association of Southeast Asian Nations
- **APEC & ASEAN**
- **COMESA:** Common Market for Eastern and Southern Africa
- **ECOWAS:** Economic Community of West African States
- **EU:** European Union
- **MERCOSUR:** Southern Common Market
- **NAFTA:** North America Free Trade Agreement & APEC
- **SAFTA:** South Asian Free Trade Area

World Water

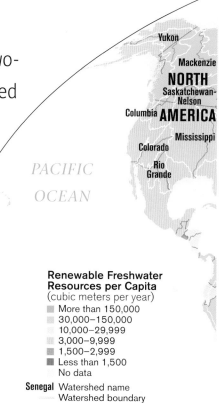

Water is Earth's most precious resource. Although more than two-thirds of the planet is covered by water, freshwater, which is needed by plants and animals—including humans—is only about 2.5 percent of all the water on Earth. Much of this is trapped deep underground or frozen in ice sheets and glaciers. Of the small amount of water that is fresh, less than one percent is available for human use.

The map at right shows each country's access to renewable freshwater supplies. Watersheds are large areas that drain into a particular river or lake. Unfortunately, human activity often puts great stress on watersheds. For example, in Brazil, plans are being made to build large dams on the Amazon. This will alter the natural flow of water in this giant watershed. In the United States, heavy use of chemical fertilizers and pesticides has created toxic runoff that threatens the health of the Mississippi watershed.

Access to clean freshwater is critical for human health. But in many places, safe water is scarce due to population pressure and pollution.

Renewable Freshwater Resources per Capita (cubic meters per year)
- More than 150,000
- 30,000–150,000
- 10,000–29,999
- 3,000–9,999
- 1,500–2,999
- Less than 1,500
- No data

Senegal Watershed name
⎯⎯ Watershed boundary

WATER FACTS

Rivers that have been dammed to generate electricity are the source of almost 90 percent of Earth's renewable energy resources.

North America's Great Lakes hold about 20 percent of Earth's available freshwater.

If all the glaciers and ice sheets on Earth's surface melted, they would raise the level of Earth's oceans by about 216 feet (66 m).

If all the world's water could be placed in a gallon jug, the freshwater available for humans to use would equal only about one tablespoon.

🌀 **BIG SPLASH!** Water sports are a favorite recreational activity, especially in hot places such as Albuquerque, New Mexico, U.S.A., where these young people cool down in a giant wave pool.

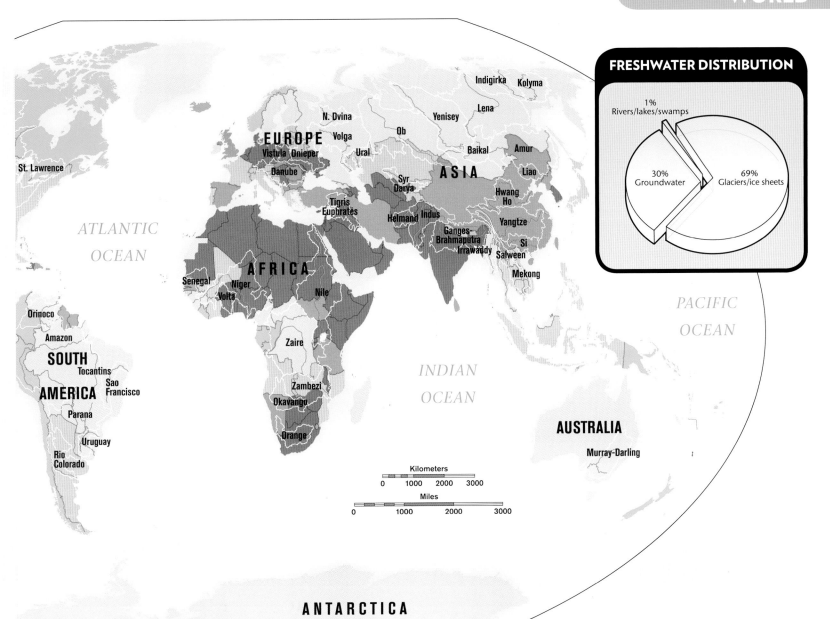

FRESHWATER DISTRIBUTION

1%
Rivers/lakes/swamps

30%
Groundwater

69%
Glaciers/ice sheets

WATER CYCLE

The amount of water on Earth has remained more or less constant over the past two billion years—only the form changes. As the sun warms Earth's surface, liquid water is changed to water vapor in a process called evaporation. Plants lose water from their leaves in a process called transpiration. As water vapor rises into the air, it cools and changes again, becoming clouds in a process called condensation. Droplets fall from clouds as precipitation, which travels as groundwater or runoff back to the lakes, rivers, and oceans, where the cycle starts again.

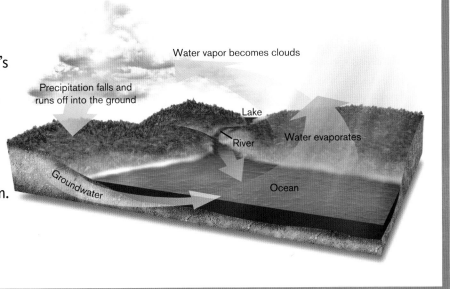

Water vapor becomes clouds

Precipitation falls and runs off into the ground

Lake

River

Water evaporates

Groundwater

Ocean

World Food

Earth produces enough food for all its inhabitants, but not everyone gets enough to eat. It's a matter of distribution. Agricultural regions (map, right) are unevenly spread around the world, and it is sometimes difficult to move food supplies from areas of surplus to areas of great need. Africa, in particular, has regions where hunger and malnourishment rob people of healthy, productive lives.

In recent decades, food production has increased, especially production of meat and cereals, such as corn, wheat, and rice, and the harvesting of fish. Grains dominate the calorie supply of people, especially in Africa and Asia. But increased yields of grain require intensive use of fertilizers and irrigation, which are not only expensive but also possibly a threat to the environment.

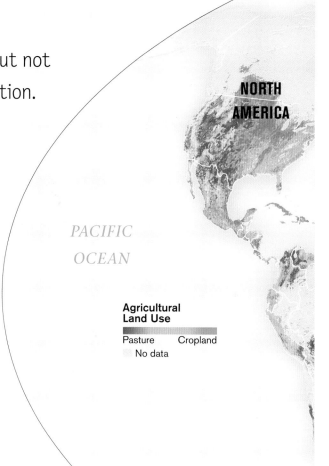

NORTH AMERICA

PACIFIC OCEAN

Agricultural Land Use

Pasture   Cropland
No data

TOP CATCH

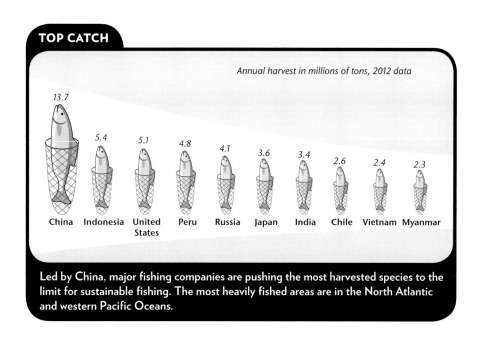

Annual harvest in millions of tons, 2012 data

China	Indonesia	United States	Peru	Russia	Japan	India	Chile	Vietnam	Myanmar
13.7	5.4	5.1	4.8	4.1	3.6	3.4	2.6	2.4	2.3

Led by China, major fishing companies are pushing the most harvested species to the limit for sustainable fishing. The most heavily fished areas are in the North Atlantic and western Pacific Oceans.

HEADED TO MARKET. A commercial fisherman uses a motorized winch to raise a net heavy with fish.

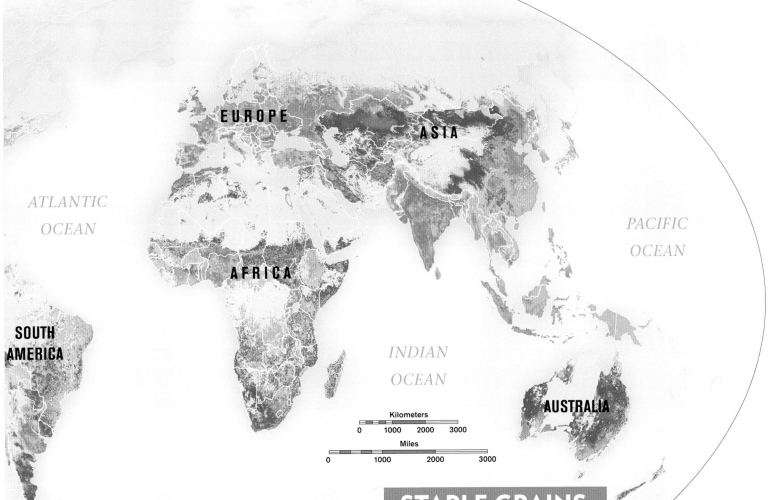

EUROPE

ASIA

ATLANTIC
OCEAN

PACIFIC
OCEAN

AFRICA

SOUTH
AMERICA

INDIAN
OCEAN

AUSTRALIA

Kilometers
0   1000   2000   3000

Miles
0   1000   2000   3000

⬭ **CASTING NETS.** Fishermen in Orissa, India, cast their nets on the Birupa River. Fish is an important source of protein in their diets. Any surplus catch can be sold in the local market.

STAPLE GRAINS

CORN. A staple in prehistoric Mexico and Peru, corn (or maize) is native to the New World. By the time Columbus's crew first tasted it, corn was already a hardy crop in much of North and South America.

WHEAT. One of the two oldest grains (barley is the other), wheat was important in ancient Mediterranean civilizations. Today, it is the most widely cultivated grain. Wheat grows best in temperate climates.

RICE. Originating in Asia many millennia ago, rice is the staple grain for about half the world's people. It is a labor-intensive crop that grows primarily in paddies (flooded fields) and thrives in the hot, humid tropics.

World Energy

Almost everything people do requires energy. But energy comes in different forms. Traditional energy sources, such as burning wood and dried animal dung, are still used by many people in the developing world. Industrialized countries and urban centers around the world rely on coal, oil, and natural gas—called fossil fuels because they formed long ago from ancient deposits of decayed plant and animal material. As the map shows, these deposits are unevenly distributed on Earth, and many countries frequently cannot afford them.

Carbon dioxide from the burning of fossil fuels along with other emissions may be contributing to climate change. Concerned scientists are looking at new ways to harness sources of renewable energy, such as water, wind, sun, and biofuels (wood, plant materials, and garbage).

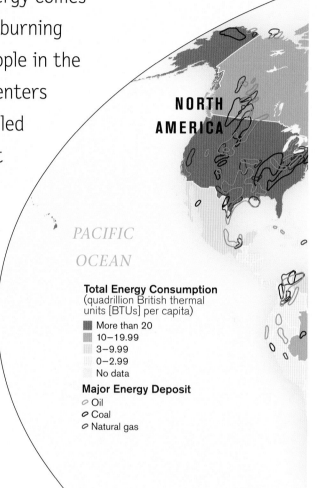

NORTH AMERICA

PACIFIC OCEAN

Total Energy Consumption
(quadrillion British thermal units [BTUs] per capita)
- More than 20
- 10–19.99
- 3–9.99
- 0–2.99
- No data

Major Energy Deposit
- Oil
- Coal
- Natural gas

OIL, GAS, AND COAL

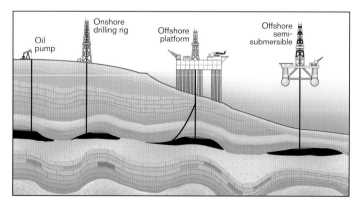

Oil pump

Onshore drilling rig

Offshore platform

Offshore semi-submersible

DRILLING FOR OIL AND GAS. The type of equipment used depends on whether the oil or natural gas is in the ground or under the ocean. This illustration shows some of the different kinds of onshore and offshore drilling equipment.

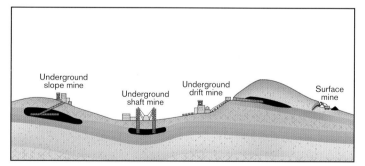

Underground slope mine

Underground shaft mine

Underground drift mine

Surface mine

COAL MINING. The mining of coal made possible the industrial revolution, which began in the mid-1700s in England, and coal still remains a major energy source. Work that was once done by people using picks and shovels now relies heavily on mechanized equipment. This diagram shows some of the various kinds of mines currently in use.

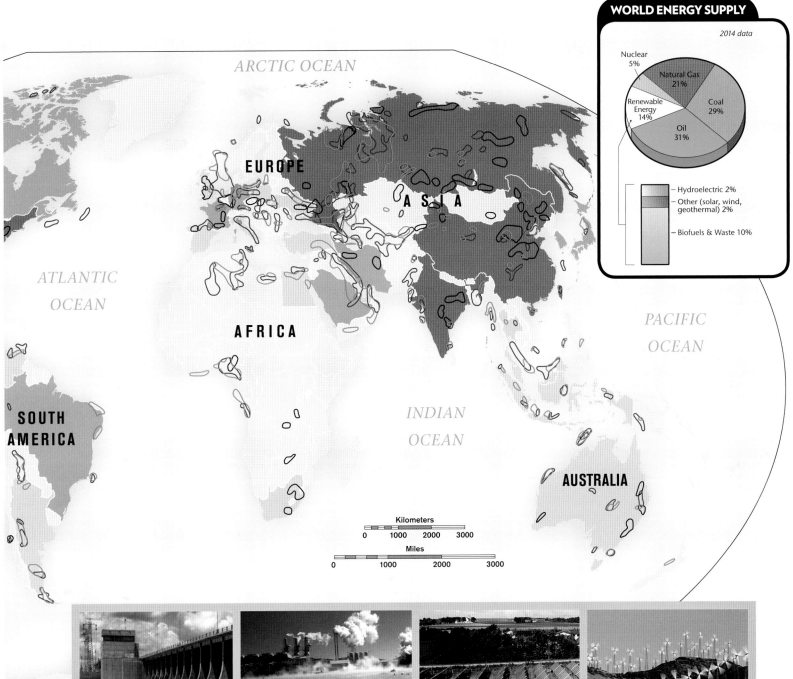

ARCTIC OCEAN

EUROPE

ASIA

ATLANTIC
OCEAN

AFRICA

PACIFIC
OCEAN

SOUTH
AMERICA

INDIAN
OCEAN

AUSTRALIA

Kilometers
0   1000   2000   3000

Miles
0   1000   2000   3000

WORLD ENERGY SUPPLY

2014 data

Nuclear
5%

Natural Gas
21%

Renewable
Energy
14%

Coal
29%

Oil
31%

– Hydroelectric 2%
– Other (solar, wind, geothermal) 2%
– Biofuels & Waste 10%

HYDROELECTRIC POWER

Hydroelectric plants, such as in Santiago del Estero, Argentina (above), use dams to harness running water to generate clean, renewable energy.

GEOTHERMAL POWER

Geothermal power, originating from groundwater heated by magma, provides energy for this power plant in Iceland. Swimmers enjoy the warm, mineral-rich waters of a lake created by the power plant.

SOLAR POWER

Solar panels on Samsø, an island in Denmark (above), capture and store energy from the sun, an environmentally friendly alternative to the use of fossil fuels.

WIND POWER

Strong winds blowing through California's mountain passes spin the blades of windmills on an energy farm (above), powering giant turbines that generate electricity for this U.S. state.

PHYSICAL			POLITICAL	
TOTAL AREA 9,449,000 sq mi (24,474,000 sq km)	**LOWEST POINT** Death Valley, California, U.S.A. -282 ft (-86 m)	**LARGEST LAKE** Lake Superior, U.S.-Canada 31,700 sq mi (82,100 sq km)	**POPULATION** 639,613,000	**LARGEST COUNTRY** Canada 3,855,081 sq mi (9,984,670 sq km)
HIGHEST POINT Denali (Mount McKinley), Alaska, U.S.A. 20,320 ft (6,194 m)	**LONGEST RIVER** Mississippi-Missouri, United States 3,780 mi (6,083 km)		**LARGEST METROPOLITAN AREA** Mexico City, Mexico Pop. 21,157,000	**MOST DENSELY POPULATED COUNTRY** Barbados 1,761.1 people per sq mi (679.9 per sq km)

NORTH AMERICA

THE CONTINENT:
NORTH AMERICA

North America

2 3 4 5 6 7 8

A

For the Aleutian Islands
and continuation of
the Bering Sea, see
inset map page 64.

ASIA

ARCTIC OCEAN

Wandel Sea

Greenland
Sea

Jan Mayen

Faroe
Islands

Chukchi
Sea

Oodaaq Island Peary
Land

Lincoln
Sea

St. Lawrence
Island

Bering Str.

Point Barrow

QUEEN
ELIZABETH
IS.

Axel Heiberg I.

Knud Rasmussen Land

GREENLAND

ICELAND

ARCTIC CIRCLE

Bering
Sea

Seward
Peninsula

North Slope

Brooks Range

Borden Island

Mackenzie King I.

Prince Patrick I.

SVERDRUP
ISLANDS

Hayes
Peninsula

Gunnbjørn +
12,119 feet
3,694 meters

B

Nunivak
Island

Yukon

ALASKA

Kuskokwim

Beaufort
Sea

Banks
Island

Melville
Island

PARRY ISLANDS

Devon I.

Baffin
Bay

Bristol
Bay

Highest point in
North America

Denali (Mt. McKinley)
20,310 ft
6,190 m

Prince of
Wales I.

Somerset I.

Qeqertarsuaq

Aleutian Range

Alaska
Range

Great
Bear L.

Victoria
Island

Boothia Pen.

Melville
Peninsula

Davis Strait

Kenai
Peninsula

King William I.

Prince Charles I.

Labrador
Sea

Kodiak I.

Gulf of
Alaska

Mt. Logan
19,551 ft
5,959 m

Mackenzie Mts.

Southampton
Island

Foxe
Basin

Cape Farewell

C

Plateau

Yukon

Mackenzie

Hudson Strait

Glacier Bay

C A N A D A

Great
Slave Lake

Hudson
Bay

Ungava
Bay

Island of
Newfoundland

Alexander
Archipelago

Coast Mountains

Slave

Peace

Ungava
Peninsula

LABRADOR

Haida
Gwaii

Lake
Athabasca

Churchill

Belcher
Islands

Laurentide Scarp

Anticosti
Island

Avalon
Peninsula

D

Vancouver
Island

Fraser
Plateau

Athabasca

Columbia Mts.

Saskatchewan

Nelson

James Bay

Gulf of St. Lawrence

Cape Breton Island

Olympic
Peninsula

ROCKY

Lake
Winnipeg

St. Lawrence

Prince Edward Island

Columbia

Missouri

Gaspé Pen.

Nova
Scotia

Cape Mendocino

Cascade Range

Coast Ranges

MOUNTAINS

Lake
Superior

Bay of
Fundy

E

Snake

Columbia Plateau

G R E A T

Lake
Michigan

Lake
Huron

L. Ontario

MOUNTAINS

Gulf of
Maine

Cape Cod

Great
Basin

Great
Salt Lake

L. Erie

Long Island

Sierra Nevada

Mt. Whitney
14,494 feet
4,418 meters

P L A I N S

CENTRAL
LOWLAND

Chesapeake Bay

F

Death Valley
-282 ft -86 m
Lowest point in
North America

Colorado
Plateau

Grand
Canyon

Colorado

U N I T E D

Platte

Missouri

Arkansas

Ozark Plateau

Ohio

APPALACHIAN

Cape
Hatteras

Bermuda
Islands

Channel
Islands

S T A T E S

Mississippi

Red

Guadalupe I.

Sonoran
Desert

Baja California

High Plains

COASTAL

G

Eugenia Point

Gulf of California

Rio Grande

Florida

Grand Bahama Island

TROPIC OF CANCER

PACIFIC

MEXICO

Sierra Madre Occidental

Sierra Madre Oriental

Gulf of
Mexico

Florida Keys

Straits of Florida

BAHAMAS

WEST

Virgin Islands

ST. KITTS & NEVIS

H

OCEAN

False Cape

Pico de Orizaba
18,855 ft
5,747 m

Yucatán
Peninsula

Cozumel
Island

Cayman
Islands

CUBA

GREATER

Hispaniola

HAITI DOMINICAN
REPUBLIC

ANTILLES

Puerto
Rico

INDIES

ANTIGUA & BARBUDA

DOMINICA Martinique

Guadeloupe

Revillagigedo Islands

Sierra Madre del Sur

Isthmus of
Tehuantepec

JAMAICA

Caribbean Sea

ST. LUCIA

BARBADOS

Lesser Antilles

ST. VINCENT &
THE GRENADINES

GRENADA

TRINIDAD & TOBAGO

Trinidad

Map Key

—— Country boundary

BELIZE

GUATEMALA

HONDURAS

Mosquito Coast

I

0   600 miles
0   600 kilometers

Azimuthal Equidistant Projection

Clipperton

Gulf of
Tehuantepec

Sierra Madre

EL SALVADOR

NICARAGUA

Lake Nicaragua

CENTRAL

COSTA RICA

Isthmus of Panama

PANAMA

SOUTH
AMERICA

Coiba I.

Gulf of Panama

AMERICA

Cocos Island

PACIFIC OCEAN

ATLANTIC OCEAN

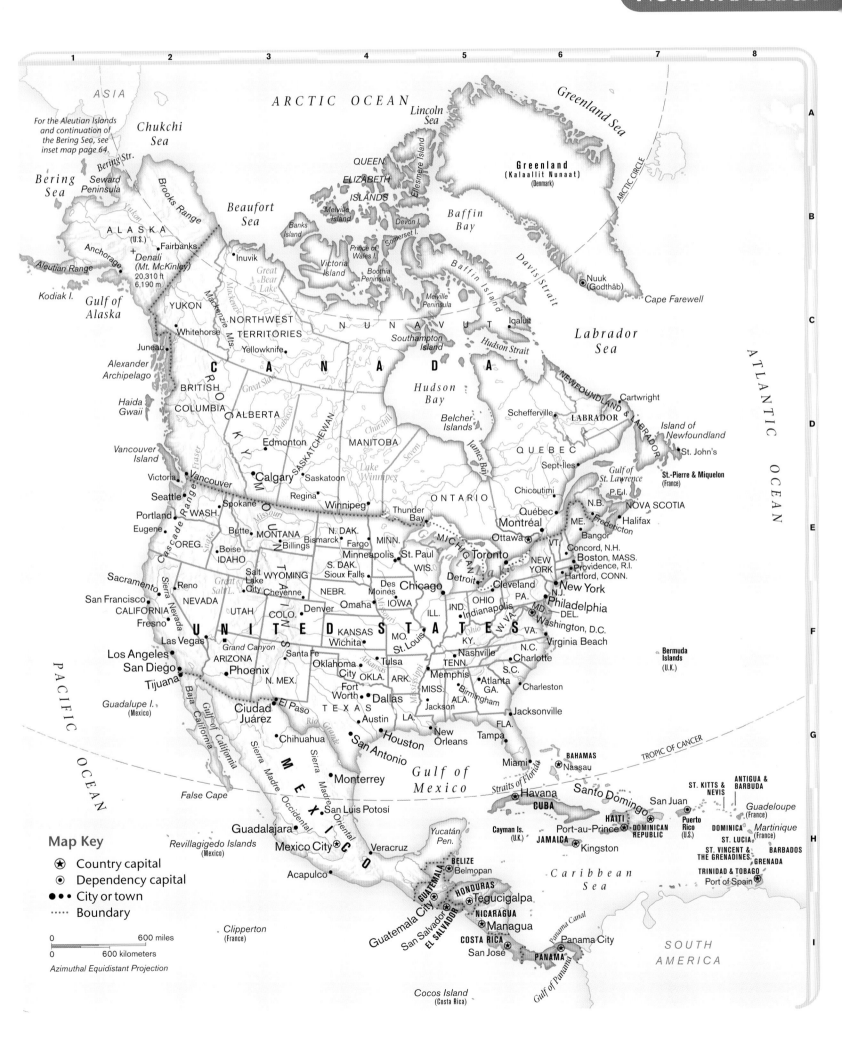

ASIA

ARCTIC OCEAN

Lincoln Sea

Greenland Sea

Chukchi Sea

For the Aleutian Islands and continuation of the Bering Sea, see inset map page 64.

Bering Str.

Bering Sea

Seward Peninsula

QUEEN ELIZABETH ISLANDS

Ellesmere Island

Greenland (Kalaallit Nunaat) (Denmark)

ARCTIC CIRCLE

ALASKA (U.S.)

• Fairbanks

Melville Island

Devon I.

Baffin Bay

Anchorage

+ Denali (Mt. McKinley) 20,310 ft 6,190 m

Banks Island

Somerset I.

Prince of Wales I.

Aleutian Range

Kodiak I.

Gulf of Alaska

YUKON

• Inuvik

Great Bear Lake

Victoria Island

Boothia Peninsula

Baffin Island

Davis Strait

Nuuk (Godthåb) ⊙

Cape Farewell

Juneau •

Whitehorse •

NORTHWEST TERRITORIES

• Yellowknife

N U N A V U T

Melville Peninsula

• Iqaluit

Southampton Island

Hudson Strait

Labrador Sea

Alexander Archipelago

C A N A D A

Haida Gwaii

BRITISH COLUMBIA

R O C K Y

• Edmonton

Great Slave Lake

ALBERTA

Athabasca

SASKATCHEWAN

MANITOBA

Churchill

Hudson Bay

Belcher Islands

Cartwright •

Schefferville •

LABRADOR

NEWFOUNDLAND & LABRADOR

Island of Newfoundland

Vancouver Island

Victoria •

Vancouver •

• Calgary

• Saskatoon

Fraser

M O U N T A I N S

Regina •

Lake Winnipeg

Winnipeg •

Severn

James Bay

O N T A R I O

Q U E B E C

Sept-Îles •

Chicoutimi •

Gulf of St. Lawrence

P.E.I.

St.-Pierre & Miquelon (France)

St. John's •

Seattle •

Spokane •

Portland •

Cascade Range

WASH.

• Butte

Missouri

Eugene •

OREG.

MONTANA

• Billings

Bismarck •

N. DAK.

Fargo •

MINN.

Great Lakes

Thunder Bay •

MICHIGAN

Québec •

Montréal ⊛

Ottawa ⊛

N.B.

Fredericton •

NOVA SCOTIA

Halifax •

ME.

Bangor •

Concord, N.H.

Boston, MASS.

Boise •

IDAHO

WYOMING

Minneapolis •

• St. Paul

S. DAK.

WIS.

Detroit •

Toronto ⊛

VT.

Providence, R.I.

Hartford, CONN.

Sacramento •

Reno •

Snake

Great Salt L.

Salt Lake City •

Cheyenne •

Sioux Falls •

NEBR.

Missouri

Des Moines •

Chicago •

IOWA

Cleveland •

OHIO

PA.

NEW YORK

New York ⊛

N.J.

Philadelphia •

San Francisco •

Sierra Nevada

NEVADA

UTAH

COLO.

Denver •

Omaha •

St. Louis •

IND.

Indianapolis •

W. VA.

MD.

DEL.

Washington, D.C. ⊛

CALIFORNIA

Fresno •

U N I T E D   S T A T E S

KANSAS

MO.

KY.

Ohio

VA.

Virginia Beach •

Las Vegas •

Grand Canyon

Wichita •

Santa Fe •

Oklahoma City •

Tulsa •

Arkansas

Nashville •

TENN.

N.C.

Charlotte •

Los Angeles •

ARIZONA

Phoenix •

N. MEX.

OKLA.

ARK.

Memphis •

MISS.

ALA.

Atlanta •

GA.

S.C.

Charleston •

San Diego •

Tijuana •

Baja California

El Paso •

TEXAS

Mississippi

Birmingham •

Jackson •

Jacksonville •

Guadalupe I. (Mexico)

Gulf of California

Ciudad Juárez •

Fort Worth •

Dallas •

Austin •

LA.

FLA.

• Chihuahua

Rio Grande

Houston •

New Orleans •

Tampa •

PACIFIC OCEAN

San Antonio •

Sierra Madre Occidental

• Monterrey

Gulf of Mexico

Miami •

BAHAMAS

Nassau •

TROPIC OF CANCER

False Cape

Sierra Madre Oriental

M E X I C O

San Luis Potosí •

Straits of Florida

Havana ⊛

CUBA

Santo Domingo ⊛

San Juan ⊙

ST. KITTS & NEVIS

ANTIGUA & BARBUDA

Guadalajara •

Mexico City ⊛

Veracruz •

Yucatán Pen.

Cayman Is. (U.K.)

Port-au-Prince ⊛

HAITI

JAMAICA

DOMINICAN REPUBLIC

Puerto Rico (U.S.)

Guadeloupe (France)

DOMINICA

Martinique (France)

Revillagigedo Islands (Mexico)

BELIZE

Belmopan •

Kingston •

Caribbean Sea

ST. LUCIA

ST. VINCENT & THE GRENADINES

BARBADOS

GRENADA

Acapulco •

GUATEMALA

Guatemala City ⊛

San Salvador ⊛

EL SALVADOR

HONDURAS

Tegucigalpa ⊛

NICARAGUA

Managua ⊛

COSTA RICA

San José ⊛

Panama Canal

Panama City ⊛

PANAMA

TRINIDAD & TOBAGO

Port of Spain ⊛

Gulf of Panama

SOUTH AMERICA

Clipperton (France)

Cocos Island (Costa Rica)

Map Key

⊛ Country capital

⊙ Dependency capital

••• City or town

····· Boundary

0 ————— 600 miles

0 ————— 600 kilometers

Azimuthal Equidistant Projection

THE CONTINENT:
NORTH AMERICA

North America
LAND OF CONTRASTS

CLASSIC CARS. American cars from the 1950s line a street in Havana, Cuba. Cuban mechanics keep old cars running by creative use of nonstandard parts.

From the windswept tundra of Alaska, U.S.A., to the rain forest of Panama, the third largest continent stretches 5,500 miles (8,850 km), spanning natural environments that support wildlife from polar bears to jaguars. Over thousands of years, Native American groups spread across these varied landscapes. But this rich mosaic of cultures largely disappeared with the arrival of European fortune hunters and land seekers. While abundant resources and fast-changing technology have brought prosperity to Canada and the United States, other countries wrestle with the most basic needs. Promise and problems abound across this contrasting realm of 23 countries and 640 million people.

DRESSED TO CELEBRATE. This boy in Mexico's southern state of Chiapas wears traditional clothing, including a brightly colored string tie and a broad-brimmed sombrero with elaborate stitching around the edge.

⬇ **HOLD TIGHT.** These daring rafters run the roaring rapids of the Kicking Horse River in British Columbia, Canada's westernmost province. Rivers tumbling down the steep slopes of the Rocky Mountains provide many recreational opportunities.

◗ **STREET MUSIC.**
People from around the world visit New Orleans, Louisiana, U.S.A., to hear jazz musicians fill the air with their music.

◗ **NIGHT SONG.**
This coyote sends his mournful howl into the dark Montana night. Members of the dog family, coyotes originated in the southwestern United States but are now found throughout North America—even in urban areas.

THE CONTINENT:
NORTH AMERICA

more about
North America

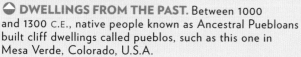

DWELLINGS FROM THE PAST. Between 1000 and 1300 C.E., native people known as Ancestral Puebloans built cliff dwellings called pueblos, such as this one in Mesa Verde, Colorado, U.S.A.

HIGH FLIER. A young Kutchin boy sails off a snowbank on snowshoes in Canada's Yukon. The Kutchin, an Athabascan tribe, live in the forested lands of eastern Alaska and western Canada. The name Kutchin means "people."

MAYA TREASURE. The Pyramid of the Magician marks the ruins of Uxmal on the Yucatan Peninsula. At least five million people of Maya descent still live in southern Mexico and Central America.

FROZEN SUMMER. Because Greenland lies so far north, even summers there are cold. Here, local people navigate their boat among icebergs in waters off the village of Augpilagtoq.

SWIMMING FREE. A variety of fish swim among colorful corals in the clear blue waters of the Caribbean Sea. Tropical waters are the habitat for many species of fish.

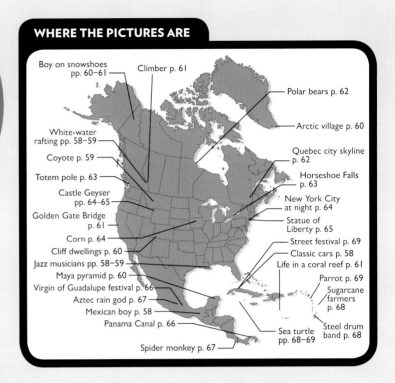

WHERE THE PICTURES ARE

Boy on snowshoes pp. 60–61
Climber p. 61
Polar bears p. 62
Arctic village p. 60
White-water rafting pp. 58–59
Quebec city skyline p. 62
Coyote p. 59
Horseshoe Falls p. 63
Totem pole p. 63
New York City at night p. 64
Castle Geyser pp. 64–65
Statue of Liberty p. 65
Golden Gate Bridge p. 61
Corn p. 64
Street festival p. 69
Cliff dwellings p. 60
Classic cars p. 58
Jazz musicians pp. 58–59
Life in a coral reef p. 61
Maya pyramid p. 60
Parrot p. 69
Virgin of Guadalupe festival p. 66
Sugarcane farmers p. 68
Aztec rain god p. 67
Mexican boy p. 58
Panama Canal p. 66
Sea turtle pp. 68–69
Steel drum band p. 68
Spider monkey p. 67

DON'T LOOK DOWN. Clinging to a sheer rock face, a young woman demonstrates great skill as she scales a steep cliff in Banff National Park in Alberta, Canada. Covering more than 2,500 square miles (6,475 sq km) in the Canadian Rockies, Banff is a major tourist attraction.

WESTERN GATEWAY. The Golden Gate Bridge marks the entrance to San Francisco Bay, U.S.A. Beyond the bridge, captured above in the warm glow of twilight, is the California port city that shares a name with the bay.

THE BASICS

STATS

Area
3,855,081 sq mi
(9,984,670 sq km)

Population
35,624,000

Predominant languages
English, French (both official)

Predominant religion
Christianity

GDP per capita
$46,400

Life expectancy
82 years

GEO WHIZ

Nunavut, Canada's newest territory, has issued license plates shaped like a polar bear for cars, motorcycles, and snowmobiles.

Canada's government is a constitutional monarchy. Britain's Queen Elizabeth II is its head of state.

Canada's Bay of Fundy, located between the eastern provinces of New Brunswick and Nova Scotia, has the highest tides in the world, with a tidal range reaching up to 53 feet (16 m).

Geologists believe the impact of a meteorite may have created Quebec's Réservoir Manicouagan more than 200 million years ago.

Canada

Topped only by Russia in area, Canada has just 36 million people. That's less than the population of the U.S. state of California. Ancient rocks yield abundant minerals. Lakes and rivers in Quebec are tapped for hydropower, and wheat farming and cattle ranching thrive across the western Prairie Provinces. Vast forests attract loggers, and mountain slopes provide a playground for nature lovers. Enormous deposits of oil sands lie waiting for technology to find a cheap way to convert them to hundreds of billions of barrels of oil. Most Canadians live within a hundred miles (161 km) of the U.S. border. Here, too, are its leading cities: Asia-focused Vancouver, ethnically diverse Toronto, national capital Ottawa, and French-speaking Montreal.

◖ **SILENT WATCHERS.** Polar bears, North America's largest land carnivores, are adapted to the extreme Arctic environment around Cape Churchill in northern Manitoba. An estimated 15,000 to 20,000 polar bears live in Canada.

LONGEST COASTLINE

Canada	151,023 miles (243,042 km)
Indonesia	33,998 miles (54,716 km)
Russia	23,397 miles (37,653 km)
Philippines	22,549 miles (36,289 km)
Japan	18,486 miles (29,751 km)
Australia	16,006 miles (25,760 km)
Norway	15,626 miles (25,148 km)
United States	12,380 miles (19,924 km)
New Zealand	9,404 miles (15,134 km)
China	9,010 miles (14,500 km)

Canada has the longest coastline in the world, and at more than 150,000 miles (243,000 km) it far surpasses the length of coastline of any other country.

◖ **FRENCH ENCLAVE.** Château Frontenac sparkles in Quebec City's nighttime skyline. Settled by the French in the early 1600s, the province of Quebec has maintained close ties to Europe and to its French heritage.

Map labels

Tuktoyaktuk
Inuvik
ALASKA (U.S.)
MACKENZIE MOUNTAINS
Yukon
YUKON
Mt. Logan 19,551 ft 5,959 m
St. Elias Mts.
Haines Junction
SELWYN MTS.
Whitehorse
PACIFIC OCEAN
ROCKY MOUNTAINS
Dawson Creek
Prince Rupert
HAIDA GWAII
BRITISH
Prince George
Grande Prairie
COLUMBIA
Campbell River
Fraser
BANFF NAT. PARK
Columbia
Vancouver Island
Kamloops
Nanaimo
Kelowna
Victoria
Vancouver
C
1   2

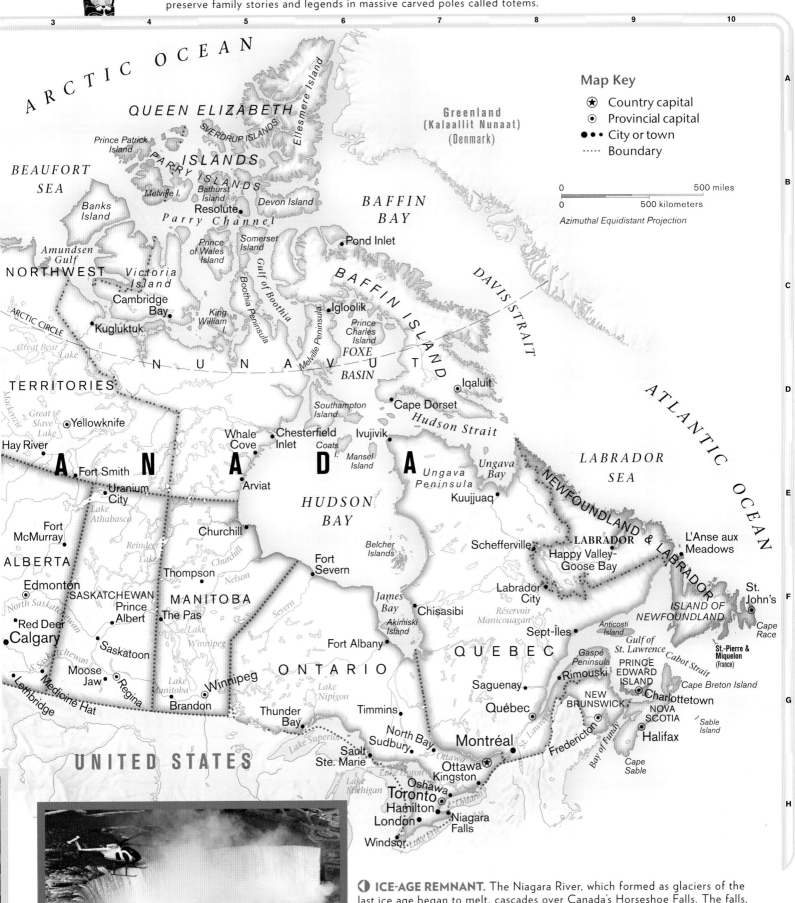

KNOWING WHO WE ARE. Native people of the Pacific Northwest preserve family stories and legends in massive carved poles called totems.

Map Key
★ Country capital
⊙ Provincial capital
•••• City or town
····· Boundary

ARCTIC OCEAN

QUEEN ELIZABETH
ISLANDS
SVERDRUP ISLANDS
Ellesmere Island
Prince Patrick Island
PARRY ISLANDS
Melville I.
Bathurst Island
Devon Island
Greenland
(Kalaallit Nunaat)
(Denmark)

BEAUFORT SEA
Banks Island
Resolute
Parry Channel
BAFFIN BAY

Amundsen Gulf
Prince of Wales Island
Somerset Island
Pond Inlet
DAVIS STRAIT

NORTHWEST
Victoria Island
Cambridge Bay
King William I.
Boothia Peninsula
Gulf of Boothia
Igloolik
BAFFIN ISLAND
ATLANTIC OCEAN

ARCTIC CIRCLE
Kugluktuk
Melville Peninsula
Prince Charles Island
FOXE BASIN

Great Bear Lake
NUNAVUT
Iqaluit

TERRITORIES
Cape Dorset
Hudson Strait

Mackenzie
Great Slave Lake
Yellowknife
Southampton Island
Ivujivik
Ungava Bay

Hay River
Whale Cove
Chesterfield Inlet
Coats I.
Mansel Island
Ungava Peninsula
Kuujjuaq
LABRADOR SEA

C A N A D A
Fort Smith
Uranium City
Arviat
HUDSON BAY
Belcher Islands
Schefferville
L'Anse aux Meadows

Fort McMurray
Lake Athabasca
Churchill
LABRADOR
Happy Valley-Goose Bay

ALBERTA
Reindeer Lake
Thompson
Churchill
Nelson
Fort Severn
Labrador City
St. John's

Edmonton
SASKATCHEWAN
Prince Albert
The Pas
James Bay
Réservoir Manicouagan
ISLAND OF NEWFOUNDLAND
Cape Race

Red Deer
North Saskatchewan
MANITOBA
Lake Winnipeg
Severn
Akimiski Island
Chisasibi
Sept-Îles
Anticosti Island
NEWFOUNDLAND & LABRADOR

Calgary
Saskatoon
Fort Albany
QUEBEC
Gaspé Peninsula
Gulf of St. Lawrence
St.-Pierre & Miquelon (France)

Moose Jaw
Regina
Lake Manitoba
ONTARIO
Saguenay
Rimouski
PRINCE EDWARD ISLAND
Cape Breton Island

Medicine Hat
Winnipeg
Lake Nipigon
Québec
NEW BRUNSWICK
Charlottetown
NOVA SCOTIA
Sable Island

Lethbridge
Brandon
Thunder Bay
Timmins
St. Lawrence
Fredericton
Halifax

UNITED STATES
Lake Superior
Sudbury
North Bay
Montréal
Bay of Fundy
Cape Sable

Sault Ste. Marie
Lake Huron
Ottawa
Kingston
Lake Michigan
Oshawa
Toronto
Hamilton
London
Lake Ontario
Niagara Falls
Lake Erie
Windsor

0   500 miles
0   500 kilometers
Azimuthal Equidistant Projection

ICE-AGE REMNANT. The Niagara River, which formed as glaciers of the last ice age began to melt, cascades over Canada's Horseshoe Falls. The falls, which stretch across the border between Canada and the United States, are a major tourist attraction.

United States

THE BASICS

STATS

Area
3,794,079 sq mi
(9,826,675 sq km)

Population
326,626,000

**Predominant
languages**
English, Spanish

**Predominant
religion**
Christianity

GDP per capita
$57,400

Life expectancy
80 years

GEO WHIZ

Florida is known as the lightning
capital of the United States.
Breezes from the Gulf of Mexico
and Atlantic Ocean collide over
the warm Florida peninsula to
create thunderstorms and the
lightning associated with them.

Hawai'i is politically part of
the United States but geograph-
ically part of Polynesia, a
cultural region of Oceania
(pages 154–155).

Lake Michigan is the only one
of the Great Lakes located
entirely within the United States.
Each of the other four lakes spans
the U.S.-Canada border.

From "sea to shining sea" the United States is blessed with a rich bounty of natural resources. Mineral treasures abound—oil, coal, iron, and gold—and its croplands are among the most productive in the world. Americans have used—and too often overused—this storehouse of raw materials to build an economic base unmatched by any other country. An array of high-tech businesses populate the Sunbelt of the South and West. By combining its natural riches and the creative ideas of its ethnically diverse population, this land of opportunity has become a leading global power.

STAPLE CROP.
Approximately 94 million acres
(38 million ha) are planted in
corn in the U.S. Most of the
crop is used as livestock feed.

WORLD CITY. The lights of Manhattan glitter around
New York City's Chrysler Building. The city's influence as
a financial and cultural center extends across the United
States and around the world.

LETTING OFF STEAM. Castle Geyser is just one of
many active geological features in Yellowstone National
Park in Wyoming. The park is part of a region that sits on
top of a major tectonic hot spot.

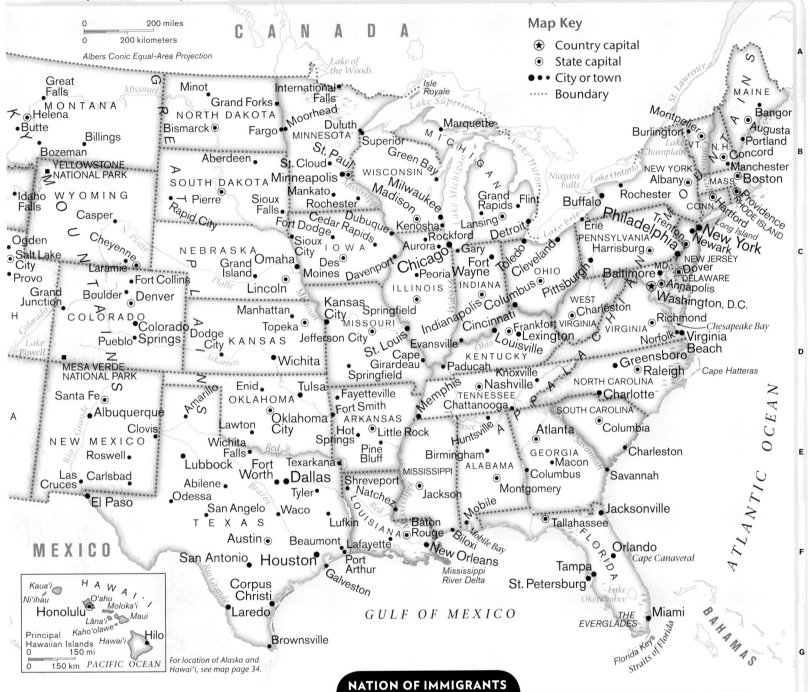

LADY LIBERTY. The Statue of Liberty, in New York City's harbor, has become a symbol of hope for millions of immigrants coming to the United States.

Map Key
- ★ Country capital
- ◉ State capital
- • • • City or town
- ⋯⋯ Boundary

0 ___ 200 miles
0 ___ 200 kilometers
Albers Conic Equal-Area Projection

CANADA

Lake of the Woods

Great Falls

MONTANA
Helena ◉
Butte
Billings
Bozeman
YELLOWSTONE NATIONAL PARK

Minot
Grand Forks
International Falls
Moorhead
Duluth
Isle Royale
Lake Superior
Marquette
MICHIGAN

MAINE
Bangor
Augusta ◉
Montpelier ◉
Portland
Burlington
VT. N.H. Concord ◉
Manchester
Boston ◉
MASS.

NORTH DAKOTA
Bismarck ◉
Fargo
MINNESOTA
St. Paul ◉
Superior
Green Bay
WISCONSIN
Milwaukee
Lake Michigan

Lake Huron
Lake Ontario
Niagara Falls
Lake Erie

NEW YORK
Albany ◉
Rochester
Buffalo
Erie

Providence
RHODE ISLAND
Hartford ◉
CONN.
Long Island
New York
Newark

SOUTH DAKOTA
Aberdeen
Pierre ◉
Rapid City

WYOMING
Idaho Falls
Casper

Sioux Falls
Mankato
Rochester
Madison ◉

Grand Rapids
Flint
Lansing ◉
Detroit

Cleveland
Toledo

PENNSYLVANIA
Harrisburg ◉
Philadelphia
Trenton ◉
NEW JERSEY

St. Cloud
Minneapolis
Cedar Rapids
Dubuque
Kenosha
Rockford

Chicago
Aurora
Gary
Fort Wayne

Pittsburgh
Baltimore
MD.
Dover ◉
DELAWARE
Annapolis ◉
Washington, D.C. ★

OGDEN
Salt Lake City ◉
Provo

Cheyenne ◉
Fort Collins
Boulder
Denver ◉

NEBRASKA
Grand Island
Omaha
Lincoln ◉
Des Moines ◉

IOWA
Davenport
Peoria
ILLINOIS
Springfield ◉

INDIANA
Indianapolis ◉
Columbus ◉
OHIO
Cincinnati

WEST VIRGINIA
Charleston ◉
Richmond ◉
VIRGINIA
Chesapeake Bay

Grand Junction
COLORADO
Colorado Springs
Pueblo

Manhattan
Topeka ◉
Dodge City
KANSAS

Kansas City
Springfield
Jefferson City ◉
MISSOURI
St. Louis

Frankfort ◉
Lexington
Louisville
KENTUCKY

Norfolk
Virginia Beach
Greensboro
Raleigh ◉
Cape Hatteras

MESA VERDE NATIONAL PARK

Santa Fe ◉
Albuquerque
Clovis

Wichita

Evansville
Cape Girardeau
Paducah

Knoxville
Nashville ◉
NORTH CAROLINA
Charlotte

NEW MEXICO
Roswell

Enid
Tulsa
OKLAHOMA
Lawton
Oklahoma City ◉

Fayetteville
Fort Smith
ARKANSAS
Hot Springs
Little Rock ◉
Pine Bluff

Memphis
TENNESSEE
Chattanooga

Huntsville

SOUTH CAROLINA
Columbia ◉
Charleston

Las Cruces
Carlsbad
El Paso

Wichita Falls
Lubbock
Abilene
Odessa

Fort Worth
Dallas
Texarkana
Tyler

Shreveport
Natchez
MISSISSIPPI
Jackson ◉

Birmingham
ALABAMA
Columbus
Montgomery ◉

GEORGIA
Atlanta ◉
Macon
Savannah

San Angelo
Waco
TEXAS
Austin ◉
San Antonio
Houston

Lufkin
LOUISIANA
Baton Rouge ◉
Beaumont
Port Arthur
Galveston
Lafayette
New Orleans

Biloxi
Mobile
Mobile Bay

Tallahassee ◉
FLORIDA
Jacksonville
Orlando
Cape Canaveral

Tampa
St. Petersburg

MEXICO

Corpus Christi
Laredo
Brownsville

GULF OF MEXICO

Mississippi River Delta

Lake Okeechobee
THE EVERGLADES
Miami

Florida Keys
Straits of Florida

BAHAMAS

ATLANTIC OCEAN

Hawaii Inset
Kaua'i
Ni'ihau
O'ahu
Honolulu
Moloka'i
Lāna'i
Kaho'olawe
Maui
Hawai'i
Hilo
HAWAI'I
Principal Hawaiian Islands
0 ___ 150 mi
0 ___ 150 km
PACIFIC OCEAN

For location of Alaska and Hawai'i, see map page 34.

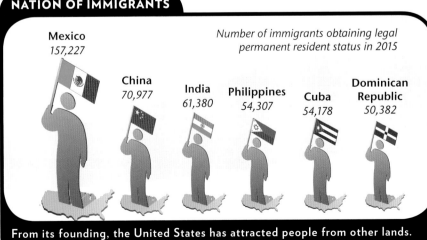

NATION OF IMMIGRANTS

Number of immigrants obtaining legal permanent resident status in 2015

Mexico 157,227
China 70,977
India 61,380
Philippines 54,307
Cuba 54,178
Dominican Republic 50,382

From its founding, the United States has attracted people from other lands. Today, most immigrants come from Latin America and Asia.

THE BASICS

STATS

Largest country
Mexico
758,445 sq mi
(1,964,375 sq km)

Smallest country
El Salvador
8,124 sq mi (21,041 sq km)

Most populous country
Mexico
124,575,000

Least populous country
Belize
360,000

Predominant languages
English, Spanish, Mayan,
indigenous languages

Predominant religion
Christianity

Highest GDP per capita
Panama
$23,000

Lowest GDP per capita
Honduras
$5,300

Highest life expectancy
Costa Rica, Panama
79 years

Lowest life expectancy
Belize
69 years

GEO WHIZ

Mexico takes its name from the word *Mexica*, another name for the Aztec, an indigenous people who ruled the land before it fell to the Spanish in 1521.

Coral colonies growing along much of the coast of Belize form the longest barrier reef in the Western Hemisphere.

Thumb-size vampire bats live throughout Central America.

◗ **CELEBRATION.**
Traditional costumes and musical instruments combine with Christian beliefs during the annual Virgin of Guadalupe festival, observed throughout Mexico. The festival marks the appearance of the Virgin Mary to a peasant in 1531.

Mexico & Central America

⬡ **VITAL LINK.** More than 17,000 oil tankers, cruise ships, and cargo vessels pass through the Panama Canal yearly, avoiding a long trip around South America.

Tijuana
Ensenada
BAJA CALIFORNIA
Mexicali
Gulf of California
Nogales
Hermosillo
Guaymas
Yaqui
Ciudad Obregón
Los Mochis
La Paz
False Cape

Mexico and most Central American countries share a backbone of mountains, a legacy of powerful Native American empires, and a largely Spanish colonial history. Deforestation has robbed the region of much of its rain forest. Mexico dwarfs its seven Central American neighbors in area, population, and natural resources. Its economy boasts a rich diversity of agricultural crops, highly productive oil fields, a growing manufacturing base, as well as strong trade with the United States and Canada. Overall, Central American countries rely on agricultural products such as bananas and coffee, though tourism is increasing. Modern-day Mexico and Central America struggle to fulfill the hopes of their people, some of whom search for better lives by migrating north to the United States.

◑ **MYTHS AND LEGENDS.** The powerful Aztec Empire dominated much of Mexico and Central America from 1427 to 1521.

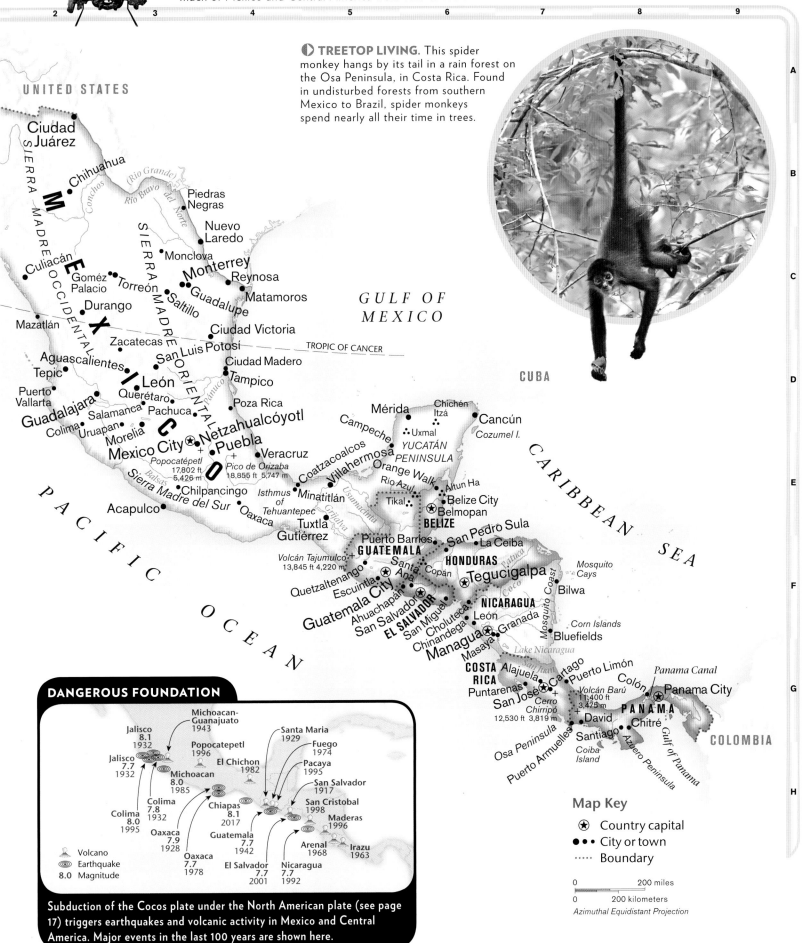

◑ **TREETOP LIVING.** This spider monkey hangs by its tail in a rain forest on the Osa Peninsula, in Costa Rica. Found in undisturbed forests from southern Mexico to Brazil, spider monkeys spend nearly all their time in trees.

UNITED STATES

Ciudad Juárez

SIERRA MADRE OCCIDENTAL

Chihuahua
(Rio Grande)
Conchos
Río Bravo del Norte

Piedras Negras

Nuevo Laredo

Culiacán
Monclova

Gomez Palacio
Torreón
Durango
Saltillo
Monterrey
Reynosa
Matamoros
Guadalupe

Mazatlán

Zacatecas
SIERRA MADRE ORIENTAL
Ciudad Victoria

Aguascalientes
San Luis Potosí

TROPIC OF CANCER

Tepic
León
Ciudad Madero
Tampico

Puerto Vallarta
Querétaro
Pachuca
Poza Rica

Guadalajara
Salamanca
Pánuco

Colima
Uruapan
Morelia
Netzahualcóyotl

MEXICO

Mexico City
Puebla
Veracruz

Popocatépetl
17,802 ft
5,426 m

Sierra Madre del Sur
Chilpancingo
Pico de Orizaba
18,855 ft 5,747 m
Coatzacoalcos

Balsas
Isthmus of Tehuantepec
Minatitlán
Villahermosa

Acapulco
Oaxaca
Tuxtla Gutiérrez

GULF OF MEXICO

CUBA

Mérida
Chichén Itzá
Cancún
Cozumel I.

Campeche
Uxmal
YUCATÁN PENINSULA

Orange Walk
Río Azul
Altun Ha

Usumacinta
Tikal
Belize City
Belmopan
BELIZE

Griljalva
Puerto Barrios
San Pedro Sula
La Ceiba

Volcán Tajumulco
13,845 ft 4,220 m
GUATEMALA
Santa Ana
Copán
HONDURAS

Patuca

Quetzaltenango
Tegucigalpa

Escuintla
Guatemala City
Ahuachapán
San Miguel
EL SALVADOR
San Salvador
Choluteca
León
NICARAGUA
Chinandega
Granada
Coco
Masaya
Managua
Lake Nicaragua

CARIBBEAN SEA

Mosquito Cays

Bilwa

Mosquito Coast

Corn Islands
Bluefields

San Juan
COSTA RICA
Alajuela
Cartago
Puerto Limón
Colón
Panama Canal

Puntarenas
San José
Volcán Barú
11,400 ft
3,475 m
David
PANAMA
Panama City

Cerro Chirripó
12,530 ft 3,819 m
Santiago
Chitré

Osa Peninsula
Puerto Armuelles
Coiba Island
Azuero Peninsula
Gulf of Panama

COLOMBIA

PACIFIC OCEAN

DANGEROUS FOUNDATION

Jalisco
8.1
1932

Michoacan-Guanajuato
1943

Santa Maria
1929

Jalisco
7.7
1932

Popocatepetl
1996

Fuego
1974

Colima
7.8
1932

Michoacan
8.0
1985

El Chichon
1982

Pacaya
1995

Colima
8.0
1995

Chiapas
8.1
2017

San Salvador
1917

Oaxaca
7.9
1928

Guatemala
7.7
1942

San Cristobal
1998

Maderas
1996

Oaxaca
7.7
1978

El Salvador
7.7
2001

Nicaragua
7.7
1992

Arenal
1968

Irazu
1963

⛰ Volcano
◎ Earthquake
8.0 Magnitude

Subduction of the Cocos plate under the North American plate (see page 17) triggers earthquakes and volcanic activity in Mexico and Central America. Major events in the last 100 years are shown here.

Map Key

⊛ Country capital
●●● City or town
····· Boundary

0 ____ 200 miles
0 ____ 200 kilometers
Azimuthal Equidistant Projection

THE CONTINENT:
NORTH AMERICA

West Indies & the Bahamas

◉ **RHYTHM OF THE TROPICS.** When traditional drums were banned in Trinidad in 1884, plantation workers looked for new instruments, including 55-gallon (208-L) oil drums, which were the origin of today's steel drums or "pans."

THE BASICS

STATS

Largest country
Cuba
42,803 sq mi (110,860 sq km)

Smallest country
St. Kitts & Nevis
101 sq mi (261 sq km)

Most populous country
Cuba
11,147,000

Least populous country
St. Kitts & Nevis
53,000

Predominant languages
Spanish, English, French, Creole

Predominant religion
Christianity

Highest GDP per capita
Trinidad & Tobago
$31,900

Lowest GDP per capita
Haiti
$1,800

Highest life expectancy
Cuba
79 years

Lowest life expectancy
Haiti
64 years

GEO WHIZ

Pico Duarte (10,417 ft/3,175 m), on Hispaniola, is the highest peak in the Caribbean.

Voodoo, which combines West African spiritualism and the worship of Roman Catholic saints, is common in Haiti. Related folk religions are found in other countries in this region.

This region of tropical islands stretches from the Bahamas, off the eastern coast of Florida, to Trinidad and Tobago, off the northern coast of South America. The Greater Antilles—Cuba, Jamaica, Hispaniola, and U.S. territory Puerto Rico—account for nearly 90 percent of the region's land area and most of its 42 million people. A necklace of smaller islands called the Lesser Antilles plus the Bahamas make up most of the rest of this region. Lush vegetation, warm waters, and scenic beaches attract tourists from across the globe. While these visitors bring much needed income, most people in this region remain poor.

◖ **WHITE GOLD.** Sugarcane is an important economic resource throughout the Caribbean. This woman carries freshly cut cane on her head in a field in Barbados.

FUN IN THE SUN

International tourist arrivals, 2014 data

Dominican Republic	Cuba	Jamaica	Bahamas	Aruba	U.S. Virgin Islands	Barbados	St. Maarten	Martinique	Haiti
5,141,377	3,001,958	2,080,181	1,421,860	1,072,082	730,367	519,598	499,920	489,561	465,174

These island countries are the region's most popular destinations for tourists seeking sandy beaches, blue waters, and warm breezes.

◀ **RARE BIRD.** The red-necked Amazon, or Jaco, parrot is found only on the island of Dominica, where it lives on flowers, seeds, and fruits.

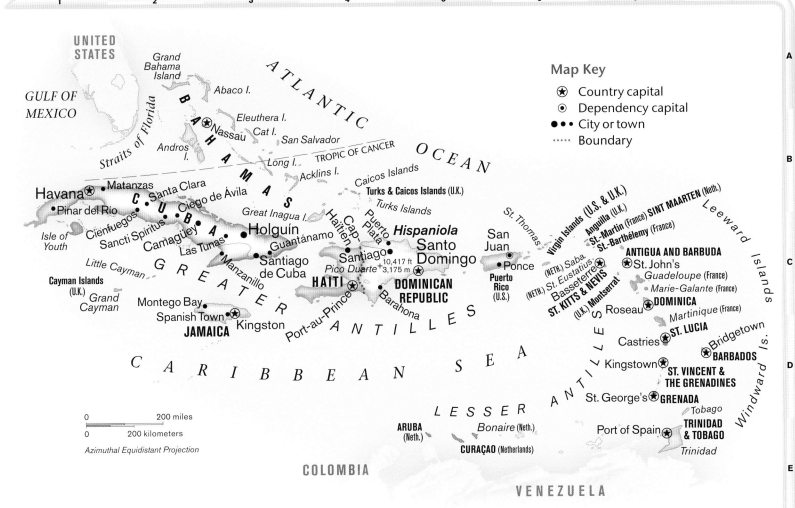

UNITED STATES

GULF OF MEXICO

Grand Bahama Island

Abaco I.

ATLANTIC OCEAN

Straits of Florida

B A H A M A S

★Nassau

Eleuthera I.
Cat I.
San Salvador

Andros I.

Long I. TROPIC OF CANCER

Acklins I.

Caicos Islands

Turks & Caicos Islands (U.K.)

Turks Islands

St. Thomas

Virgin Islands (U.S. & U.K.)

Anguilla (U.K.)

St-Martin (France) **SINT MAARTEN** (Neth.)
St-Barthélemy (France)

Leeward Islands

●Matanzas
Havana ★
●Pinar del Rio

C● ●Santa Clara

U ●Ciego de Ávila

San Juan

●Ponce

(NETH.) Saba.
(NETH.) St. Eustatius ★
Basseterre
ST. KITTS & NEVIS

(U.K.) Montserrat

ANTIGUA AND BARBUDA
★St. John's
Guadeloupe (France)
● *Marie-Galante* (France)

Cienfuegos
Isle of Youth

B A

Sancti Spíritus
Camagüey ● ●Holguín

Las Tunas

Manzanillo ●Santiago de Cuba

Guantánamo

Cap-Haïtien

Puerto Plata

Hispaniola
Santiago ● **Santo Domingo**

10,417 ft
Pico Duarte +3,175 m ●

Puerto Rico (U.S.)

★**DOMINICA**
Roseau ●
Martinique (France)

Little Cayman

G R E A T E R

HAITI ★

DOMINICAN REPUBLIC

Castries ★**ST. LUCIA**

Cayman Islands (U.K.) *Grand Cayman*

Montego Bay ●
Spanish Town ★
JAMAICA Kingston

Port-au-Prince
Barahona

A N T I L L E S

Kingstown ★
**ST. VINCENT &
THE GRENADINES**

★**Bridgetown**
BARBADOS

Windward Is.

C A R I B B E A N   S E A

St. George's ★**GRENADA**
Tobago

L E S S E R   A N T I L L E S

0   200 miles
0   200 kilometers

Azimuthal Equidistant Projection

ARUBA
(Neth.)

Bonaire (Neth.)

Port of Spain ● **TRINIDAD
& TOBAGO**

CURAÇAO (Netherlands)

Trinidad

COLOMBIA

VENEZUELA

Map Key
★ Country capital
◉ Dependency capital
●●● City or town
····· Boundary

A
B
C
D
E

◆ **WATER WORLD.** The clear waters of the Caribbean allow face-to-face interaction with sea life, such as this green sea turtle. Adult sea turtles can remain underwater for two hours without breathing.

◆ **CELEBRATION.** Stilt walkers in brightly colored costumes tower above this street in Old Havana, Cuba, during the annual celebration of Carnival. Introduced by Catholic colonizers from Spain, this festival occurs prior to the beginning of the religious season of Lent.

PHYSICAL

TOTAL AREA	LOWEST POINT	LARGEST LAKE
6,880,000 sq mi (17,819,000 sq km)	Laguna del Carbón, Argentina -344 ft (-105 m)	Lake Titicaca, Bolivia-Peru 3,200 sq mi (8,290 sq km)
HIGHEST POINT	**LONGEST RIVER**	
Cerro Aconcagua, Argentina 22,831 ft (6,959 m)	Amazon 4,150 mi (6,679 km)	

POLITICAL

POPULATION	LARGEST COUNTRY
418,538,000	Brazil 3,287,594 sq mi (8,514,877 sq km)
LARGEST METROPOLITAN AREA	**MOST DENSELY POPULATED COUNTRY**
São Paulo, Brazil Pop. 21,297,000	Ecuador 148.8 people per sq mi (57.5 per sq km)

SOUTH AMERICA

South America

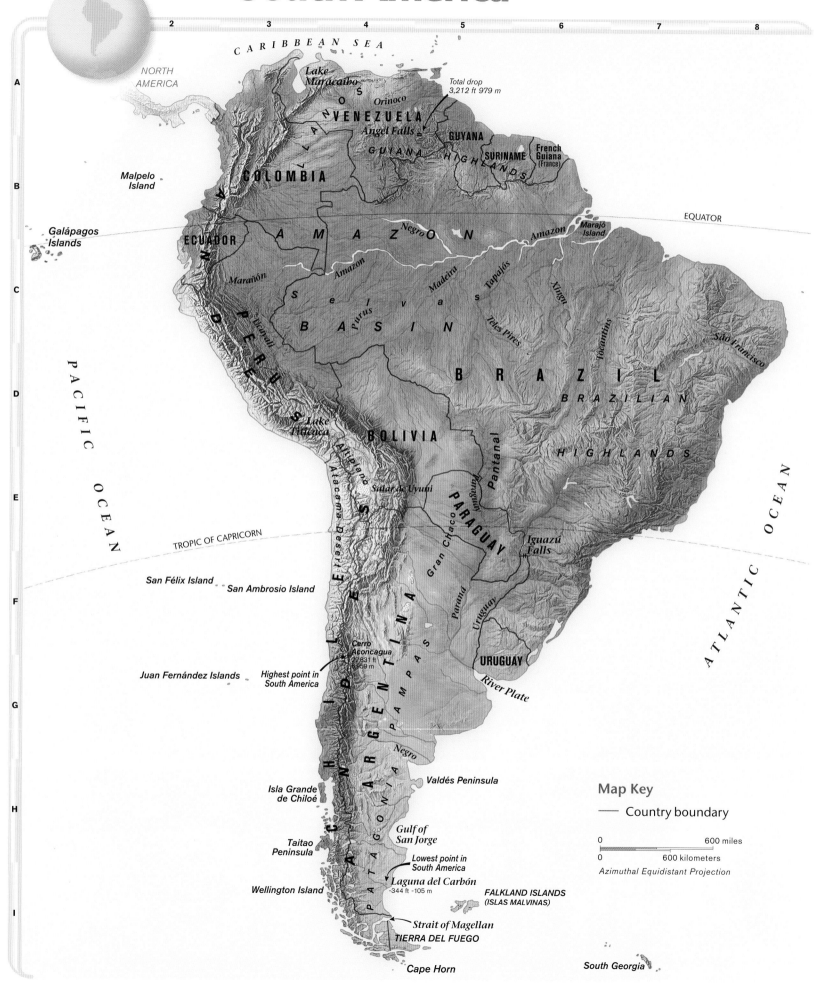

CARIBBEAN SEA

NORTH
AMERICA

A

Lake
Maracaibo

Orinoco

Total drop
3,212 ft 979 m

VENEZUELA

Angel Falls

GUYANA

GUIANA HIGHLANDS

SURINAME

French
Guiana
(France)

COLOMBIA

B

Malpelo
Island

A M A Z O N

Negro

Amazon

Marajó
Island

EQUATOR

Galápagos
Islands

ECUADOR

Marañón

Amazon

Madeira

Tapajós

Xingu

São Francisco

C

Ucayali

S e l v a s

B A S I N

Purus

Teles Pires

Tocantins

P E R U

BRAZIL

BRAZILIAN

D

PACIFIC

Lake
Titicaca

BOLIVIA

HIGHLANDS

Altiplano

Salar de Uyuni

Pantanal

E

OCEAN

Atacama Desert

Paraguay

PARAGUAY

TROPIC OF CAPRICORN

Gran Chaco

Iguazú
Falls

ATLANTIC

San Félix Island

San Ambrosio Island

Paraná

Uruguay

F

Juan Fernández Islands

A N D E S

Cerro Aconcagua
22,831 ft
6,959 m

Highest point in
South America

ARGENTINA

PAMPAS

URUGUAY

River Plate

OCEAN

G

Negro

Valdés Peninsula

Isla Grande
de Chiloé

Map Key

—— Country boundary

H

Taitao
Peninsula

Gulf of
San Jorge

PATAGONIA

Lowest point in
South America

Laguna del Carbón
-344 ft -105 m

0   600 miles

0   600 kilometers

Azimuthal Equidistant Projection

Wellington Island

FALKLAND ISLANDS
(ISLAS MALVINAS)

I

Strait of Magellan

TIERRA DEL FUEGO

Cape Horn

South Georgia

2   3   4   5   6   7   8

CARIBBEAN SEA

NORTH
AMERICA

Santa Marta
Barranquilla
Cartagena
Lake Maracaibo
Maracaibo
Barquisimeto
Caracas
Maracay
Ciudad Guayana
Cúcuta
Valencia
San Cristóbal
VENEZUELA
Georgetown
Paramaribo
Bucaramanga
Angel Falls
GUYANA
Cayenne
Medellín
SURINAME
French
Guiana
(France)
Manizales
Bogotá
GUIANA HIGHLANDS
Ibagué
COLOMBIA
Boa Vista
Amapá
Malpelo Island
(Colombia)
Cali
Boundary claimed
by Suriname

Esmeraldas
Pasto
EQUATOR

A   M   A   Z   O   N
Negro
Amazon
Marajó
Island
Belém

Galápagos
Islands
(Ecuador)
Quito
ECUADOR
Manaus
Santarém
São Luís
Parnaíba

Guayaquil
Cuenca
Iquitos
Amazon (Solimões)
Madeira
Marabá
Fortaleza

Piura
Marañón
S   e   l   v   a   s
Teresina

Chiclayo
B   A   S   I   N
Tapajós
Xingu
Natal
João Pessoa

Trujillo
Rio
Branco
Porto Velho
Campina Grande

Chimbote
P
Tocantins
Recife

Callao
E
Teles Pires
B   R   A   Z   I   L
Maceió

Lima
R
Machu Picchu
Aracaju

Ayacucho
U
Cusco
Trinidad
B   R   A   Z   I   L   I   A   N
Feira de Santana

Arequipa
S
L. Titicaca
Salvador
(Bahia)

La Paz
BOLIVIA
Brasília
Ilhéus

Arica
Oruro
Cochabamba
Santa Cruz
Goiânia
H   I   G   H   L   A   N   D   S
São Francisco

Altiplano
Sucre
Uberlândia
Governador Valadares

Iquique
Salar
de Uyuni
Campo
Grande
Uberaba

Tarija
São José do
Rio Preto
Belo Horizonte
Ribeirão Preto
Nova Iguaçu

PARAGUAY
Pantanal
Londrina
Campinas
Rio de Janeiro

TROPIC OF CAPRICORN
Antofagasta
Salta
Gran Chaco
São Paulo
Santos

Asunción
Iguazú Falls
Curitiba

San Félix Island
(Chile) *San Ambrosio Island*
San Miguel
de Tucumán
Resistencia
Corrientes
Passo
Fundo
Florianópolis

La Serena
Uruguaiana
Santa
Maria
Porto Alegre

Cerro
Aconcagua
22,831 ft
6,959 m
Córdoba
A
URUGUAY

Valparaíso
Santiago
Mendoza
R
Santa Fe
Rosario
Montevideo

Juan Fernández Islands
(Chile)
Talca
G
Buenos
Aires
River Plate

Concepción
E
La Plata

Temuco
N
Mar del Plata

Puerto Montt
T
Bahía Blanca

Isla Grande
de Chiloé
I
Viedma

Valdés Peninsula

N
Negro

Comodoro Rivadavia
Gulf of San Jorge

Taitao
Peninsula

Laguna del Carbón
-344 ft -105 m

Wellington I.
Stanley
Falkland Islands *(Islas Malvinas)*
(United Kingdom)

Strait of Magellan
Río Gallegos
Punta Arenas
TIERRA DEL FUEGO
Ushuaia

Cape Horn
South Georgia
(U.K.)

P   A   C   I   F   I   C   O   C   E   A   N

A   T   L   A   N   T   I   C   O   C   E   A   N

Map Key
✪ Country capital
◉ Dependency capital
● ● ● City or town
····· Boundary
····· Claimed boundary

0   600 miles
0   600 kilometers
Azimuthal Equidistant Projection

South America

A MIX OF OLD AND NEW

South America stretches from the warm waters of the Caribbean to the frigid ocean near Antarctica. Draining a third of the continent, the mighty Amazon carries more water than the world's next 10 biggest rivers combined. Its basin contains the planet's largest rain forest. The Andes tower along the continent's western edge from Colombia to southern Chile. The indigenous people who lived in the Andes were no match for the gold-seeking Spanish who arrived in 1532. The Spanish, along with the Portuguese, ruled most of the continent for almost 300 years. Centuries of ethnic blending have woven indigenous, European, African, and Asian heritage into South America's rich cultural fabric.

⬯ **SILENT STALKER.** The jaguar, an at-risk species, is the largest member of the cat family native to the Americas. These cats are most numerous in remote areas of Central and South America.

◖ **ROYAL CITY.** Built by an Inca ruler between 1460 and 1470, Machu Picchu reveals the Inca's skill as stone masons. Massive blocks of granite were carved so carefully that all seams fit tightly without the use of mortar.

🌐 **SOUTHERN METROPOLIS.** A 1,300-foot (396-m)-high block of granite called Sugar Loaf dominates the harbor of Brazil's second largest city, Rio de Janeiro. Rio was Brazil's capital until 1960 and remains the country's most popular tourist destination.

◑ **NATURAL HERITAGE.**
Extending 2.5 miles (4 km) along the border between Brazil and Argentina, Iguazú Falls, which means "great water" in the local Guaraní language, is clouded in mist as the water drops 296 feet (90 m) into the Iguazú River.

◑ **MOUNTAIN BUDDIES.**
An Aymara woman, with her llama, follows a traditional mountain lifestyle in the Andes of Peru.

more about
South America

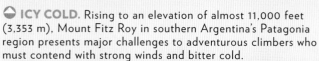

ICY COLD. Rising to an elevation of almost 11,000 feet (3,353 m), Mount Fitz Roy in southern Argentina's Patagonia region presents major challenges to adventurous climbers who must contend with strong winds and bitter cold.

QUIET VIGIL. A young Panare Indian sits beside a rushing stream in Venezuela, ready to catch a fish with his spear. Many groups of native people live in relative isolation from the modern world.

GLEAMING SANDS. The white sands of Rio de Janeiro's 2.5-mile (4-km)-long Copacabana and Leme Beaches are among the most famous in the world, attracting tourists year-round. The beaches, which are now lined with upscale hotels that overlook Guanabara Bay, were once the site of thriving fishing villages.

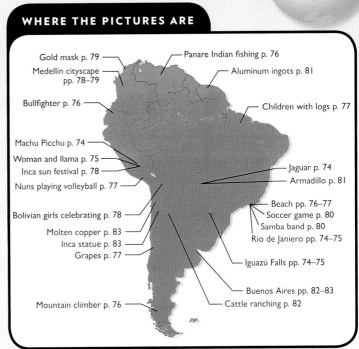

JUICY HARVEST. Grapes hang in heavy clusters ready for harvest near Santiago, Chile. A leading exporter of table grapes, Chile is the major supplier of these grapes for the United States and European Union during winter months.

WHERE THE PICTURES ARE

Gold mask p. 79
Medellín cityscape pp. 78–79
Panare Indian fishing p. 76
Aluminum ingots p. 81
Bullfighter p. 76
Children with logs p. 77
Machu Picchu p. 74
Woman and llama p. 75
Inca sun festival p. 78
Jaguar p. 74
Armadillo p. 81
Nuns playing volleyball p. 77
Bolivian girls celebrating p. 78
Beach pp. 76–77
Soccer game p. 80
Molten copper p. 83
Samba band p. 80
Inca statue p. 83
Rio de Janiero pp. 74–75
Grapes p. 77
Iguazú Falls pp. 74–75
Buenos Aires pp. 82–83
Mountain climber p. 76
Cattle ranching p. 82

BREAK TIME. Colonization of South America by Spain and Portugal in the 16th century brought a new religion—Roman Catholicism—to the region. Here, Catholic nuns in Arequipa, Peru, take a break from prayers to engage in a game of volleyball.

ENVIRONMENTAL TRAGEDY. These giants of the rain forest dwarf two children in the Amazon village of Paragominas in Brazil. Harvesting such trees provides income for villagers but poses a serious long-term threat to the environment.

EL TORRO! Introduced to South America during Spanish colonization, bullfighting is a popular sport and the focus of many festivals. Here, in Cayambe, Ecuador, a matador flashes his red cape before the bull.

THE CONTINENT:
SOUTH AMERICA

THE BASICS

STATS

Largest country
Peru 496,222 sq mi
(1,285,216 sq km)

Smallest country
Ecuador
109,483 sq mi (283,561 sq km)

Most populous country
Colombia 47,699,000

Least populous country
Bolivia 11,138,000

Predominant languages
Spanish, indigenous languages,
English

Predominant religion
Christianity

Highest GDP per capita
Colombia $14,100

Lowest GDP per capita
Bolivia $7,200

Highest life expectancy
Ecuador 77 years

Lowest life expectancy
Bolivia 69 years

GEO WHIZ

On the llanos of Venezuela, capybaras, the world's largest rodents, are hunted by anacondas. These snakes can weigh as much as 550 pounds (250 kg).

Colombia is the source of some of the world's finest emeralds, a gemstone sacred to the Inca. Mines once operated by the Inca still yield quality stones.

Marine iguanas live only on Ecuador's Galapagos Islands.

Northwestern South America

⊝ **HAIL THE SUN.** The ancient Inca celebrated the new year in June with the festival of Inti Raymi. The tradition continues today in Cusco, Peru, with the Festival of the Sun, when the celestial body is honored through music and dance.

Like a huge letter "C," five countries crest the continent's northwest—Venezuela, Colombia, Ecuador, Peru, and Bolivia. Each has a seacoast, except for landlocked Bolivia. Dominated by the volcano-studded Andes range, the region contains huge rain forests in the upper Amazon and Orinoco River basins. Colombia and Venezuela share an extensive tropical grassland called Los Llanos. Though the Spanish defeated the Inca in the 16th century, Quechua, their language, is still spoken in the altiplanos—high plateaus of the Andes. Despite rich oil reserves around Lake Maracaibo, many people remain poor. Venezuela has been plagued by demonstrations and civil unrest due to high prices and shortages of basic goods.

◐ **FOLKLORE CENTER.** Founded as a mining town, Oruro, Bolivia, is a UNESCO World Heritage site. Each November traditional Andean culture is celebrated with ancient dances, music, and rituals.

INDIGENOUS PEOPLE

Estimated populations, 2009–2010

Bolivia	55%
Peru	45%
Ecuador	25%
Guyana	9%
Chile	5%
Argentina	3%
Suriname	2%
Colombia	1%
Brazil	0%
Paraguay	0%
Uruguay	0%
Venezuela	0%

Amerindians are concentrated largely in Andean countries. More than half of Bolivia's population is made up of these indigenous people.

◐ **OLD MEETS NEW.** Against a backdrop of skyscrapers, a train speeds past the old government palace in Medellín, Colombia. The city is working hard to change its image as a center of illegal drug traffic by introducing economic and social changes.

ANCIENT ARTISANS. Early cultures of Colombia left no great stone monuments, but distinguished themselves with fine gold work, such as this mask.

Map Key

⭐ Country capital
●●● City or town
⋯⋯ Boundary

0 ——— 600 miles
0 ——— 600 kilometers

Azimuthal Equidistant Projection

For the Galápagos Islands (Ecuador), see maps on pages 72, 73.

CARIBBEAN SEA
Aruba (Neth.)
Bonaire (Netherlands)
Curaçao (Neth.)

Santa Marta
Barranquilla
Cartagena
Valledupar
Sincelejo
Montería

PANAMA

Gulf of Venezuela
Maracaibo
Cabimas
Ciudad Ojeda
Mérida
Lake Maracaibo
Barinas
Pico Bolívar 16,427 ft 5,007 m
Cúcuta
San Cristóbal

Puerto Cabello
Maracay
Los Teques
Caracas
Cumaná
Valencia
Barcelona
Barquisimeto
Maturín
Puerto La Cruz

TRINIDAD & TOBAGO

ATLANTIC OCEAN

Barrancabermeja
Bucaramanga

VENEZUELA

Ciudad Guayana

Medellín
Manizales
Pereira
Armenia
Tuluá
Ibagué
Sogamoso
Tunja
Bogotá
Villavicencio

Ciudad Bolívar

Orinoco

Angel Falls Total drop 3,212 ft 979 m

GUIANA HIGHLANDS

Mt. Roraima 8,986 ft 2,739 m

GUYANA

Buenaventura
Cali
Palmira
Neiva

COLOMBIA

San José del Guaviare

Orinoco

Popayán
Pasto
Florencia

Ibarra
Cayambe
Portoviejo
Quito
Manta

EQUATOR

Chimborazo 20,551 ft 6264 m
Riobamba

ECUADOR

Putumayo

AMAZON

Negro

Guayaquil
Milagro
Machala
Cuenca
Loja

Iquitos

Amazon (Solimões)

A N D E S

BASIN

Talara
Sullana
Piura

Marañón
Ucayali
Amazon

BRAZIL

Chiclayo
Cajamarca

Trujillo
Chimbote
Nevado Huascarán 22,205 ft 6,768 m

PERU

Pucallpa

Purus

PACIFIC OCEAN

Huánuco

Madre de Dios
Madeira

Callao
Lima
Huancayo

Machu Picchu
Cusco
Ica

Apurímac
Mamoré
Iténez

Puno
Lake Titicaca

Trinidad

Arequipa
La Paz (administrative capital)

BOLIVIA

Cochabamba
Oruro
Santa Cruz

Tacna
Nevado Sajama 21,463 ft 6,542 m

Altiplano

Sucre (constitutional capital)
Potosí

Salar de Uyuni

Tarija

Pantanal

CHILE

ARGENTINA

PARAGUAY

Northeastern South America

THE BASICS

STATS

Largest country
Brazil
3,287,594 sq mi
(8,514,877 sq km)

Smallest country
Suriname
63,251 sq mi (163,820 sq km)

Most populous country
Brazil 207,353,000

Least populous country
Suriname 592,000

Predominant languages
Portuguese, English, Dutch, Hindi

Predominant religions
Christianity, Hinduism, Islam

Highest GDP per capita
Brazil $15,200

Lowest GDP per capita
Guyana $7,900

Highest life expectancy
Brazil 74 years

Lowest life expectancy
Guyana 68 years

GEO WHIZ

Guyana's roughly 300 species of catfish are hunted for the international aquarium trade.

Brazil's Pantanal is the world's largest freshwater wetland.

Paramaribo, Suriname's capital, is a melting pot of Dutch, Hindu, Chinese, East Indian, and Javanese cultures. Dutch is the only official language.

GOAL! Maracanã Stadium in Rio de Janeiro is packed with enthusiastic soccer fans. Brazil has a long history of producing world-class soccer teams, winning the coveted World Cup five times as of 2017.

Brazil dominates the region as well as the continent in size and population. It is the world's fifth largest country in area, and it is home to half of South America's 419 million people. São Paulo and Rio de Janeiro are among the world's largest cities, and the country's vast agricultural lands make it a top global exporter of coffee, soybeans, beef, orange juice, and sugar. The vast Amazon rain forest, once a dense wilderness of unmatched biodiversity, is now threatened by farmers, loggers, and miners. Lands colonized by the British, Dutch, and French make up sparsely settled Guyana and Suriname as well as French Guiana, a French overseas department. Formerly known as the Guianas, these lands are populated by people of African, South Asian, and European heritage.

VAST WATERSHED

The United States and South America are shown at the same scale.

Amazon Basin

SOUTH AMERICA

The Amazon River basin includes 2.4 million square miles (6.1 million sq km). It would cover much of the contiguous, or lower 48, U.S. states.

NATIONAL RHYTHM. Samba, often called Brazil's national music, combines the music traditions of the country's populations—Amerindian, Portuguese, and African. Here a samba band practices on Rio de Janeiro's Ipanema Beach.

THE SIX-BANDED ARMADILLO, found throughout the dry grassland areas of the region, lives on plants and insects. Unlike others of its species, it remains active during the day.

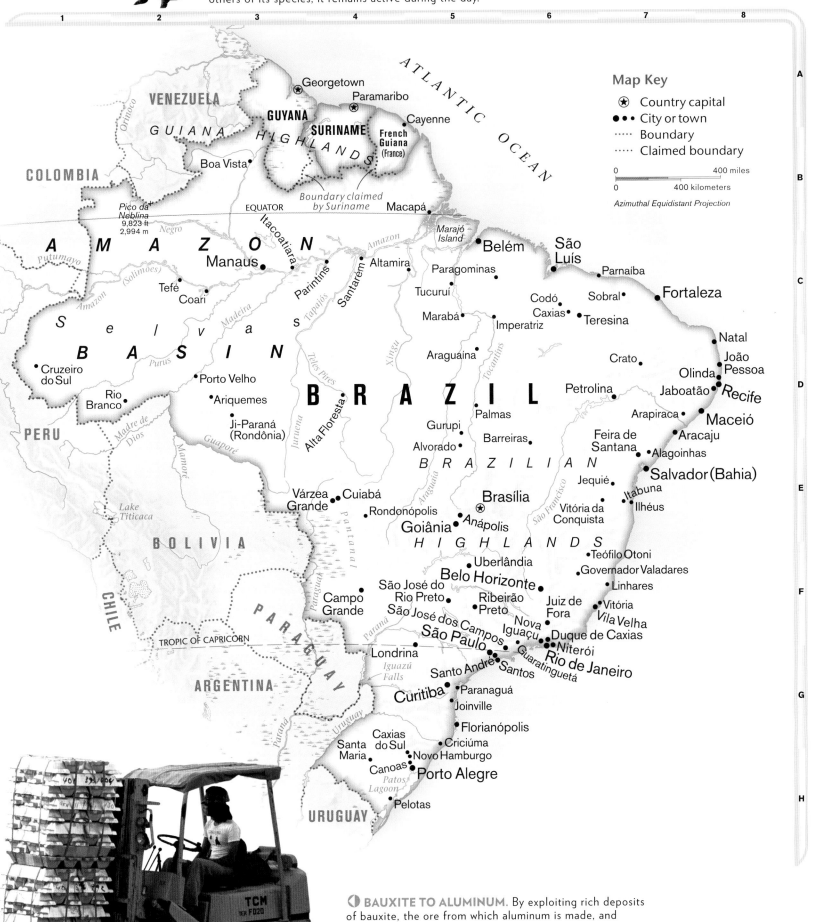

Map Key

⊛ Country capital
●●● City or town
····· Boundary
····· Claimed boundary

0 ————— 400 miles
0 ————— 400 kilometers
Azimuthal Equidistant Projection

ATLANTIC OCEAN

VENEZUELA
Georgetown
Paramaribo
GUYANA
SURINAME
French Guiana (France)
Cayenne
GUIANA HIGHLANDS
Boa Vista
COLOMBIA
Boundary claimed by Suriname
EQUATOR
Macapá
Pico da Neblina 9,823 ft 2,994 m
Negro
Marajó Island
Belém
São Luís
Parnaíba
AMAZON
Itacoatiara
Amazon
Altamira
Paragominas
Sobral
Fortaleza
Manaus
(Solimões)
Parintins
Santarém
Tucuruí
Codó
Caxias
Teresina
Amazon
Tefé
Coari
Tapajós
Marabá
Imperatriz
Natal
Selvas
Araguaína
Crato
João Pessoa
BASIN
Madeira
Xingu
Olinda
Jaboatão
Recife
Cruzeiro do Sul
Purus
Porto Velho
B R A Z I L
Petrolina
Arapiraca
Maceió
Rio Branco
Ariquemes
Palmas
Aracaju
PERU
Madre de Dios
Ji-Paraná (Rondônia)
Alta Floresta
Gurupi
Barreiras
Feira de Santana
Alagoinhas
Guaporé
Mamoré
Juruena
Teles Pires
Alvorado
B R A Z I L I A N
Jequié
Salvador (Bahia)
Lake Titicaca
Várzea Grande
Cuiabá
Itabuna
Brasília
Vitória da Conquista
Ilhéus
BOLIVIA
Rondonópolis
Anápolis
H I G H L A N D S
Goiânia
São Francisco
Teófilo Otoni
CHILE
Pantanal
Uberlândia
Governador Valadares
Belo Horizonte
Linhares
São José do Rio Preto
Ribeirão Preto
Juiz de Fora
Vitória
Campo Grande
São José dos Campos
Nova Iguaçu
Vila Velha
TROPIC OF CAPRICORN
São Paulo
Guaratinguetá
Duque de Caxias
Niterói
Rio de Janeiro
Londrina
Paraná
Santo André
Santos
Iguaçú Falls
Curitiba
Paranaguá
ARGENTINA
PARAGUAY
Joinville
Florianópolis
Uruguay
Criciúma
Caxias do Sul
Santa Maria
Novo Hamburgo
Canoas
Porto Alegre
Patos Lagoon
Pelotas
URUGUAY

BAUXITE TO ALUMINUM. By exploiting rich deposits of bauxite, the ore from which aluminum is made, and inexpensive hydropower, Suriname produces aluminum ingots, such as these headed for global markets.

THE CONTINENT:
SOUTH AMERICA

THE BASICS
STATS

Largest country
Argentina
1,073,512 sq mi
(2,780,400 sq km)

Smallest country
Uruguay
68,037 sq mi (176,215 sq km)

Most populous country
Argentina 44,293,000

Least populous country
Uruguay 3,360,000

Predominant languages
Spanish, Guaraní, English, Italian, German, French

Predominant religion
Christianity

Highest GDP per capita
Chile $24,100

Lowest GDP per capita
Paraguay $9,400

Highest life expectancy
Chile 79 years

Lowest life expectancy
Argentina, Paraguay, Uruguay 77 years

GEO WHIZ

The Itaipú Dam, which spans the Paraná River between Paraguay and Brazil, is currently the world's second largest operating hydro-electric power plant.

Guanacos, llama-like animals that live mainly in the Patagonia region of Argentina and Chile, keep enemies at bay by spitting at them.

Southern South America

Four countries make up this region, which is sometimes called the Southern Cone because of its shape. Long north-south distances in Chile and Argentina result in varied environments. Chile's Atacama Desert in the north contrasts with much cooler, moister lands in the country's south, where there are fjords and glaciers. Almost half of Chileans live in and around the country's booming capital, Santiago. Similarly, most neighboring Argentinians live in the central Pampas region, where wheat and cattle flourish on the fertile plains. Farther south lie the arid, windswept plateaus of Patagonia. Landlocked Paraguay is small in comparison, less urbanized, and one of South America's poorest countries. Uruguay is smaller still, but it possesses a strong agricultural economy, including cattle- and sheep-raising.

◗ **COWBOYS OF THE PAMPAS.** Cattle are herded by gauchos, the Argentine term for cowboys. The country's pampas, extensive grass-covered plains, support grain and cattle production on ranches called estancias.

◗ **GATEWAY CITY.** Skyscrapers in the modern skyline rise above Buenos Aires, capital of Argentina and second largest metropolitan area in South America. Situated on the Rio de la Plata, the city was established in 1536 by Spanish explorers. Its port is one of the busiest in South America.

WORLD BEEF EXPORTS

2016 data

Brazil	India	Australia	United States	New Zealand	Canada	Paraguay	Uruguay	European Union	Mexico
20%	20%	15%	12%	6%	5%	4%	4%	4%	3%

Almost 30 percent of world beef exports originate in South America. Uruguay is the leading consumer of beef, at more than 124 pounds (56 kg) per capita annually.

INCA TREASURE. Near the frozen summit of Argentina's Cerro Llullaillaco, archaeologists uncovered well-preserved Inca mummies and 20 clothed statues, such as this one.

DESERT RICHES. Molten copper is poured into molds at a refinery near Chuquicamata, a mine that has operated since 1910 in Chile's Atacama Desert. Chile produces 28 percent of the world's copper.

PERU

BOLIVIA

BRAZIL

Arica

Iquique

Puerto
Bahía Negra

Chuquicamata

La Esmeralda

Calama

TROPIC OF CAPRICORN

PARAGUAY

Antofagasta

San Salvador
de Jujuy

Cerro Llullaillaco
22,057 ft
6,723 m

Salta

Asunción

Ciudad
del Este

Itaipú Dam

Iguazú
Falls

Formosa

San Miguel
de Tucumán

Villarrica

Copiapó

Resistencia

Gran Chaco

Santiago
del Estero

Corrientes

Posadas

Catamarca

Paraná

La Rioja

La Serena

Concordia

Rivera

Patos
Lagoon

Coquimbo

San
Juan

Córdoba

Santa Fe

Salto

San
Nicolás

Uruguay

Cerro Aconcagua
22,831 ft 6,959 m

Río Cuarto

Paraná

Viña del Mar

Rosario

URUGUAY

Valparaíso

Mendoza

San Luis

Santiago

Godoy Cruz

Buenos Aires

Rancagua

San Justo

La Plata

River Plate

Montevideo

Curicó

Talca

ARGENTINA

Chillán

Concepción

Bahía
Blanca

Mar del Plata

Los Ángeles

Temuco

Neuquén

Colorado

Valdivia

Negro

Osorno

San Matías Gulf

Puerto Montt

Valdés
Peninsula

Isla Grande
de Chiloé

Comodoro Rivadavia

Gulf of San Jorge

PACIFIC
OCEAN

ATLANTIC OCEAN

PATAGONIA

Wellington
Island

Laguna
del Carbón
-344 ft -105 m

Río Gallegos

Strait of Magellan

Punta Arenas

TIERRA DEL
FUEGO

Ushuaia

Cape Horn

ANDES

ATACAMA DESERT

Map Key

⊛ Country capital
◉ Dependency capital
•• City or town
····· Boundary

0 ____ 200 miles
0 ____ 200 kilometers

Azimuthal Equidistant Projection

Falkland Islands
(Islas Malvinas)
(United Kingdom)

Stanley

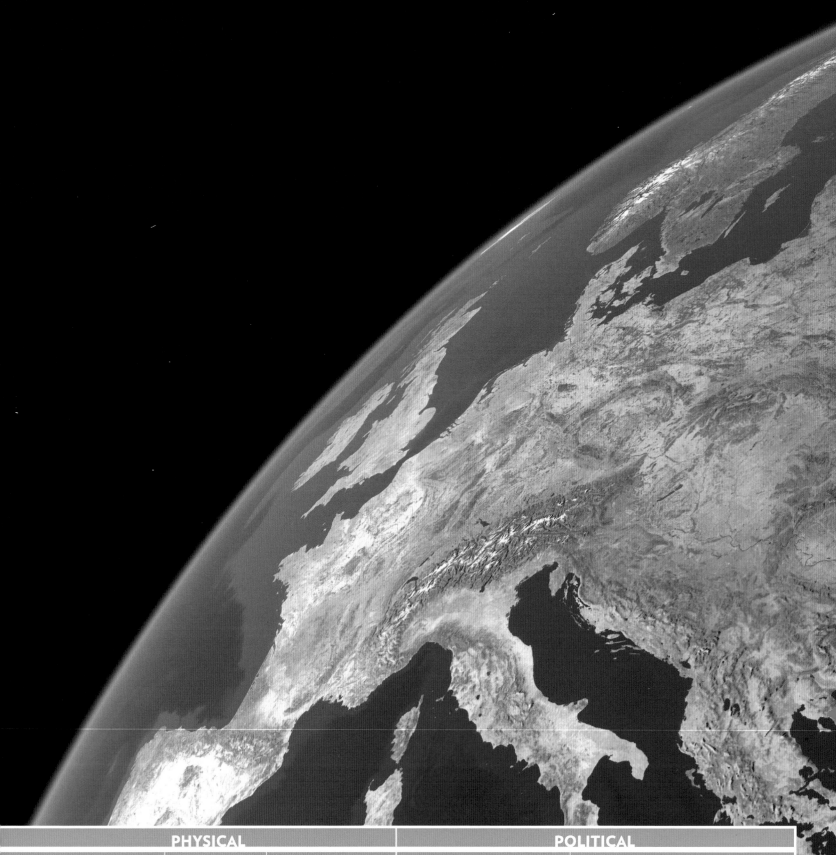

PHYSICAL

TOTAL AREA	LOWEST POINT	LARGEST LAKE ENTIRELY IN EUROPE
3,841,000 sq mi (9,947,000 sq km)	Caspian Sea -92 ft (-28 m)	Ladoga, Russia 6,835 sq mi (17,703 sq km)
HIGHEST POINT El'brus, Russia 18,510 ft (5,642 m)	**LONGEST RIVER** Volga, Russia 2,290 mi (3,685 km)	

POLITICAL

POPULATION	LARGEST COUNTRY ENTIRELY IN EUROPE
683,816,000	Ukraine 233,031 sq mi (603,550 sq km)
LARGEST METROPOLITAN AREA Moscow, Russia Pop. 12,260,000	**MOST DENSELY POPULATED COUNTRY** Monaco 30,645.0 people per sq mi (15,322.5 per sq km)

EUROPE

Europe

Map Key

—— Country boundary

- - - - Disputed or undefined boundary

400 miles
400 kilometers
Azimuthal Equidistant Projection

ARCTIC OCEAN

BARENTS SEA

NORWEGIAN SEA

ARCTIC CIRCLE

Jan Mayen

ICELAND
Vatnajökull

North Cape

Kola Peninsula

WHITE SEA

Pechora

Northern Dvina

URAL MOUNTAINS

RUSSIA

EUROPE-ASIA BOUNDARY

Ural

KAZAKHSTAN

Caspian Depression

Ural

Caspian

Lowest point in Europe
-92 ft -28 m

CASPIAN SEA

Volga

Volga

Kama

El'brus
18,510 ft
5,642 m
Highest point in Europe

Caucasus Mountains

AZERBAIJAN

ARMENIA

GEORGIA

EUROPE-ASIA BOUNDARY

TURKEY

CYPRUS

Rhodes

Crete

AEGEAN SEA

Bosporus

Dardanelles

BLACK SEA

SEA OF AZOV

Crimea

Don

Don

Dnieper

CENTRAL RUSSIAN UPLAND

EUROPEAN PLAIN

Oka

Volga

Lake Onega

Lake Ladoga

Lake Region

FINLAND

Gulf of Bothnia

Gulf of Finland

ESTONIA

LATVIA

LITHUANIA

Western Dvina

BELARUS

Dnieper

UKRAINE

MOLDOVA

Dniester

Carpathian Mountains

Danube

ROMANIA

Tisza

Prut

BULGARIA

Balkan Mountains

BALKAN PENINSULA

GREECE

Peloponnesus

IONIAN SEA

ALBANIA

MACEDONIA

KOSOVO

SERBIA

MONTENEGRO

BOSNIA & HERZEGOVINA

Sava

Drava

CROATIA

SLOVENIA

HUNGARY

Danube

SLOVAKIA

POLAND

Vistula

Oder

NORTHERN

GERMANY

Elbe

CZECHIA (CZECH REP.)

AUSTRIA

Po

SAN MARINO

ITALY

APENNINES

ALPS

Mont Blanc
15,781 ft
4,810 m

Danube

Rhine

SWITZ.

LIECH.

VATICAN CITY

Sicily ✦ Etna
10,995 ft
3,330 m

MALTA

TYRRHENIAN SEA

Sardinia

Corsica

Balearic Islands

ADRIATIC SEA

Riviera

MONACO

Rhône

Massif Central

FRANCE

Loire

Seine

LUX.

BELGIUM

NETHERLANDS

NORTH SEA

BALTIC SEA

SWEDEN

NORWAY

SCANDINAVIA

DENMARK

Jutland

Sjælland

Shetland Islands

Orkney Islands

Faroe Islands

Highlands

Outer Hebrides

Great Britain

The Pennines

UNITED KINGDOM

IRISH SEA

IRELAND

BRITISH ISLES

Ireland

English Channel

Brittany

Bay of Biscay

ATLANTIC OCEAN

Pyrenees

ANDORRA

Cantabrian Mountains

SPAIN

IBERIAN PENINSULA

PORTUGAL

Douro

Tagus

Ebro

Baetic Mountains

Strait of Gibraltar

AFRICA

MEDITERRANEAN SEA

SEA

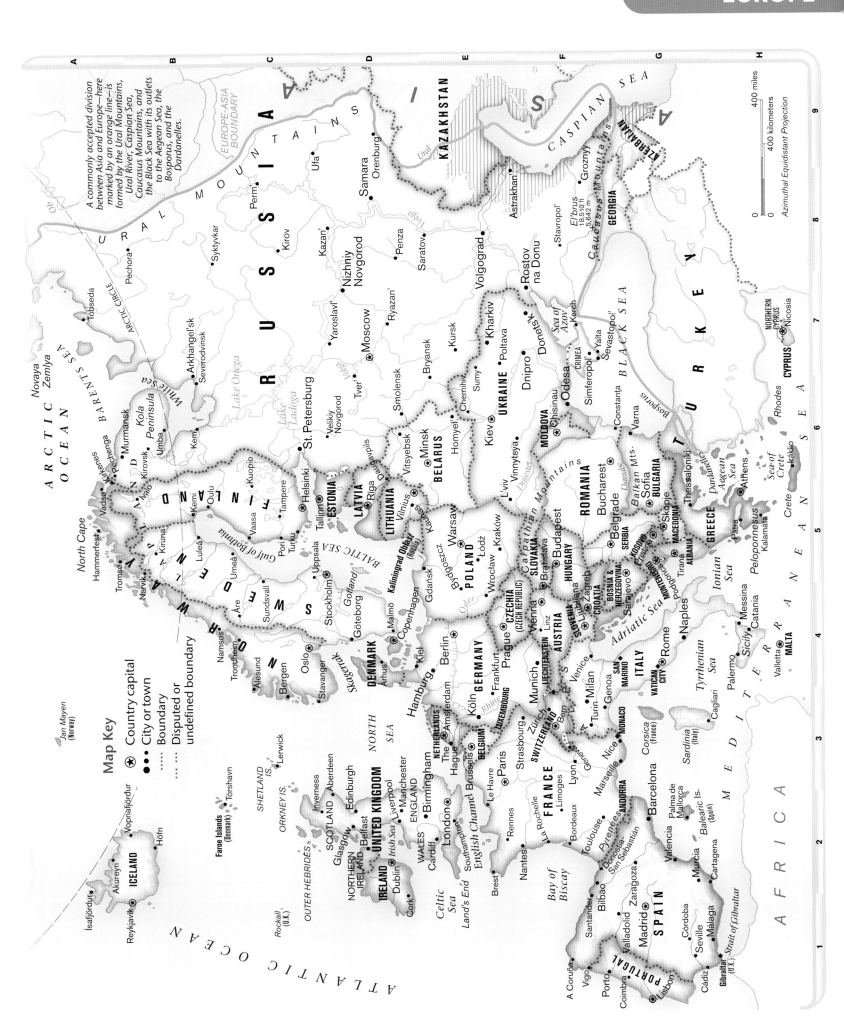

A commonly accepted division between Asia and Europe—here marked by an orange line—is formed by the Ural Mountains, Ural River, Caspian Sea, Caucasus Mountains, and the Black Sea with its outlets to the Aegean Sea, the Bosporus, and the Dardanelles.

Map Key
⊛ Country capital
● City or town
••• Boundary
••••• Disputed or undefined boundary

400 miles
400 kilometers
Azimuthal Equidistant Projection

THE CONTINENT:
EUROPE

Europe
SMALL SPACES, DIVERSE PLACES

WIND POWER.
A traditional windmill stands silent in Spain, calling to mind scenes from the classic Spanish novel *Don Quixote*. Modern windmills are used to generate electricity and to pump water.

A cluster of islands and peninsulas jutting west from Asia, Europe is bordered by two oceans and more than a dozen seas, which are linked to inland areas by canals and navigable rivers such as the Rhine and Danube. The fertile Northern European Plain sweeps west from the Urals. Rugged uplands form part of Europe's western coast, while the Alps shield Mediterranean lands from frigid northern winds. Here, first Greek and then Roman civilizations laid Europe's cultural foundation. Its colonial powers built wealth from vast empires, while its inventors and thinkers revolutionized world industry, economy, and politics. Today, the European Union seeks to achieve political and economic cooperation among member countries.

CHEERY GREETINGS. Laughing children clown for the camera in Klaipėda, Lithuania. The city is the northernmost ice-free port on the eastern coast of the Baltic Sea.

⬤ **WATCHFUL GUARDIAN.** A gargoyle stares out across the Paris skyline from a ledge of Notre Dame Cathedral. Gargoyles were first used in Gothic architecture as waterspouts but later were decorative additions meant to ward off evil spirits.

⬤ **ROCKY SENTINEL.** Towering 14,692 feet (4,478 m) in elevation, the Matterhorn, on the border between Switzerland and Italy, is one of Europe's most famous mountains. Frequent avalanches on its steep slopes pose challenges for mountain climbers.

⬤ **WINDOW ON THE PAST.** The brightly painted houses of Nyhavn (New Harbor), once the homes and warehouses of wealthy Copenhagen merchants, are now shops and restaurants and one of the most popular tourist attractions in Denmark's capital city.

THE CONTINENT:
EUROPE

more about
Europe

AGELESS TIME. This famous astronomical clock, built in 1410 in Prague, Czechia, has an astronomical dial on top of a calendar dial. Together, they keep track of time as well as the movement of the sun, moon, and stars.

CITY AT NIGHT. A winged victory statue atop the Metropolis Building, a classic example of early 20th-century architecture, appears to watch the evening traffic on the Gran Via in Madrid, Spain.

CLIFF DWELLERS. The town of Positano clings to the rocky hillside along Italy's Amalfi coast. In the mid-19th century, more than half the town's population emigrated, mainly to the United States. The economy today is based on tourism.

SEABIRDS OF THE NORTH. Colorful Atlantic puffins perch on a grass-covered cliff in Iceland, Europe's westernmost country. These unusual birds are skilled fishers but have difficulty becoming airborne and often crash as they attempt to land.

◑ **GLIMPSE OF THE PAST.** Rome's Colosseum is a silent reminder of a once powerful empire that stretched from the British Isles to Persia (now Iran). The concrete, stone, and brick structure could seat as many as 50,000 people.

WHERE THE PICTURES ARE

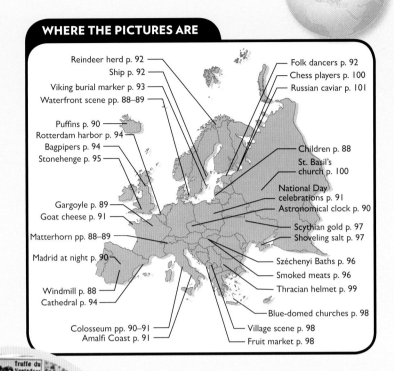

Reindeer herd p. 92
Ship p. 92
Viking burial marker p. 93
Waterfront scene pp. 88–89

Puffins p. 90
Rotterdam harbor p. 94
Bagpipers p. 94
Stonehenge p. 95

Gargoyle p. 89
Goat cheese p. 91

Matterhorn pp. 88–89

Madrid at night p. 90

Windmill p. 88
Cathedral p. 94

Colosseum pp. 90–91
Amalfi Coast p. 91

Folk dancers p. 92
Chess players p. 100
Russian caviar p. 101

Children p. 88
St. Basil's church p. 100
National Day celebrations p. 91
Astronomical clock p. 90
Scythian gold p. 97
Shoveling salt p. 97
Széchenyi Baths p. 96
Smoked meats p. 96
Thracian helmet p. 99
Blue-domed churches p. 98
Village scene p. 98
Fruit market p. 98

◐ **LUNCHTIME!** Varieties of creamy, fresh goat cheese are displayed in a market in the Brittany region of northern France.

◑ **NATIONAL PRIDE.** Young women carry banners in a parade marking Poland's National Day. Celebrated each year on May 3, it is the anniversary of the 1997 proclamation of the Polish Constitution.

THE BASICS

STATS

Largest country
Sweden
173,859 sq mi (450,295 sq km)

Smallest country
Denmark
16,639 sq mi (43,094 sq km)

Most populous country
Sweden 9,960,000

Least populous country
Iceland 340,000

Predominant languages
Swedish, Danish, Finnish,
Norwegian, Lithuanian, Latvian,
Estonian, Russian, Icelandic

Predominant religion
Christianity

Highest GDP per capita
Norway $69,200

Lowest GDP per capita
Latvia $25,700

Highest life expectancy
Iceland 83 years

Lowest life expectancy
Latvia, Lithuania 75 years

GEO WHIZ

Vatnajökull, in Iceland, is the largest glacier in Europe.

The national symbol of Denmark is a statue of Hans Christian Andersen's Little Mermaid, in Copenhagen's harbor.

During Iceland's Thorrablot winter festival, locals eat *hákarl*, a Viking dish made of rotten shark meat.

Northern Europe

This region lies in latitudes similar to Canada's Hudson Bay, but the warm North Atlantic Drift current moderates temperatures from volcanically active Iceland to Denmark and Norway. Sparsely populated but mostly urban, northern Europe is home to slightly more than 33 million people. The region's better farmlands lie in southern Sweden and Denmark's lowlands. Forested Finland shares a border with Russia. Estonia, Latvia, and Lithuania—the so-called Baltic States—are former republics of the Soviet Union.

◐ **NORDIC HERDERS.** The Sami, indigenous people of northern Europe, herd their reindeer across the borders of Norway, Sweden, Finland, and Russia. Some use snowmobiles instead of horses.

◐ **MIGHTY WARSHIP.** In 1628 the Swedish warship *Vasa* sank in the cold waters of Stockholm Harbor on its maiden voyage. After 333 years it was raised and reconstructed.

◐ **COLORFUL TRADITION.** Costumed folk dancers perform traditional dances at an open-air museum in Tallinn, Estonia's capital city.

NORTHERN FISHERIES

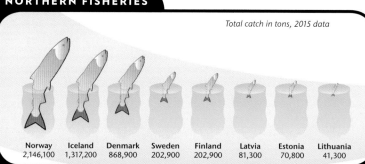

Total catch in tons, 2015 data

Norway	Iceland	Denmark	Sweden	Finland	Latvia	Estonia	Lithuania
2,146,100	1,317,200	868,900	202,900	202,900	81,300	70,800	41,300

Large schools of fish thrive in the cold waters off northern Europe. Norway harvests the most, bringing in more than two million tons of fish annually.

🌓 **MARKER FROM THE PAST.** This stone memorial in Sweden marks the burial site of Viking warriors. Although known for their fierce raids, Vikings were mainly farmers and traders.

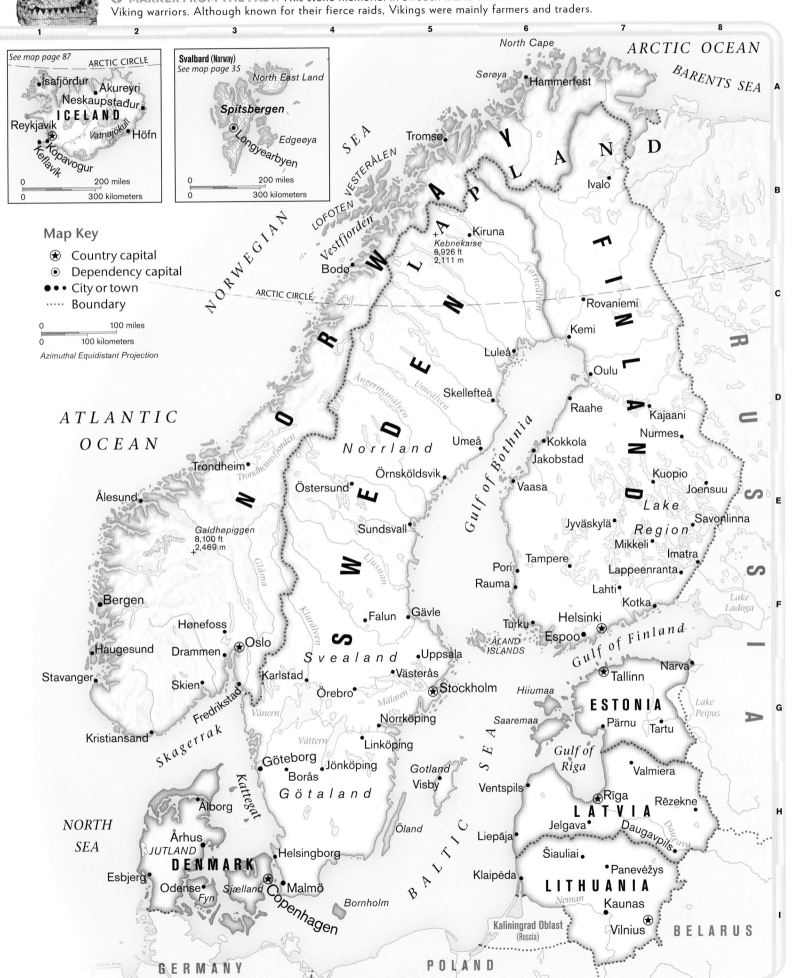

See map page 87

ARCTIC CIRCLE

Ísafjördur Akureyri

Neskaupstadur

ICELAND

Reykjavik   Vatnajökull   Höfn

Kópavogur

Keflavik

0 ___ 200 miles
0 ___ 300 kilometers

Svalbard (Norway)
See map page 35

North East Land

Spitsbergen

⊙ Longyearbyen   Edgeøya

0 ___ 200 miles
0 ___ 300 kilometers

Map Key

⭐ Country capital
⊙ Dependency capital
●●● City or town
········ Boundary

0 ___ 100 miles
0 ___ 100 kilometers

Azimuthal Equidistant Projection

North Cape

ARCTIC OCEAN

BARENTS SEA

Søroya   Hammerfest

Tromsø

Ivalo

NORTH EAST LAND

LOFOTEN   VESTERÅLEN

Vestfjorden

Bodø

Kebnekaise
6,926 ft
2,111 m

Kiruna

Rovaniemi

Kemi

Luleå

ARCTIC CIRCLE

NORWEGIAN SEA

NORDEN

Ångermanälven   Umeälven

Skellefteå

Raahe

Kajaani

Nurmes

Oulu

Kokkola

Jakobstad

Kuopio

Joensuu

Umeå

Vaasa

Lake Region

Savonlinna

ATLANTIC OCEAN

Norrland

Örnsköldsvik

Östersund

Jyväskylä

Mikkeli

Imatra

Trondheim   Trondheimsfjorden

Ålesund

Sundsvall

Galdhøpiggen
8,100 ft
2,469 m

Ljusnan

Pori   Tampere

Rauma

Lappeenranta

Lahti

Kotka

Bergen

Glåma

Falun   Gävle

Hønefoss

Turku   Helsinki

Espoo ⊛

Drammen

Oslo ⊛

S W E D E N

Svealand

Uppsala

ÅLAND ISLANDS

Stavanger

Skien

Karlstad

Örebro   Västerås

Narva

Stockholm ⊛

Tallinn ⊛

Haugesund

Vänern

Hiiumaa

Kristiansand

Fredrikstad

Norrköping

Saaremaa

ESTONIA

Lake Peipus

Pärnu

Tartu

Skagerrak

Vättern

Linköping

Götaland

Gotland

Visby

Gulf of Riga

Valmiera

Göteborg

Jönköping

Ventspils

Rīga ⊛

Rēzekne

Borås

Ålborg

Kattegat

Öland

LATVIA

NORTH SEA

Århus

JUTLAND

Helsingborg

Daugava

Jelgava

Liepāja

Daugavpils

DENMARK

Odense

Esbjerg

Fyn

Malmö

Sjælland

Šiauliai

Panevėžys

Klaipėda

LITHUANIA

Bornholm

Copenhagen ⊛

Neman

Kaunas

Kaliningrad Oblast
(Russia)

Vilnius ⊛

BELARUS

Gulf of Bothnia

F I N L A N D

L A P L A N D

N O R W A Y

R U S S I A

Torneälven

Lake Ladoga

Gulf of Finland

BALTIC SEA

Mälaren

GERMANY   **POLAND**

THE CONTINENT:
EUROPE

THE BASICS

STATS

Largest country
France
248,572 sq mi (643,801 sq km)

Smallest country
Vatican City
0.2 sq mi (0.4 sq km)

Most populous country
Germany 80,594,000

Least populous country
Vatican City 1,000

Predominant languages
German, French, English, Italian, Spanish, Dutch, Portuguese

Predominant religion
Christianity

Highest GDP per capita
Liechtenstein $139,100

Lowest GDP per capita
Portugal $28,900

Highest life expectancy
Monaco 90 years

Lowest life expectancy
Portugal 79 years

GEO WHIZ

Turiasaurus riodevensis is the largest dinosaur ever found in Europe. The fossil was discovered in northern Spain in 2006.

Mount Etna, on Sicily, is known as the home of Zeus, ruler of all Greek gods. It is also Europe's highest active volcano.

Antwerp, Belgium, is the center of the world's diamond industry.

Western Europe

Eighteen countries crowd this diverse region, which has enjoyed a central role in world affairs for centuries. The past half-century has seen bitter rivals become allies, with today's European Union growing out of the need to rebuild economic and political stability after World War II. Fertile soil in the many river valleys across the Northern European Plain and on Mediterranean hillsides gives rise to abundant harvests of a wide variety of crops. France leads in agricultural production and area, while Germany is the most populous country.

⬤ **MONUMENT TO FAITH.** The towering spires of La Sagrada Familia (The Holy Family) rise above Barcelona, Spain. This massive Roman Catholic church has been under construction for more than a century.

⬤ **HIGHLAND TUNE.** Bagpipers in formal dress parade through the streets of Edinburgh, Scotland, in the United Kingdom. Bagpipes may have arrived centuries ago with Roman invaders, but today they are most associated with the Scottish Highlands.

⬤ **MODERN SPAN.** Tall red arches support the Willem Bridge across the Maas River in Rotterdam, Netherlands. The Maas, which flows into the North Sea, is a major trade and transport artery, linking the Netherlands to the rest of Europe.

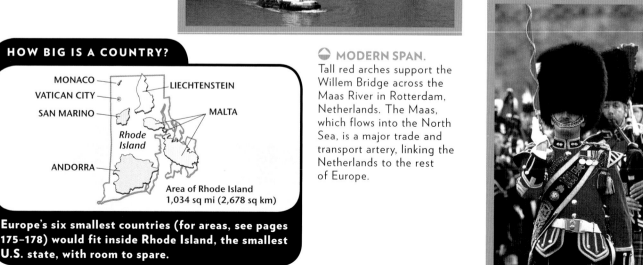

HOW BIG IS A COUNTRY?

MONACO
VATICAN CITY
SAN MARINO
Rhode Island
ANDORRA

LIECHTENSTEIN
MALTA

Area of Rhode Island
1,034 sq mi (2,678 sq km)

Europe's six smallest countries (for areas, see pages 175–178) would fit inside Rhode Island, the smallest U.S. state, with room to spare.

◖ **CELTIC POWER.** These rock pillars, part of Stonehenge in southern England, United Kingdom, were erected more than 5,000 years ago and may be associated with sun worship.

0 — 200 miles
0 — 200 kilometers
Azimuthal Equidistant Projection

Map Key

⊛ Country capital
⊙ Capital of a political division of the United Kingdom
••• City or town
····· Boundary

FINLAND
ESTONIA

NORWAY
SWEDEN

Shetland Islands
Orkney Islands

Rockall (United Kingdom)

ATLANTIC OCEAN

Outer Hebrides
Inner Hebrides

Inverness
SCOTLAND Aberdeen
Perth Dundee
Glasgow Edinburgh
Londonderry
NORTHERN IRELAND
Belfast
Isle of Man

NORTH SEA

DENMARK
BALTIC SEA
POLAND

IRELAND (ÉIRE)
IRISH SEA
Limerick Dublin
Waterford Liverpool Manchester
Cork Birmingham
WALES
Cardiff
Bristol
CELTIC SEA
Plymouth
Southampton
ENGLISH CHANNEL
Channel Islands (U.K.)
Brest

Newcastle
Sunderland
Leeds
KINGDOM
Kingston upon Hull
Sheffield
Nottingham
ENGLAND
London
Thames
Brugge
Strait of Dover
Le Havre
Caen
Rouen
Reims
Amiens
Lille

GREAT BRITAIN
UNITED

Kiel Rostock
Lübeck
Groningen Oldenburg Hamburg
NETHERLANDS Bremen Berlin
The Amsterdam Hannover
Hague Utrecht Bielefeld Magdeburg
Rotterdam Dortmund Leipzig
Antwerp Essen Erfurt Dresden
Köln GERMANY Chemnitz
BELGIUM Bonn Frankfurt CZECHIA (CZECH REPUBLIC)
Brussels
Charleroi
LUXEMBOURG
Luxembourg Mainz Mannheim Nürnberg
Metz Karlsruhe Stuttgart
Nancy Strasbourg Augsburg Linz Vienna
Frisian Islands
Elbe
Oder
Elbe
SLOVAKIA

Paris
Le Mans Orléans
Rennes
Angers Tours
Nantes
Loire
FRANCE
Limoges
Clermont-Ferrand
MASSIF CENTRAL
Bordeaux
Garonne

Seine
Marne
Seine
Besançon
Dijon
Lausanne
Geneva
Lyon
Vichy
Loire
St-Étienne
Mont Blanc 15,781 ft 4,810 m
Rhône

Mulhouse
Basel
Bern
SWITZERLAND
Zürich
LIECHTENSTEIN
Matterhorn 14,692 ft 4,478 m
Freiburg
Munich
Salzburg
AUSTRIA
Innsbruck
Graz
Bolzano
Trento
SLOVENIA
Trieste

HUNGARY

A L P S
Milan Verona Venice
Turin Padova
Genoa Modena Ferrara Bologna
Florence
Pisa
Po

CROATIA
BOSNIA & HERZEGOVINA
SERBIA

BAY OF BISCAY

Donostia-San Sebastián
A Coruña Gijón Santander Bilbao
Oviedo
Santiago de Compostela
Vigo León Vitoria-Gasteiz
Braga Burgos
Porto Valladolid
Bragança
Viseu Zaragoza
Douro Duero
Coimbra Salamanca
PORTUGAL Madrid
Tagus Toledo
Lisbon SPAIN
Guadiana
Setúbal Castelló de la Plana
Badajoz
SIERRA MORENA
Huelva Córdoba Jaén
Jerez Seville Granada
Cádiz Málaga
Algeciras Gibraltar (U.K.)
Strait of Gibraltar
Ceuta (Spain)
ALBORAN SEA
Melilla (Spain)
MOROCCO

Toulouse
Nîmes
Montpellier
Marseille
Perpignan
PYRENEES
ANDORRA
Andorra la Vella
Pamplona
Lleida
Sabadell
Martaró
Barcelona
Tarragona
Valencia
Albacete
Murcia
Alicante
Cartagena
Almería
Ebro
BALEARIC SEA
Palma de Mallorca
Minorca
Majorca
BALEARIC ISLANDS

Avignon
Aix-en-Provence
Nice
Toulon
MONACO
LIGURIAN SEA
CORSICA
Ajaccio
Bastia
Sassari
SARDINIA
Cagliari
TYRRHENIAN SEA

APENNINES
Perugia Ancona
SAN MARINO
VATICAN CITY Rome Pescara
Terni
Foggia Bari
Naples Salerno
Vesuvius 4,203 ft 1,281 m
Taranto
Gulf of Taranto
Lecce
Cosenza
IONIAN SEA
Messina Reggio di Calabria
Palermo Mt. Etna 10,925 ft 3,330 m Taormina
Marsala SICILY Catania
Syracuse

ITALY
ADRIATIC SEA
MONTENEGRO
ALBANIA

MEDITERRANEAN SEA

ALGERIA TUNISIA

MALTA Valletta

A B C D E F G H I

1 2 3 4 5 6 7 8

THE BASICS

STATS

Largest country
Ukraine
233,031 sq mi (603,550 sq km)

Smallest country
Moldova
13,070 sq mi (33,851 sq km)

Most populous country
Ukraine 44,034,000

Least populous country
Moldova 3,474,000

Predominant languages
Ukrainian, Russian, Polish, Hungarian, Czech, Belarusian, Slovak, Moldovan

Predominant religions
Christianity, Judaism, Islam

Highest GDP per capita
Czechia $33,200

Lowest GDP per capita
Moldova $5,300

Highest life expectancy
Czechia 79 years

Lowest life expectancy
Moldova 71 years

GEO WHIZ

The Wieliczka salt mine is known as the underground salt cathedral of Poland. It features historical, religious, and mythical figures, chambers, a chapel, and an exhibit about how salt is mined—all carved in salt!

Budapest became a united city in 1873 after Count István Széchenyi built a bridge connecting Buda on the west bank of the Danube River and Pest on the east bank.

The Pinsk Marshes, one of Europe's largest wetlands, are still contaminated by radioactive waste from a 1986 nuclear reactor explosion in Chernobyl, Ukraine.

Eastern Europe

⬤ **TIME TO EAT.** Smoked sausages and bacon, ready for purchase in the market, are an important part of the diet in the countries of eastern Europe.

Eastern Europe stretches from the Baltic Sea southeast to the Black Sea. Before 1991, Ukraine, Belarus, and Moldova were part of the Soviet Union, with the region's other countries largely under its control. Kaliningrad, a small region of Russia separated from the main country, lies just north of Poland. Much of the region has a continental climate similar to that of the U.S. Midwest. Nearly the size of Texas, Ukraine is the region's largest country in both population and area. Like Poland, it holds rich agricultural and industrial resources. Warsaw is the region's largest city, while historic Prague and Budapest are popular tourist stops. With the exceptions of Hungarians and Moldovans, most people in these lands are linked by branches of Slavic language and ethnicity.

◖ **HEALING WATERS.**
Budapest's Széchenyi Baths, built between 1909 and 1913, are famous for their medicinal thermal waters, discovered in 1879. A total of 15 baths, as well as saunas and steam rooms, are housed in buildings decorated with sculptures and mosaics by Hungary's leading artists.

BALTIC

Koszalin
Szczecin
Gorzów
Wielkopolski
Poznań
Zielona
Góra
P O
Kalisz
GERMANY
Legnica
Wrocław
Liberec
Wałbrzych
Opole
Prague
Pilsen
CZECHIA
(CZECH REPUBLIC)
Ostrava
České
Budějovice
Olomouc
Brno
Danube
S L
Bratislava
AUSTRIA
Győr
Székesfehérvár
SLOVENIA
H U
Pécs
Drava
Danube
CROATIA

ANCIENT GOLD. Scythians, who occupied the area from what is now Ukraine into Russia from the third century B.C.E. to the second century C.E., crafted this gold collar.

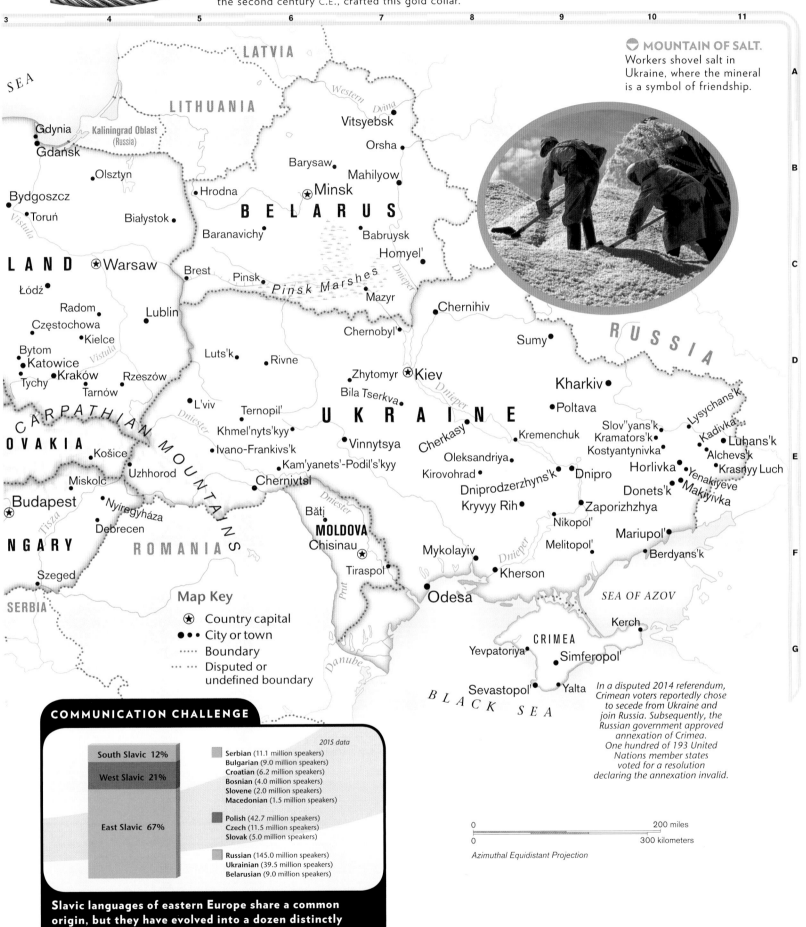

MOUNTAIN OF SALT. Workers shovel salt in Ukraine, where the mineral is a symbol of friendship.

LATVIA

SEA

LITHUANIA

Western Dvina

Vitsyebsk

Gdynia
Gdańsk
Kaliningrad Oblast
(Russia)

Orsha

Olsztyn

Barysaw
Mahilyow

Bydgoszcz

Hrodna
★ Minsk

Toruń

B E L A R U S

Vistula

Białystok

Baranavichy
Babruysk

L A N D
★ Warsaw

Brest
Pinsk
Pinsk Marshes
Mazyr

Homyel'

Łódź

Dnieper

Radom
Lublin

Częstochowa
Kielce

Chernihiv

Bytom
Katowice

Vistula

Chernobyl'

Tychy
Kraków
Rzeszów

Luts'k
Rivne

Sumy

R U S S I A

Tarnów

L'viv
Ternopil'

Zhytomyr ★ Kiev

Kharkiv

C A R P A T H I A N

Dniester

Khmel'nyts'kyy

Bila Tserkva

U K R A I N E

Poltava

O V A K I A
Košice

Ivano-Frankivs'k

Vinnytsya

Cherkasy

Kremenchuk

Slov"yans'k
Kramators'k
Lysychans'k
Kadivka

M O U N T A I N S

Uzhhorod

Kam'yanets'-Podil's'kyy

Oleksandriya

Kostyantynivka
Horlivka
Luhans'k
Alchevs'k

Miskolc
Chernivtsi

Kirovohrad

Dnipro

Yenakiyeve
Krasnyy Luch

★ Budapest

Kirovohrad

Dniprodzerzhyns'k

Donets'k
Makiyivka

Nyiregyháza

Dniester

Bălţi

Kryvyy Rih

Zaporizhzhya

N G A R Y
Debrecen

MOLDOVA
Chisinau ★

Nikopol'
Melitopol'

Mariupol'

R O M A N I A

Mykolayiv

Dnieper

Berdyans'k

Tisza

Tiraspol

Kherson

SEA OF AZOV

Szeged

Odesa

SERBIA

Prut

Kerch

Map Key

★ Country capital
●●● City or town
···· Boundary
···· Disputed or undefined boundary

CRIMEA

Yevpatoriya
Simferopol'

Danube

Sevastopol'
Yalta

B L A C K   S E A

In a disputed 2014 referendum, Crimean voters reportedly chose to secede from Ukraine and join Russia. Subsequently, the Russian government approved annexation of Crimea. One hundred of 193 United Nations member states voted for a resolution declaring the annexation invalid.

COMMUNICATION CHALLENGE

2015 data

South Slavic 12%	**Serbian** (11.1 million speakers)
	Bulgarian (9.0 million speakers)
West Slavic 21%	**Croatian** (6.2 million speakers)
	Bosnian (4.0 million speakers)
	Slovene (2.0 million speakers)
	Macedonian (1.5 million speakers)
East Slavic 67%	**Polish** (42.7 million speakers)
	Czech (11.5 million speakers)
	Slovak (5.0 million speakers)
	Russian (145.0 million speakers)
	Ukrainian (39.5 million speakers)
	Belarusian (9.0 million speakers)

Slavic languages of eastern Europe share a common origin, but they have evolved into a dozen distinctly different languages.

0 ————— 200 miles
0 ————— 300 kilometers

Azimuthal Equidistant Projection

EUROPE

THE BASICS
STATS

Largest country
Romania
92,043 sq mi (238,391 sq km)

Smallest country
Cyprus
3,572 sq mi (9,251 sq km)

Most populous country
Romania 21,530,000

Least populous country
Montenegro 643,000

Predominant languages
Romanian, Greek, Serbian, Croatian, Bulgarian, Albanian, Turkish, English

Predominant religions
Christianity, Islam

Highest GDP per capita
Cyprus $35,000

Lowest GDP per capita
Kosovo $9,600

Highest life expectancy
Greece 81 years

Lowest life expectancy
Bulgaria, Romania
75 years

GEO WHIZ

The Dalmatian, a popular breed of dog, is named for the region where it originated: Dalmatia, along the Adriatic coast of the Balkan Peninsula.

Dracula tours are popular in Romania, home of Vlad Dracula (Vlad the Impaler), who ruled the region between the Danube and the Transylvanian Alps in the 15th century.

The Balkans & Cyprus

The Balkans—named for a Bulgarian mountain range—make up a rugged land with a rough history. Ethnic and religious conflicts have long troubled the area. After 1991, seven new countries stretching from Slovenia to Macedonia emerged as a result of the breakup of Yugoslavia. Kosovo is the most recent. The

⬤ **TRADITIONAL LIFE.** Villagers walk down a cobbled street in Gusinje, a rural town in northeastern Montenegro. A place of rugged mountains, Montenegro is one of the countries that emerged from the former Yugoslavia.

Danube River winds east across the Balkans, separating Bulgaria from Romania, the region's largest country. Rimmed by four seas—the Black, Aegean, Ionian, and Adriatic— the Balkans, particularly Greece, have a long maritime history. In 2004, Cyprus, which has been uneasily divided for three decades into Turkish and Greek sections, joined the European Union along with Greece.

⬤ **VIOLENT PAST.**
Blue domes of Greek Orthodox churches on the island of Thira (Santorini) cling to cliffs above the remains of a volcano that erupted more than 3,000 years ago.

⬤ **COLORFUL BOUNTY.** An open-air fruit market overflows with grapes, plums, apples, and other produce that thrive in the moderate climate of the Mediterranean region. Warm, dry summers and cool, rainy winters provide ideal growing conditions for a variety of fruits, many of which had their origins in the region.

◑ **ANCIENT WARRIORS.** Soldiers and horsemen from Thrace, an ancient territory in present-day Bulgaria and Greece, wore battle masks, such as this one.

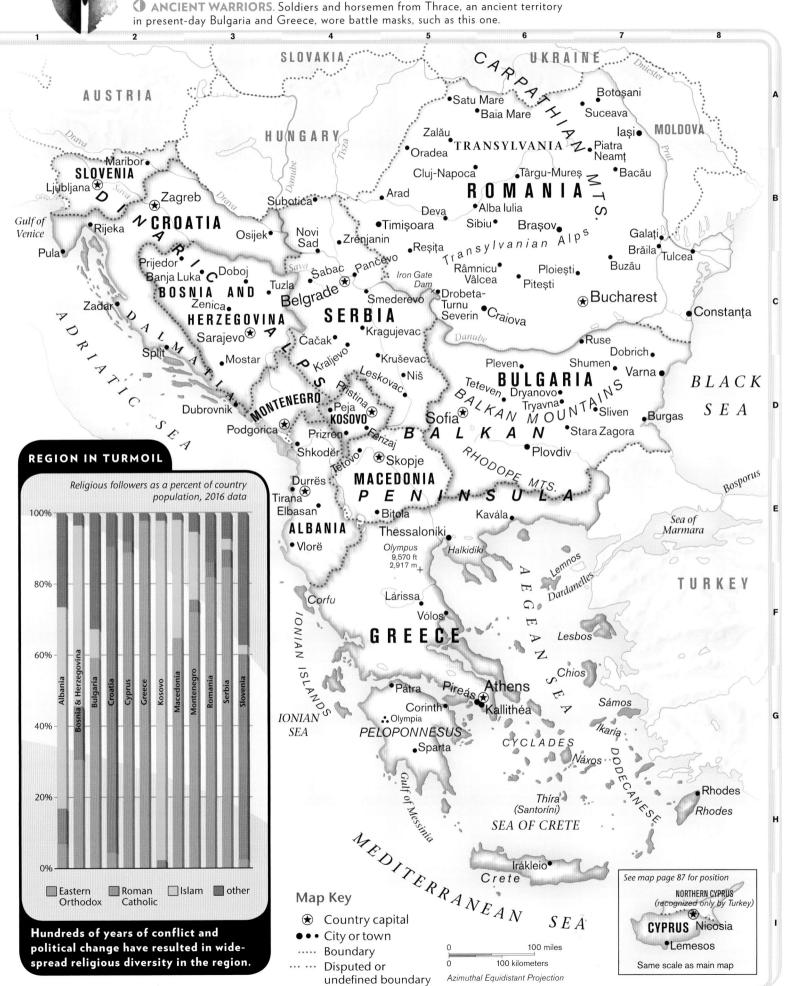

SLOVAKIA

UKRAINE

Dniester

AUSTRIA

Drava

HUNGARY

Satu Mare

Botoşani

Baia Mare

Suceava

Zalău

TRANSYLVANIA

Iaşi

MOLDOVA

Maribor

SLOVENIA

Oradea

Piatra Neamţ

Ljubljana

Sava

Zagreb

Subotica

Cluj-Napoca

Târgu-Mureş

Bacău

Prut

DINARIC

CROATIA

Drava

Arad

ROMANIA

Gulf of Venice

Rijeka

Osijek

Novi Sad

Deva

Alba Iulia

Timişoara

Sibiu

Braşov

Transylvanian Alps

Galaţi

Pula

Zrenjanin

Reşiţa

Râmnicu Vâlcea

Ploieşti

Brăila

Prijedor

Doboj

Sava

Šabac

Pancevo

Iron Gate Dam

Buzău

Tulcea

Banja Luka

Tuzla

Belgrade

Smederevo

Drobeta-Turnu Severin

Pitești

Bucharest

BOSNIA AND

Zenica

SERBIA

Craiova

Danube

Constanţa

Zadar

HERZEGOVINA

Sarajevo

Čačak

Kragujevac

Ruse

Dobrich

BLACK

Split

Mostar

Kraljevo

Kruševac

Niš

Pleven

Shumen

Varna

SEA

DALMATIA

Leskovac

BULGARIA

Teteven

Dryanovo

ALPS

Pristina

Stara Zagora

Tryavna

Sliven

Dubrovnik

MONTENEGRO

Peja

KOSOVO

Sofia

BALKAN MOUNTAINS

Burgas

ADRIATIC SEA

Podgorica

Prizren

Ferizaj

BALKAN

Plovdiv

Shkodër

Tetovo

Skopje

RHODOPE MTS.

Durrës

MACEDONIA

Bitola

PENINSULA

Bosporus

Tirana

Kavála

Elbasan

Thessaloníki

Sea of Marmara

ALBANIA

Olympus 9,570 ft 2,917 m

Halkidikí

Vlorë

Lemnos

TURKEY

Corfu

Lárissa

Dardanelles

IONIAN ISLANDS

Vólos

AEGEAN SEA

Lesbos

GREECE

Chios

IONIAN SEA

Pátra

Pireás

Athens

Sámos

Corinth

Kallithéa

Ikaría

Olympia

DODECANESE

PELOPONNESUS

CYCLADES

Sparta

Náxos

Rhodes

Rhodes

Thíra (Santoríni)

Gulf of Messinia

SEA OF CRETE

MEDITERRANEAN

Irákleio

Crete

SEA

REGION IN TURMOIL

Religious followers as a percent of country population, 2016 data

100%

80%

60%

40%

20%

0%

Albania | Bosnia & Herzegovina | Bulgaria | Croatia | Cyprus | Greece | Kosovo | Macedonia | Montenegro | Romania | Serbia | Slovenia

▨ Eastern Orthodox   ▨ Roman Catholic   ▨ Islam   ▨ other

Hundreds of years of conflict and political change have resulted in widespread religious diversity in the region.

Map Key

⊛ Country capital

●●● City or town

····· Boundary

····· Disputed or undefined boundary

0 ___ 100 miles
0 ___ 100 kilometers

Azimuthal Equidistant Projection

See map page 87 for position

NORTHERN CYPRUS
(recognized only by Turkey)

CYPRUS   ⊛ Nicosia

Lemesos

Same scale as main map

European Russia

🔵 **CHECKMATE!** Bystanders watch intently as one player prepares to make his move in this chess game in a park in St. Petersburg. In Russia, chess is a national pastime, popular with people from all walks of life.

THE BASICS

STATS*

Area
6,601,631 sq mi
(17,098,242 sq km)

Population
142,258,000

Predominant language
Russian (official)

Predominant religions
Christianity, Islam

GDP per capita
$26,500

Life expectancy
71 years

*Note: These figures are for all of Russia. For Asian Russia, see pages 110–111.

GEO WHIZ

St. Petersburg's many canals and hundreds of bridges have earned the city the nickname Venice of the North.

The fertile Northern European Plain, west of the Urals, is home to most of Russia's population and industry, whereas most of its mineral resources lie east of the Urals in the Asian portion of the country.

Arkhangel'sk, founded in 1584, is Russia's oldest Arctic port. The timber resources that are its chief export have been nicknamed "green gold."

The Kremlin is a walled fortress in Moscow, Russia's capital city, that houses the official residence of the country's president.

Home to four-fifths of Russia's 142 million people, European Russia contains most of the country's agriculture and industry. Here also is Moscow, its capital and Europe's largest city. Far to the north, Murmansk provides a year-round seaport—a gift of the warming currents of the North Atlantic Drift. This funnel-shaped portion of Russia, spanning 1,600 miles (2,575 km) from the Arctic to the Caucasus Mountains, is home to the Volga, Europe's longest river, and Mount El'brus, its highest peak. The Caucasus and Urals form a natural boundary between Europe and Asia. Although parts of Azerbaijan, Georgia, and Kazakhstan span the continental boundary, only Russia is counted as part of Europe.

🔵 **CATHEDRAL ON THE SQUARE.** The onion-shaped domes atop the towers of St. Basil's are a key landmark on Red Square in Moscow. Built between 1555 and 1561 to commemorate military campaigns led by Ivan the Terrible, the building is rich in Christian symbolism.

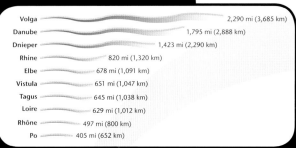

EUROPE'S GREAT RIVERS

River	Length
Volga	2,290 mi (3,685 km)
Danube	1,795 mi (2,888 km)
Dnieper	1,423 mi (2,290 km)
Rhine	820 mi (1,320 km)
Elbe	678 mi (1,091 km)
Vistula	651 mi (1,047 km)
Tagus	645 mi (1,038 km)
Loire	629 mi (1,012 km)
Rhône	497 mi (800 km)
Po	405 mi (652 km)

Europe's rivers, many linked by canals, form a transportation network that connects the continent's people and places to each other and the world beyond.

◖ **RUSSIAN DELICACY.** Caviar is the eggs (called roe) of sturgeon fish caught in the Caspian Sea. The eggs are aged in a salty brine, then packaged in cans (left) for export.

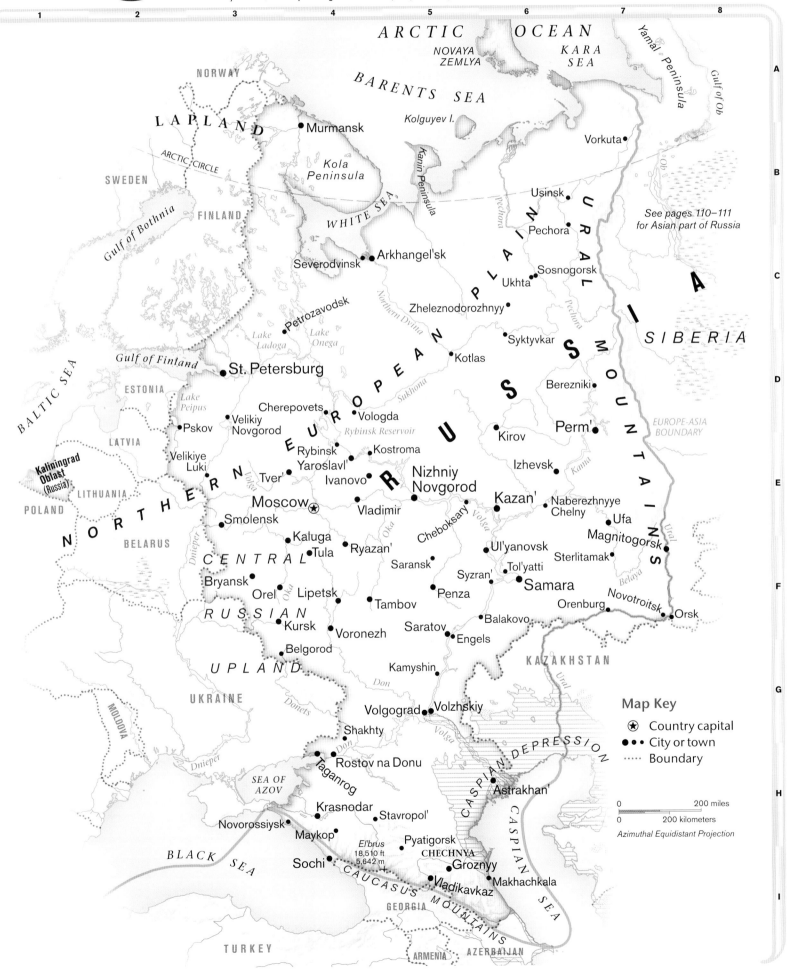

ARCTIC OCEAN

NORWAY

NOVAYA ZEMLYA

KARA SEA

Yamal Peninsula

Gulf of Ob

BARENTS SEA

LAPLAND

Kolguyev I.

Murmansk

Vorkuta

ARCTIC CIRCLE

Kola Peninsula

Kanin Peninsula

Usinsk

See pages 110–111 for Asian part of Russia

SWEDEN

FINLAND

WHITE SEA

Pechora

Pechora

U R A L   M O U N T A I N S

Gulf of Bothnia

Arkhangel'sk

Ukhta

Sosnogorsk

S I B E R I A

Severodvinsk

Northern Dvina

Zheleznodorozhnyy

Syktyvkar

A

Petrozavodsk

Kotlas

Lake Ladoga

Lake Onega

Sukhona

Berezniki

Gulf of Finland

St. Petersburg

Cherepovets

Vologda

Rybinsk Reservoir

Kirov

Perm'

EUROPE-ASIA BOUNDARY

BALTIC SEA

ESTONIA

Lake Peipus

Velikiy Novgorod

Kostroma

Izhevsk

Kama

Pskov

Rybinsk

Yaroslavl'

Velikiye Luki

Tver'

Ivanovo

Nizhniy Novgorod

Kazan'

Naberezhnyye Chelny

Ufa

Kaliningrad Oblast (Russia)

LITHUANIA

Moscow

Vladimir

Volga

Cheboksary

Magnitogorsk

POLAND

Smolensk

Oka

Ul'yanovsk

Sterlitamak

Ural

BELARUS

Kaluga

Tula

Ryazan'

Saransk

Syzran'

Tol'yatti

CENTRAL

Bryansk

Orel

Lipetsk

Oka

Tambov

Penza

Samara

Novotroitsk

Belaya

RUSSIAN

Kursk

Voronezh

Saratov

Balakovo

Orenburg

Orsk

Belgorod

Engels

KAZAKHSTAN

UPLAND

Kamyshin

Don

UKRAINE

Ural

Volgograd

Volzhskiy

Map Key

MOLDOVA

Dnieper

Donets

Shakhty

Volga

★ Country capital

●●● City or town

······ Boundary

Dnieper

Rostov na Donu

CASPIAN DEPRESSION

Taganrog

SEA OF AZOV

Don

0   200 miles

Krasnodar

Stavropol'

Astrakhan'

0   200 kilometers

Novorossiysk

Maykop

El'brus 18,510 ft 5,642 m

Pyatigorsk

CASPIAN SEA

Azimuthal Equidistant Projection

BLACK SEA

Sochi

CHECHNYA

Groznyy

Makhachkala

CAUCASUS MOUNTAINS

Vladikavkaz

GEORGIA

TURKEY

ARMENIA

AZERBAIJAN

THE CONTINENT:
ASIA

PHYSICAL

TOTAL AREA	LOWEST POINT	LARGEST LAKE
17,208,000 sq mi	Dead Sea, Israel-Jordan	ENTIRELY IN ASIA
(44,570,000 sq km)	-1,388 ft (-423 m)	Lake Baikal
HIGHEST POINT	**LONGEST RIVER**	12,200 sq mi (31,500 sq km)
Mount Everest, China-Nepal	Yangtze (Chang), China	
29,035 ft (8,850 m)	3,880 mi (6,244 km)	

POLITICAL

POPULATION	LARGEST COUNTRY ENTIRELY IN ASIA
4,405,052,000	China 3,705,386 sq mi (9,596,960 sq km)
LARGEST METROPOLITAN AREA	**MOST DENSELY POPULATED COUNTRY**
Tokyo, Japan	Singapore
Pop. 38,140,000	21,891.9 people per sq mi (8,449.0 per sq km)

ASIA

Asia

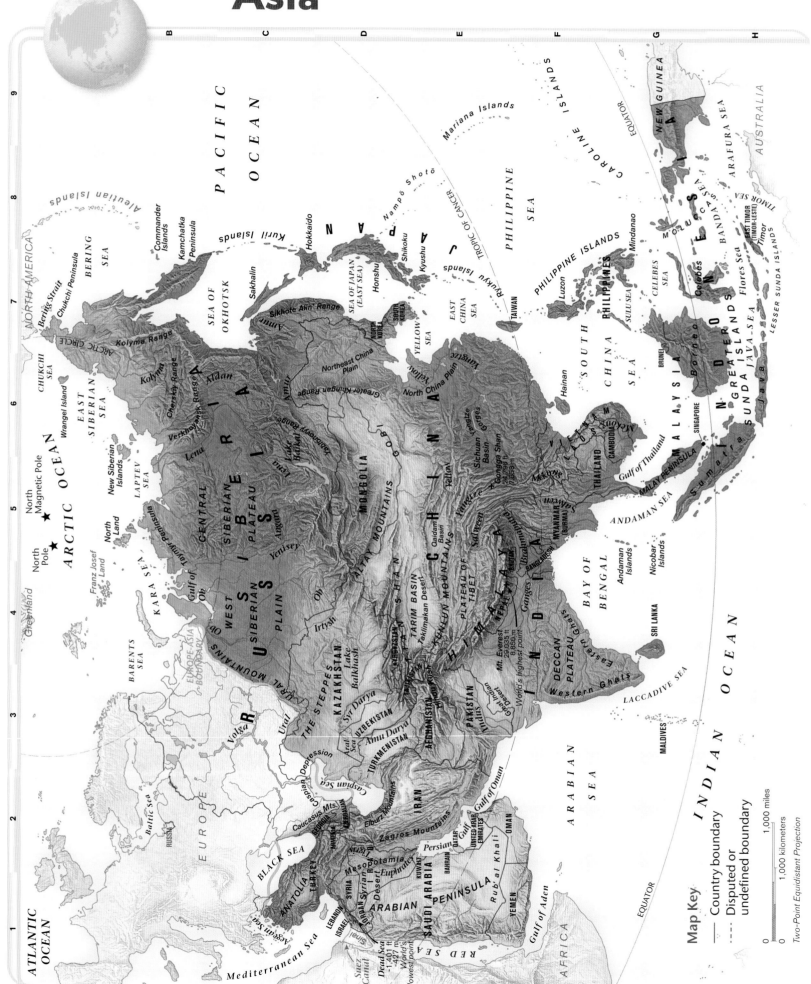

Map Key:
— Country boundary
--- Disputed or undefined boundary

0 — 1,000 miles
0 — 1,000 kilometers

Two-Point Equidistant Projection

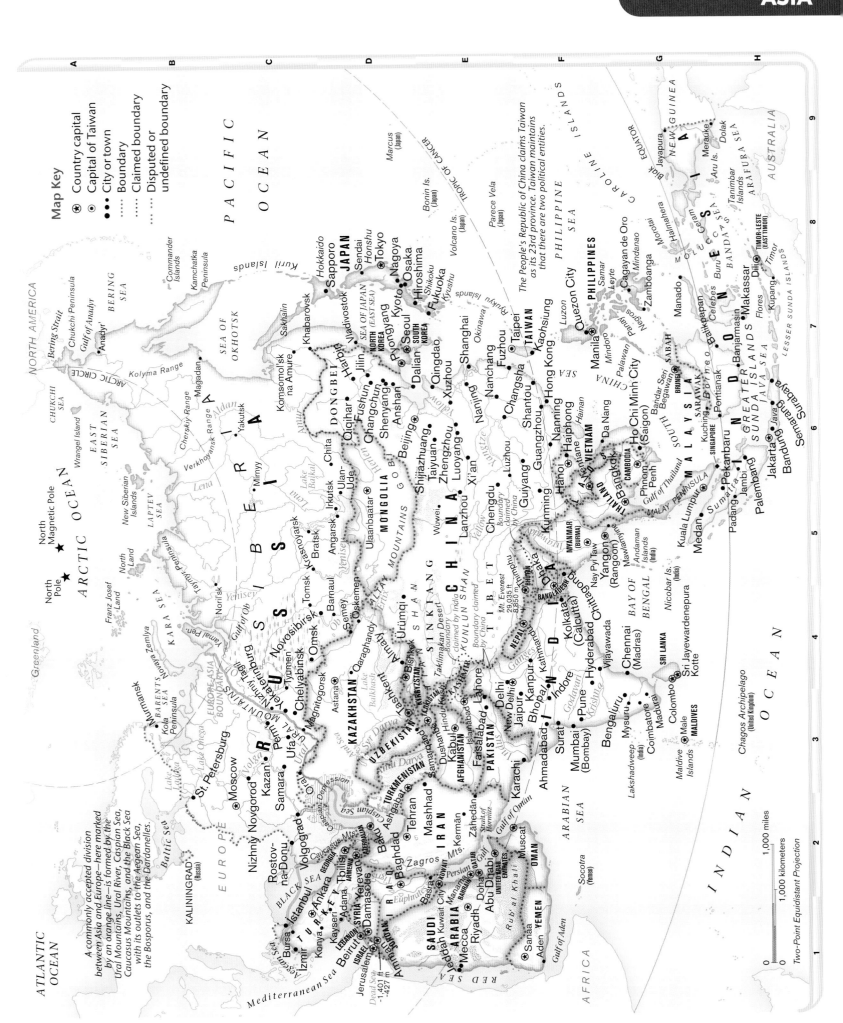

Map Key

⊛ Country capital
⊙ Capital of Taiwan
• City or town
••• Boundary
•••• Claimed boundary
•••• Disputed or
undefined boundary

A commonly accepted division
between Asia and Europe—here marked
by an orange line—is formed by the
Ural Mountains, Ural River, Caspian Sea,
Caucasus Mountains, and the Black Sea,
with its outlets to the Aegean Sea,
the Bosporus, and the Dardanelles.

The People's Republic of China claims Taiwan
as its 23rd province. Taiwan maintains
that there are two political entities.

Two-Point Equidistant Projection

Asia

WORLD CHAMPION

⬤ **TASTY SNACK.** This black-and-white giant panda, native to China, munches on a stalk of bamboo, the mainstay of its diet.

From Turkey to the eastern tip of Russia, Asia sprawls across nearly 180 degrees of longitude—almost half the globe! It boasts the highest (the Himalaya) and lowest (the Dead Sea) places on Earth's surface. Then there are Asia's people—more than four billion of them. That's more people than live on all the other continents put together. Asia has both the most farmers and the most million-plus cities. The world's first civilization arose in Sumer, in what is now southern Iraq. Rich cultures also emerged along rivers in present-day India and China, strongly influencing the world ever since.

⬤ **NEW VS. OLD.** An Afghan woman, completely covered by a traditional burka, sits among young girls dressed in Western clothes in Kabul.

◖ LUNAR NEW YEAR.
Young men carry a writhing paper dragon on poles in this Chinese New Year's parade in Singapore.

◖ WINGED HUNTER.
A Kazakh falconer sits astride his pony as he releases his golden eagle to pursue prey on the dry Asian steppe.

◖ NEON AVENUE.
Bright lights and neon signs highlight bustling Nanjing Lu, Shanghai's main shopping street. With a population of more than 24 million, Shanghai is China's largest city.

more about
Asia

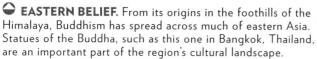 **EASTERN BELIEF.** From its origins in the foothills of the Himalaya, Buddhism has spread across much of eastern Asia. Statues of the Buddha, such as this one in Bangkok, Thailand, are an important part of the region's cultural landscape.

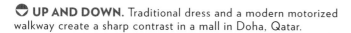 **UP AND DOWN.** Traditional dress and a modern motorized walkway create a sharp contrast in a mall in Doha, Qatar.

FINAL TOUCH. A silk kimono and perfectly applied makeup identify a *maiko*, or apprentice geisha, in Kyoto, Japan.

STONE BARRIER. Construction on China's Great Wall began in 220 B.C.E. as a defense against invasion from the north and continued until the 1600s C.E.

WHERE THE PICTURES ARE

Kyrgyz goat herder p. 112
Samarkand market p. 113
Baikonur Cosmodrome p. 112
Saiga antelope p. 113
Girls talking p. 118
Stone head p. 117
Galata Bridge p. 116
Swimmers p. 117
Petra p. 116
Ring p. 119
Horse and car p. 118
Mall scene p. 108
Drummer p. 118
Afghan girls p. 106
Taj Mahal p. 120
Hindu god Shiva p. 121
Elephant at work p. 122
Tigers p. 109
Mountain climbers p. 121

Natural gas well p. 111
Ger and yak p. 115
Falconer p. 107

Nenet woman and child p. 110
Lenin's head p. 111
Brown bears p. 110
Great Wall of China pp. 108–109
Woman in lab p. 114
Tokyo city street pp. 114–115
Geisha p. 108
Shanghai city lights pp. 106–107
Terra-cotta soldiers p. 115
Panda p. 106
Jeepney p. 123
Buddhist monk p. 122
Container terminal p. 122
Rain forest p. 125
Boy with flag p. 124
Orangutan p. 125
Terraced rice fields p. 109
Ceremonial mask p. 125

Golden Buddha p. 108
Petronas Twin Towers p. 123
Lunar New Year pp. 106–107
Man and his cow p. 120   Jakarta at night p. 124

MOUNTAIN STAIRWAY. Terraces cut into a steep mountainside create fields for rice on the island of Bali, in Indonesia. Rice is a staple grain crop in much of eastern Asia. In the foreground, a man nimbly climbs a palm tree to harvest coconuts.

MOTHER KNOWS BEST.
A Bengal tiger gently moves her cub to a safe hiding place before stalking her prey in India's Bandhavgarh National Park. Tigers are an endangered species.

THE BASICS

STATS*

Area
6,601,631 sq mi
(17,098,242 sq km)

Population
142,258,000

Predominant language
Russian (official)

Predominant religions
Christianity, Islam

GDP per capita
$26,500

Life expectancy
71 years

*These figures are for all of
Russia. For European Russia,
see pages 100–101.

GEO WHIZ

The name Siberia comes from
the Turkic language and means
"Sleeping Land."

It takes at least six days to travel
6,000 miles (9,656 km) on the
Trans-Siberian Railway from
Moscow to the Pacific port of
Vladivostok. The trip crosses
eight time zones.

Lake Baikal, nicknamed Siberia's
"blue eye," is home to 1,500
unique species of plants and
animals, including the nerpa,
the world's only freshwater seal.

The Chukchi, the largest group
of native people in Siberia, take
their name from a word meaning
"rich in reindeer." They share
their name with their homeland,
a peninsula bordered by the
Arctic and Pacific Oceans.

A region of northern coniferous
forest called taiga stretches
across northern Russia as far
as Norway.

Asian Russia

⊖ **NOMADIC HERDERS.**
A Nenet woman and her grandson
prepare to follow the family reindeer herd to northern Siberia for
spring and summer grazing.

Forming more than half of Russia, this region stretches from the Ural Mountains east to the Pacific, and from the Arctic Ocean south to mountains and deserts along borders with central Asia, Mongolia, China, and North Korea. Siberia, as this region is commonly known, has limited croplands but bountiful forests (the taiga) and rich mineral resources such as oil, natural gas, and gold. The Trans-Siberian Railway, built between 1891 and 1905, opened up the region for settlement, but not too much. Fewer than 39 million people—27 percent of Russia's popula-tion—live in sprawling Siberia.

See page 101 for
European part of Russia

◖ **FISHING FOR A MEAL.**
A brown bear and her cubs
hunt for fish in a river below the
slopes of a volcano on Russia's
Kamchatka Peninsula. Part of the
Pacific Ring of Fire, this peninsula
has 29 active volcanoes.

◖ **REVOLUTIONARY LEADER.** Vladimir Ilyich Lenin, a founder of the Soviet Union, was honored with many statues. This one in Siberia is the largest still standing in Russia.

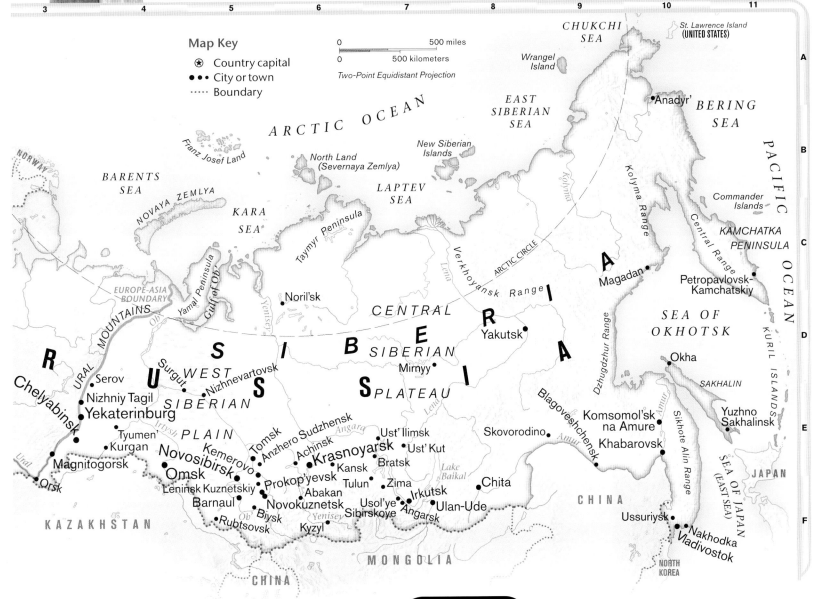

Map Key

⯨ Country capital
●●● City or town
⋯⋯ Boundary

0 ———— 500 miles
0 ———— 500 kilometers
Two-Point Equidistant Projection

ARCTIC OCEAN

NORWAY

BARENTS SEA

NOVAYA ZEMLYA

Franz Josef Land

North Land (Severnaya Zemlya)

New Siberian Islands

CHUKCHI SEA

St. Lawrence Island (UNITED STATES)

Wrangel Island

EAST SIBERIAN SEA

•Anadyr'

BERING SEA

PACIFIC OCEAN

KARA SEA

LAPTEV SEA

Taymyr Peninsula

Kolyma

Kolyma Range

Commander Islands

Verkhoyansk Range

ARCTIC CIRCLE

Lena

Central Range

KAMCHATKA PENINSULA

EUROPE-ASIA BOUNDARY

Yamal Peninsula

Gulf of Ob

Ob

Yenisey

•Noril'sk

CENTRAL

SIBERIAN

PLATEAU

Lena

•Yakutsk

Magadan•

Dzhugdzhur Range

Petropavlovsk-Kamchatskiy•

SEA OF OKHOTSK

KURIL ISLANDS

URAL MOUNTAINS

R

U

S

S

I

B

E

R

I

A

Serov•

Surgut•

WEST

SIBERIAN

•Nizhnevartovsk

SIBERIAN

PLATEAU

Mirnyy•

Okha•

SAKHALIN

Chelyabinsk•

Nizhniy Tagil•

Yekaterinburg

Tyumen'•

•Kurgan

PLAIN

Irtysh

Tomsk•

Kemerovo•

Anzhero Sudzhensk•

Achinsk•

Angara

Krasnoyarsk

Ust'Ilimsk•

Ust' Kut•

Skovorodino•

Blagoveshchensk•

Amur

Komsomol'sk na Amure•

Khabarovsk•

Yuzhno-Sakhalinsk•

Magnitogorsk•

Ural

Novosibirsk

Omsk•

Leninsk Kuznetskiy•

Prokop'yevsk•

Barnaul•

Novokuznetsk•

Kansk•

Bratsk•

Tulun•

Zima•

Abakan•

Usol'ye•

Sibirskoye

Irkutsk•

Lake Baikal

Angarsk•

Ulan-Ude•

•Chita

CHINA

Sikhote Alin Range

SEA OF JAPAN (EAST SEA)

JAPAN

Orsk•

KAZAKHSTAN

Ob'

Biysk•

Rubtsovsk•

Kyzyl•

Yenisey

MONGOLIA

CHINA

Ussuriysk•

Nakhodka•

Vladivostok•

NORTH KOREA

DEEPEST LAKES

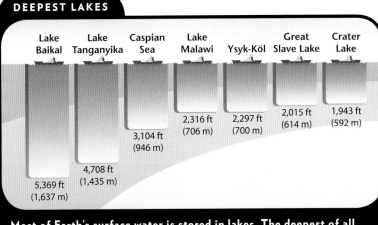

Lake Baikal	Lake Tanganyika	Caspian Sea	Lake Malawi	Ysyk-Köl	Great Slave Lake	Crater Lake
5,369 ft (1,637 m)	4,708 ft (1,435 m)	3,104 ft (946 m)	2,316 ft (706 m)	2,297 ft (700 m)	2,015 ft (614 m)	1,943 ft (592 m)

Most of Earth's surface water is stored in lakes. The deepest of all is Lake Baikal, which contains about 20 percent of Earth's total surface freshwater.

◖ **COLD POWER.** A liquefied natural gas well in the Yamal Peninsula in northwestern Siberia taps into Russia's largest gas reserves. Bitterly cold Arctic winters are a major challenge to this project.

THE BASICS

STATS

Largest country
Kazakhstan 1,052,084 sq mi
(2,724,900 sq km)

Smallest country
Tajikistan 55,251 sq mi
(143,100 sq km)

Most populous country
Uzbekistan 29,749,000

Least populous country
Turkmenistan 5,351,000

Predominant languages
Russian, Kazakh, Uzbek, Kyrgyz,
Tajik, Turkmen

Predominant religions
Islam, Christianity

Highest GDP per capita
Kazakhstan $25,100

Lowest GDP per capita
Tajikistan $3,000

Highest life expectancy
Uzbekistan 74 years

Lowest life expectancy
Tajikistan 68 years

GEO WHIZ

The main musical instrument of
the steppes in Kazakhstan is the
dombra, a long-necked lute with
two strings.

Uzbekistan, one of the world's
top gold-producing countries,
has the world's largest open-pit
gold mine. Muruntau Mine is said
to hold more gold reserves than
any other mine in the world.

Mountains, including the Pamir
and Tian Shan, cover more than
90 percent of Tajikistan.

Central Asia

Located along the historic Silk Road, central Asia is made up of five former Soviet republics, often referred to as the stans, or "homelands." This region has a largely Muslim population that includes Kazakhs, Turkmen, Uzbeks, Tajiks, and Kyrgyz, but Russians are also still present. Kazakhstan's short-grass steppes give way to deserts, arid plateaus, and rugged mountains to the south. The Amu Darya and the Syr Darya provide water for irrigating wheat, rice, cotton, and fruit crops. Although this landlocked region lies far from any ocean, it includes several large bodies of water, including the Caspian Sea, which is actually a saltwater lake.

◑ **BEST FRIENDS.** A boy carries his goat in mountainous Kyrgyzstan, where almost half the land is used for pasture and hay to support herds of goats and sheep.

◑ **INTO SPACE.** Russia's Baikonur Cosmodrome, located east of the Aral Sea in Kazakhstan's desert, has been the launch site for Russian space missions since Sputnik 1 in 1957. U.S. astronauts have flown from here to the International Space Station.

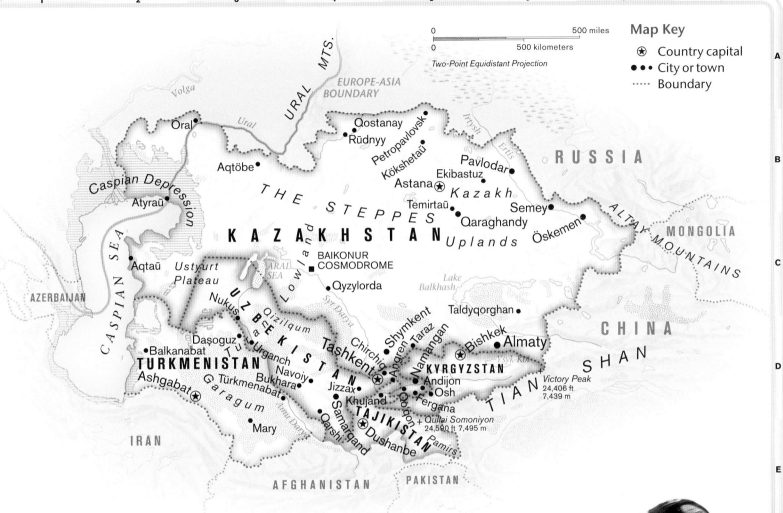

◑ **CRITICALLY ENDANGERED.** Loss of habitat, illegal hunting, and disease have put the saiga antelope, found mainly in Kazakhstan, at risk.

Map Key

⊛ Country capital
●•• City or town
····· Boundary

0 ————————— 500 miles
0 ————————— 500 kilometers
Two-Point Equidistant Projection

◑ **WHERE BARGAINING IS AN ART.**
Two men haggle over the price of cherries in a bazaar in Samarqand, Uzbekistan. Located on the fabled Silk Road, the country relies on agriculture, especially cotton production, to support its economy.

VANISHING SEA

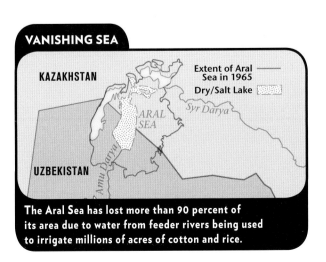

KAZAKHSTAN

Extent of Aral
Sea in 1965
Dry/Salt Lake

ARAL
SEA

Syr Darya

Amu Darya

UZBEKISTAN

The Aral Sea has lost more than 90 percent of its area due to water from feeder rivers being used to irrigate millions of acres of cotton and rice.

Eastern Asia

THE BASICS

STATS

Largest country
China 3,705,386 sq mi
(9,596,960 sq km)

Smallest country
South Korea
38,502 sq mi (99,720 sq km)

Most populous country
China 1,379,303,000

Least populous country
Mongolia 3,068,000

Predominant languages
Standard Chinese (Mandarin),
Japanese, Korean, Mongol

Predominant religions
Daoism, Buddhism, Shintoism,
Christianity, Confucianism

Highest GDP per capita
Japan $41,300

Lowest GDP per capita
North Korea $1,700

Highest life expectancy
Japan 85 years

Lowest life expectancy
Mongolia, North Korea 70 years

GEO WHIZ

The only surviving breed of
wild horse, the Przewalski, is
named for the count who
"discovered" it in Mongolia in
the 1880s. Careful breeding has
saved it from extinction. About
1,500 remain.

Each year on October 9, people
in South Korea celebrate their
alphabet, which was created in
1446 to increase literacy.

China, Mongolia, the Koreas, and Japan make up eastern Asia. Rich river valleys have supported Chinese civilization for more than four millennia. The Tibetan Plateau, dry basins, and the towering Himalaya border China to the west. Mongolia, the land of Genghis Khan, lies to China's north. Despite rugged uplands that limit living space, Japan and South Korea have used technology and manufacturing to become economic powerhouses, while North Korea remains poor and isolated. China's gradual shift toward capitalism has made it a leader in global markets.

HIGH TECH. This young South Korean woman works in a laboratory that makes microcircuits in a semiconductor plant in Seoul.

NIGHTLIGHTS.
Tokyo's Shinjuku is both a shopping center and a theater district as well as the city's busiest train station. It averages more than 3.6 million passengers daily.

AUTO GIANTS

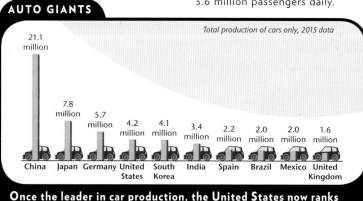

Total production of cars only, 2015 data

China	21.1 million
Japan	7.8 million
Germany	5.7 million
United States	4.2 million
South Korea	4.1 million
India	3.4 million
Spain	2.2 million
Brazil	2.0 million
Mexico	2.0 million
United Kingdom	1.6 million

Once the leader in car production, the United States now ranks
fourth. Holding first place, China's production is almost triple that
of second-ranked Japan.

◗ **HOME ON THE STEPPE.** A *ger* is the traditional Mongolian dwelling. The cowlike yak works as a pack animal and is a source of milk.

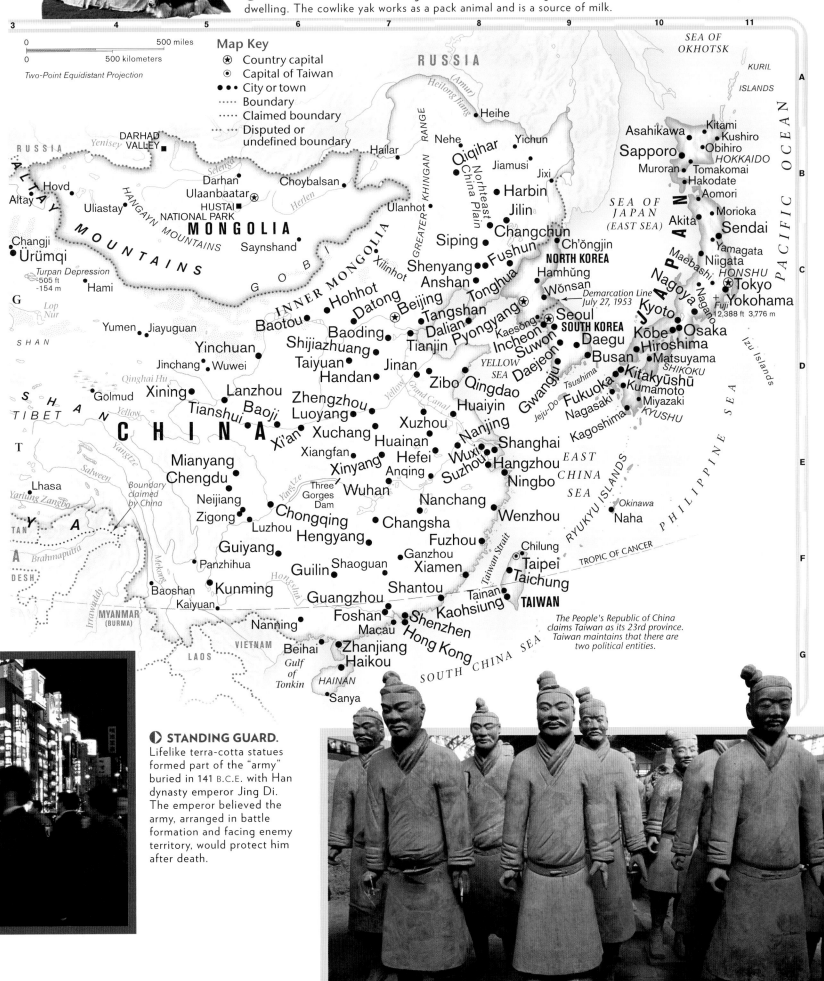

0 ————— 500 miles
0 ————— 500 kilometers

Two-Point Equidistant Projection

Map Key
★ Country capital
◉ Capital of Taiwan
• • • City or town
····· Boundary
····· Claimed boundary
····· Disputed or undefined boundary

◗ **STANDING GUARD.** Lifelike terra-cotta statues formed part of the "army" buried in 141 B.C.E. with Han dynasty emperor Jing Di. The emperor believed the army, arranged in battle formation and facing enemy territory, would protect him after death.

The People's Republic of China claims Taiwan as its 23rd province. Taiwan maintains that there are two political entities.

Eastern Mediterranean

THE BASICS

STATS

Largest country
Turkey
302,533 sq mi (783,562 sq km)

Smallest country
Lebanon
4,015 sq mi (10,400 sq km)

Most populous country
Turkey 80,845,000

Least populous country
Armenia 3,045,000

Predominant languages
Turkish, Arabic, Azerbaijani, Hebrew, Georgian, Armenian, English, French, Kurdish

Predominant religions
Islam, Judaism, Christianity

Highest GDP per capita
Israel $35,200

Lowest GDP per capita
Syria $2,900

Highest life expectancy
Israel 82 years

Lowest life expectancy
Azerbaijan 73 years

GEO WHIZ

Mount Ararat, near Turkey's border with Iran and Armenia, is believed by some to be the resting place for the ark that—according to the Bible—Noah built to survive the great flood.

Israelis capture runoff from seasonal rains to support crops in the Negev, a desert region that extends across more than half their country.

☁ **ANCIENT MYSTERY.**
A camel walks past Al-Khazneh in Petra, a World Heritage site in Jordan. Carved out of the mountainside more than 2,500 years ago, Petra was the capital of the Nabateans.

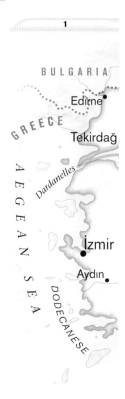

This region forms a bridge between Europe and Asia, from the Caucasus Mountains to the desert lands of Jordan. Turkey, framed by the Black, Aegean, and Mediterranean Seas, leads the region in population and area. The historic and life-giving Tigris and Euphrates Rivers begin in Turkey and flow southeast through arid Syria and Iraq. Israel, Lebanon, Syria, and Turkey share the Mediterranean shore. While Islam claims the majority of followers across these lands, Judaism, Christianity, and other faiths are present. The holiest places to Christians and Jews occupy Israeli soil in Jerusalem, adjacent to the third holiest site for Muslims, which continues to cause tension and conflict.

BELOW SEA LEVEL

sea level

Empire State Building (U.S.A.)

-1,401 ft
(-427 m)

1,250 ft
(381 m)

Dead Sea

Not every place with an elevation below sea level is under the ocean. The Dead Sea, in western Asia, plunges to -1,401 feet (-427 m) below sea level. That's deeper than the Empire State Building is tall.

◑ **WATCHERS FROM THE PAST.** Giant stone heads, representing Greek gods, guard the first-century B.C.E. burial site of King Antiochus I in southeastern Turkey.

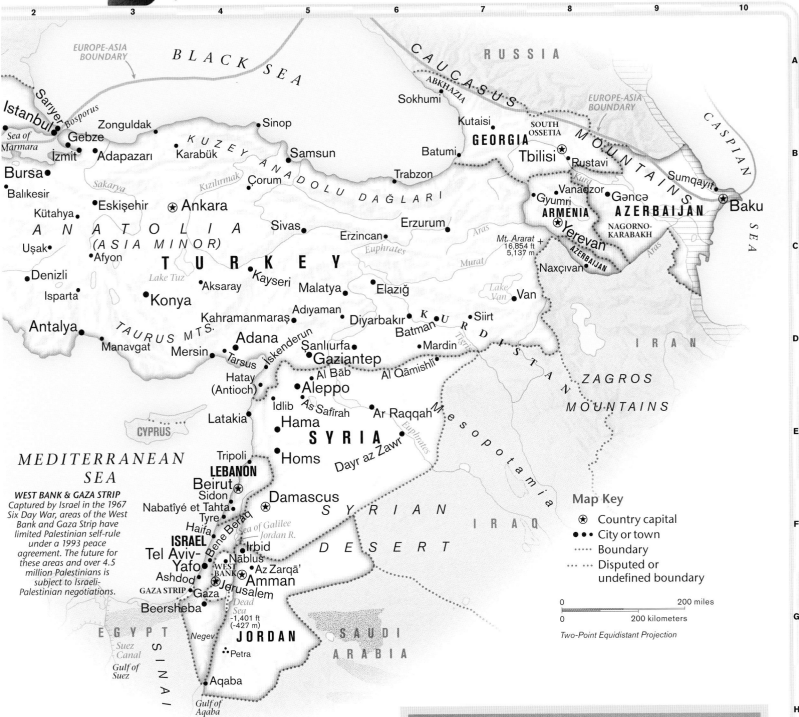

EUROPE-ASIA BOUNDARY

BLACK SEA

RUSSIA

CAUCASUS

Sokhumi
ABKHAZIA

Istanbul
Sarıyer
Bosporus
Zonguldak
Sinop
Kutaisi
EUROPE-ASIA BOUNDARY
CASPIAN

Sea of Marmara
Gebze
İzmit
Adapazarı
Karabük
Samsun
Batumi
SOUTH OSSETIA
GEORGIA
Tbilisi
Rustavi

Bursa
Balıkesir
Sakarya
Kızılırmak
Çorum
Trabzon
Vanadzor
Gyumri
Gəncə
Sumqayıt
Baku

Kütahya
Eskişehir
Ankara
KUZEY ANADOLU DAĞLARI
Erzurum
ARMENIA
AZERBAIJAN

ANATOLIA
(ASIA MINOR)
Sivas
Erzincan
Mt. Ararat
16,854 ft
5,137 m
Yerevan
NAGORNO-KARABAKH

Uşak
Afyon
TURKEY
Euphrates
Murat
AZERBAIJAN
Naxçıvan
IRAN

Denizli
Lake Tuz
Kayseri
Malatya
Elazığ
Lake Van
Van

Isparta
Konya
Aksaray
Adıyaman
Diyarbakır
K
Siirt
ZAGROS

Antalya
TAURUS MTS.
Kahramanmaraş
Batman
U
Mardin
MOUNTAINS

Manavgat
Adana
İskenderun
Şanlıurfa
R
Al Qāmishlī
Tigris

Mersin
Tarsus
Gaziantep
Al Bāb
D
Mesopotamia

Hatay
(Antioch)
Aleppo
I
S

Latakia
Idlib
As Safirah
Ar Raqqah
T
Euphrates

CYPRUS
Hama
SYRIA
A

MEDITERRANEAN SEA
Tripoli
Homs
Dayr az Zawr
N

LEBANON
Beirut
Sidon
Damascus
SYRIAN
IRAQ

WEST BANK & GAZA STRIP
Captured by Israel in the 1967 Six Day War, areas of the West Bank and Gaza Strip have limited Palestinian self-rule under a 1993 peace agreement. The future for these areas and over 4.5 million Palestinians is subject to Israeli-Palestinian negotiations.

Nabatîyé et Tahta
Tyre
Sea of Galilee
Jordan R.
Irbid
DESERT

Haifa
Bene Beraq
Nablus
Az Zarqā'

ISRAEL
Tel Aviv-Yafo
WEST BANK
Amman

Ashdod
Jerusalem
GAZA STRIP
Gaza
Dead Sea
-1,401 ft
(-427 m)

Beersheba
Negev
JORDAN
SAUDI ARABIA

EGYPT
SINAI
Suez Canal
Petra

Gulf of Suez
Aqaba

Gulf of Aqaba

Map Key
⊛ Country capital
●●● City or town
····· Boundary
···· Disputed or undefined boundary

0 ————— 200 miles
0 ————— 200 kilometers
Two-Point Equidistant Projection

◑ **BETWEEN TWO WORLDS.** The Galata Bridge crosses the Golden Horn, connecting the Asian part of Istanbul, Turkey (foreground), to the Galata area in the city's European part.

◑ **SALTY EXTREME.** The land between Israel and Jordan plunges down to the surface of the Dead Sea. The water of the sea is almost six times saltier than the ocean.

THE CONTINENT:
ASIA

Southwestern Asia

THE BASICS

STATS

Largest country
Saudi Arabia 829,995 sq mi
(2,149,690 sq km)

Smallest country
Bahrain 293 sq mi (760 sq km)

Most populous country
Iran 82,022,000

Least populous country
Bahrain 1,411,000

Predominant languages
Arabic, Persian (Farsi), Kurdish

Predominant religion
Islam

Highest GDP per capita
Qatar $127,700

Lowest GDP per capita
Yemen $2,400

Highest life expectancy
Bahrain, Qatar 79 years

Lowest life expectancy
Yemen 66 years

GEO WHIZ

The Rub' al Khali, or Empty Quarter, is the world's largest sand desert. It covers an area larger than France.

More than 4,000 years ago, the Sumerians built the world's first cities on the plain between the Tigris and Euphrates Rivers in what is now Iraq.

The ancient Romans called Yemen "Arabia Felix," meaning "Happy Arabia."

GIRL TALK. Young Iranian girls get together at a film festival in Tehran. The scarves they are wearing are part of the Islamic dress code, hijab, which says that women and girls must cover their heads and dress modestly.

This region, made up largely of deserts and mountains, includes the countries of the Arabian Peninsula and those that border the Persian Gulf. Islam is the dominant religion, and the two holiest places for Muslims—Mecca and Medina—are here. Arabic is the principal language everywhere but Iran, where most people speak Farsi. While water has been the most important natural resource here for millennia, global attention has focused in recent decades on the region's extensive oil reserves. Ongoing conflict and political tensions also have kept this region in headlines around the world.

HE'S GOT THE BEAT.
This Omani drummer plays at a dance in the Arabian Sea port of Qurayyāt. Oman works hard to preserve its traditional culture.

DIFFERENT WORLDS. This roadside meeting in Qatar displays a contrast between horse and horsepower and between traditional Arab and Western clothing styles. Qatar has a rich history of Arabian horse breeding.

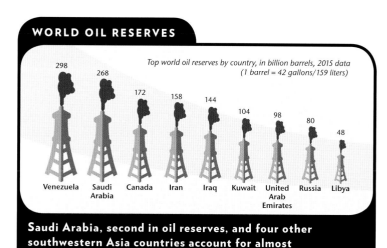

WORLD OIL RESERVES

Top world oil reserves by country, in billion barrels, 2015 data
(1 barrel = 42 gallons/159 liters)

298	268	172	158	144	104	98	80	48
Venezuela	Saudi Arabia	Canada	Iran	Iraq	Kuwait	United Arab Emirates	Russia	Libya

Saudi Arabia, second in oil reserves, and four other southwestern Asia countries account for almost 25 percent of all oil production.

LOST AND FOUND. Ancient treasures were destroyed, lost, or stolen during the 2003 invasion of Iraq. This ring is among the few items recovered.

BLACK SEA

GEORGIA

ARMENIA

AZERBAIJAN

TURKEY

CASPIAN SEA

TURKMENISTAN

Tigris

K U R D I S T A N

L. Urmia

Euphrates

Orūmiyeh
Marand
Tabrīz • Ardabīl
Bojnūrd
Gondad-e Kāvūs
Zakho • Dihok
Tall 'Afar • Nineveh
Miāndoāb • Rasht • Gorgān
Sārī
Mashhad
Sabzevār

MEDITERRANEAN SEA

SYRIA

LEBANON

ISRAEL

Mosul • Erbil
Kirkuk
As Sulaymānīyah
Zanjān
Qazvīn
Elburz Mts.
Semnān
Tehran ⊛
Kūh-e Damāvand 18,605 ft 5,671 m

KHORĀSĀN

Gonābād

Tikrīt • Kermānshāh
Sāmarrā'
Sanandaj
Hamadān
Arāk
Qom
Dasht-e Kavīr (Kavir Desert)
Bīrjand

I R A Q

M E S O P O T A M I A

Ar Ramādī ⊛ Baghdad
Turaybīl
Al Fallūjah
Karbalā'
Nippur
Dezfūl
Isfahan
Qomsheh
Yazd

I R A N

Dasht-e Lūt

Zābol
Noṣratābād

JORDAN

D E S E R T

Z A G R O S M O U N T A I N S

Al Hillah
An Najaf
Ur
An Nāṣirīyah
Al 'Amārah
Ahvāz
Shīrāz
Persepolis

FĀRS

Kermān
Zāhedān
Bam

PAKISTAN

EGYPT

Al Qurayyāt
'Ar'ar
Sakākā
Al Jawf

S Y R I A N

Az Zubayr
Al Baṣrah
Ābādān
KUWAIT ★
Marv Dasht
Būshehr
Fasā
Jahrom
Sa'īdābād
Tārom

Irānshahr

BALUCHISTAN

Gulf of Aqaba
Tabūk

An Nafūd

Ḥā'il

Ad Dahnā'

Kuwait City ⊛

Bandar-e 'Abbās
Qeshm
Strait of Hormuz
Angohrān
Chāh Bāhar

R E D

A L Ḥ I J Ā Z

Buraydah
Al Jubayl
Ad Dammām

BAHRAIN ⊛
Manama
Al Mubarraz
Ra's al-Khaimah
OMAN
Sharjah
Dubai
Suḥār
GULF OF OMAN

S A U D I

Medina

Riyadh ★

Doha ⊛
QATAR
Al Hufūf

Abu Dhabi ⊛ Al Ain
'Ibrī

Muscat ⊛
Qurayyāt
TROPIC OF CANCER

A R A B I A

UNITED ARAB EMIRATES

Nizwá
Ṣūr

S E A

Yanbu' al Bahr

Al Hillah

ARABIAN PENINSULA

Jabal Tuwayq

Al Ḥadīdah × (meteorite craters)

Rub' al Khali (Empty Quarter)

O M A N

Khalūf

Jeddah
Mecca • Aṭ Ṭā'if
Qal'at Bīshah
Al Qunfudhah

Duqm

Masira

Z U F Ā R

ARABIAN SEA

SUDAN

Abā as Sa'ūd
Jīzān

Ḥaḍramawt

Mirbāṭ
Ṣalālah
Hawf

ERITREA

Sanaa ⊛
Dhamār
Ridā'
Al Ḥudaydah
Ibb
Ash Shiḥr

Nishtūn

Socotra (Yemen)

Y E M E N

Ta'izz
Lahij
Al Mukallā

ETHIOPIA

Aden

GULF OF ADEN

DJIBOUTI

Map Key
⊛ Country capital
••• City or town
······ Boundary

0 ——— 300 miles
0 ——— 300 kilometers

Two-Point Equidistant Projection

S O M A L I A

Southern Asia

THE BASICS

STATS

Largest country	India 1,269,212 sq mi (3,287,263 sq km)
Smallest country	Maldives 115 sq mi (298 sq km)
Most populous country	India 1,281,936,000
Least populous country	Maldives 393,000
Predominant languages	Hindi, English, Punjabi, Bangla, Dari, Burmese, Pashto, Urdu, Sinhala, Nepali, Dzongkha
Predominant religions	Hinduism, Islam, Buddhism
Highest GDP per capita	Maldives $15,500
Lowest GDP per capita	Afghanistan $1,900
Highest life expectancy	Sri Lanka 77 years
Lowest life expectancy	Afghanistan 51 years

GEO WHIZ

India's rail system transports 8.4 billion passengers each year across nearly 40,660 miles (65,436 km) of track.

Bhutan, a Himalayan country known as Land of the Thunder Dragon, is the world's only Buddhist kingdom.

◐ **TAJ MAHAL.** In 1631 in Agra, India, the Mughal emperor Shah Jehan began construction of this magnificent marble memorial to his deceased wife.

This region is home to the world's highest peaks. Three of the world's storied rivers—the Indus, Ganges, and Brahmaputra—support the hundreds of millions of people who live here. India is at the center, greater in area than the other countries combined and more than double their population. Hinduism and Buddhism originated in India where Hinduism continues to be the main religion. There are large numbers of Buddhists in Bhutan, Nepal, Sri Lanka, and Myanmar, and Muslims form the majority in Afghanistan, Pakistan, and Bangladesh. Poverty and prosperity live side by side across the region, with streams of migrants flowing from rural areas to mushrooming cities.

◑ **GOLDEN GRAIN.** A man leads his cow past a rice field south of Rangpur, Bangladesh. Rice is the staple food for 158 million Bangladeshis and provides employment for almost half the rural population.

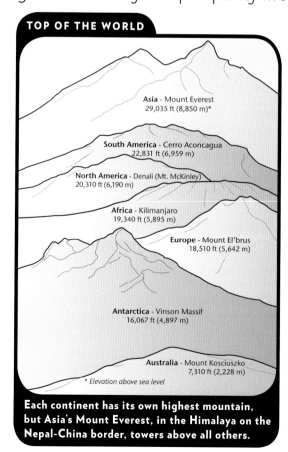

TOP OF THE WORLD

Asia - Mount Everest
29,035 ft (8,850 m)*

South America - Cerro Aconcagua
22,831 ft (6,959 m)

North America - Denali (Mt. McKinley)
20,310 ft (6,190 m)

Africa - Kilimanjaro
19,340 ft (5,895 m)

Europe - Mount El'brus
18,510 ft (5,642 m)

Antarctica - Vinson Massif
16,067 ft (4,897 m)

Australia - Mount Kosciuszko
7,310 ft (2,228 m)

* Elevation above sea level

Each continent has its own highest mountain, but Asia's Mount Everest, in the Himalaya on the Nepal-China border, towers above all others.

EASTERN BELIEF. The god Shiva (left) is part of the Hindu trinity, which also includes the gods Brahma and Vishnu. Hinduism is the world's third largest religion (after Christianity and Buddhism), with more than a billion followers.

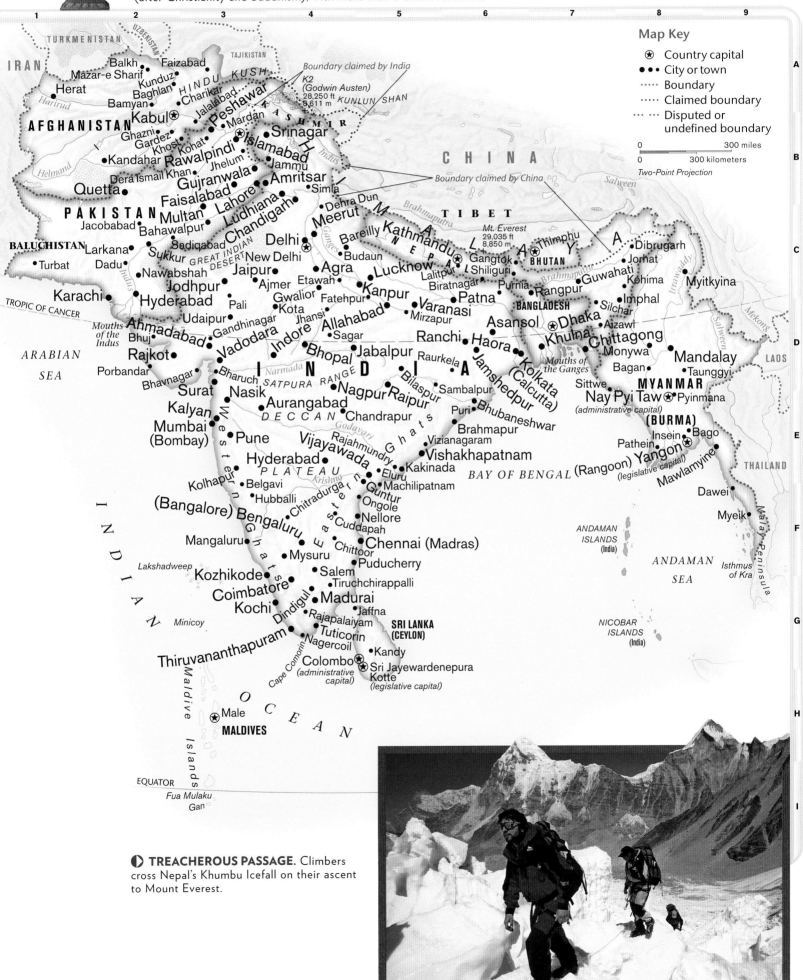

Map Key

★ Country capital
● ● ● City or town
······ Boundary
······ Claimed boundary
······ Disputed or undefined boundary

0   300 miles
0   300 kilometers
Two-Point Projection

TREACHEROUS PASSAGE. Climbers cross Nepal's Khumbu Icefall on their ascent to Mount Everest.

THE CONTINENT:
ASIA

Southeastern Asia

The countries of southeastern Asia have long been influenced by neighboring giants India and China. The result is a dazzling mix of cultures, rich histories, terrible conflicts, and future promise. Cambodia's spectacular 12th-century Angkor Wat provides a glimpse of former greatness. Colonial rule brought division and change, and struggles for independence took a heavy toll, as in Vietnam. Mainland countries are largely Buddhist, whereas peninsular Malaysia is mostly Muslim, and Christians dominate the Philippines. All but Laos have ocean access, with fisheries providing jobs and food for millions. Rivers like the Chao Phraya and the mighty Mekong provide transport and water-rich croplands dominated by rice growing. Tiny Singapore has gained global importance with its bustling port operations and high-tech focus.

◯ SMILING BUDDHA.
A Buddhist monk admires a
sculpture in Cambodia's Angkor
temple complex. Built by the
Khmer between 800 and 1200
C.E., the complex includes
Buddhist and Hindu temples.

◯ WILLING WORKER.
Smaller and more easily
tamed than the African
variety, Asian elephants
have been a part of the
workforce for centuries.
They are found from
India to Indonesia.

◐ SHIPPING HUB.
Huge container terminals, such
as this one at Tanjong Pagar,
make Singapore the world's
busiest transshipment center,
connected to 600 ports in 123
countries around the world.

◖ FLASHY RIDE. Colorful Philippine taxis, called jeepneys because of their origin as rebuilt World War II jeeps, are a common sight on the streets of Manila.

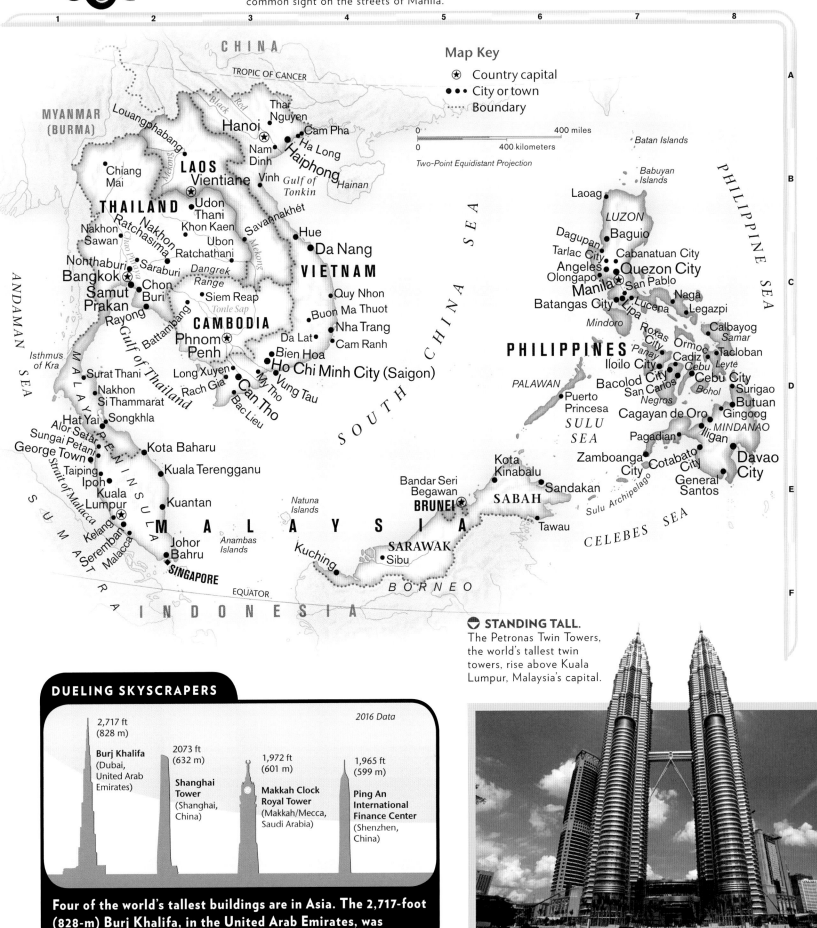

CHINA

TROPIC OF CANCER

MYANMAR (BURMA)

Louangphabang

Black River   Red River

Thai Nguyen

Hanoi

Cam Pha

Ha Long

Nam Dinh

Haiphong

Hainan

Chiang Mai

LAOS

Vientiane

Vinh

Gulf of Tonkin

THAILAND

Udon Thani

Khon Kaen

Savannakhet

Hue

Nakhon Sawan

Nakhon Ratchasima

Ubon Ratchathani

Da Nang

Nonthaburi

Saraburi

Dangrek Range

Mekong

VIETNAM

Bangkok

Chon Buri

Siem Reap

Quy Nhon

Samut Prakan

Rayong

Tonle Sap

Battambang

CAMBODIA

Buon Ma Thuot

Nha Trang

ANDAMAN SEA

Isthmus of Kra

Phnom Penh

Da Lat

Cam Ranh

Surat Thani

Long Xuyen

Bien Hoa

Ho Chi Minh City (Saigon)

Nakhon Si Thammarat

Rach Gia

Can Tho

My Tho

Vung Tau

Hat Yai

Songkhla

Bac Lieu

Gulf of Thailand

SOUTH CHINA SEA

Alor Setar

Sungai Petani

George Town

Taiping

Kota Baharu

Ipoh

Kuala Terengganu

Kuala Lumpur

Kuantan

MALAY PENINSULA

Kelang

Johor Bahru

Anambas Islands

Seremban

Malacca

MALAYSIA

Natuna Islands

Strait of Malacca

SUMATRA

SINGAPORE

EQUATOR

Kuching

Sibu

SARAWAK

BORNEO

INDONESIA

Map Key
- ✪ Country capital
- ••• City or town
- ····· Boundary

0   400 miles
0   400 kilometers
Two-Point Equidistant Projection

Batan Islands

Babuyan Islands

Laoag

LUZON

Baguio

Dagupan

Tarlac City

Cabanatuan City

Angeles

Quezon City

Olongapo

Manila

San Pablo

Batangas City

Lipa

Naga

Lucena

Legazpi

Mindoro

Roxas City

Panay

Calbayog

Samar

PHILIPPINES

Ormoc

Cadiz

Tacloban

Iloilo City

Cebu

Leyte

PALAWAN

Bacolod City

San Carlos

Cebu City

Bohol

Surigao

Puerto Princesa

Negros

Butuan

Cagayan de Oro

Gingoog

SULU SEA

Pagadian

Iligan

MINDANAO

Kota Kinabalu

Zamboanga City

Cotabato City

Davao City

Sandakan

General Santos

SABAH

Sulu Archipelago

Bandar Seri Begawan

BRUNEI

Tawau

CELEBES SEA

PHILIPPINE SEA

◖ STANDING TALL.
The Petronas Twin Towers, the world's tallest twin towers, rise above Kuala Lumpur, Malaysia's capital.

DUELING SKYSCRAPERS

2016 Data

2,717 ft (828 m)
Burj Khalifa (Dubai, United Arab Emirates)

2073 ft (632 m)
Shanghai Tower (Shanghai, China)

1,972 ft (601 m)
Makkah Clock Royal Tower (Makkah/Mecca, Saudi Arabia)

1,965 ft (599 m)
Ping An International Finance Center (Shenzhen, China)

Four of the world's tallest buildings are in Asia. The 2,717-foot (828-m) Burj Khalifa, in the United Arab Emirates, was completed in 2010.

THE BASICS

STATS

Largest country
Indonesia 735,354 sq mi
(1,904,569 sq km)

Smallest country
Timor-Leste 5,743 sq mi
(14,874 sq km)

Most populous country
Indonesia 260,581,000

Least populous country
Timor-Leste 1,291,000

Predominant languages
Indonesian, English, Dutch,
Javanese, Tetum, Portuguese

Predominant religions
Islam, Christianity

Highest GDP per capita
Indonesia $11,700

Lowest GDP per capita
Timor-Leste $4,200

Highest life expectancy
Indonesia 73 years

Lowest life expectancy
Timor-Leste 68 years

GEO WHIZ

In 2006, two species of sharks
that use their fins to "walk"
on coral reefs were discovered
off the northwestern coast of
Indonesia's Papua province.

When seen from the air, Timor
Island resembles a crocodile.
According to local legend, a crocodile turned itself into the island
as a way of saying thank you to a
boy who saved its life.

Komodo dragons, the world's
heaviest lizard, live only on
Indonesia's Lesser Sunda Islands.
They eat all types of prey—even
people sometimes!

Indonesia & Timor-Leste

Stretching more than 2,200 miles (3,520 km) from Sumatra to New Guinea, Indonesia is the world's largest island nation and the fourth most populous country. Most of its 261 million people live on the volcanically active island of Java. Indonesia shares rain-forested Borneo with Malaysia and Brunei. Most Indonesians are of Malay ethnicity, though there are large numbers of Melanesians (see page 154), Chinese, and East Indians. Arab traders brought Islam to the islands in the 13th century, and today six of seven Indonesians are Muslim. Timor-Leste gained independence from Indonesia in 2002. It and the Philippines are Asia's only mainly Catholic countries.

(see page 154)

◒ **PROUD CITIZEN.**
A young boy smiles broadly
as he waves the flag of Timor-
Leste (also known as East
Timor) in Díli, the capital city.

◖ **CITY ON THE MOVE.**
Skyscrapers and a busy freeway
are just one face of Jakarta,
Indonesia's national capital and
center of trade and industry. In
this city of more than 10 million
people, the modern and traditional, the rich and poor, live side
by side. Like the country, the city
has a very diverse population.

THE CONTINENT:
ASIA

SPIRIT WORLD. Masks, such as this one from Bali, Indonesia, were probably originally created for traditional dance and storytelling rituals.

3   4   5   6   7   8   9   10   11

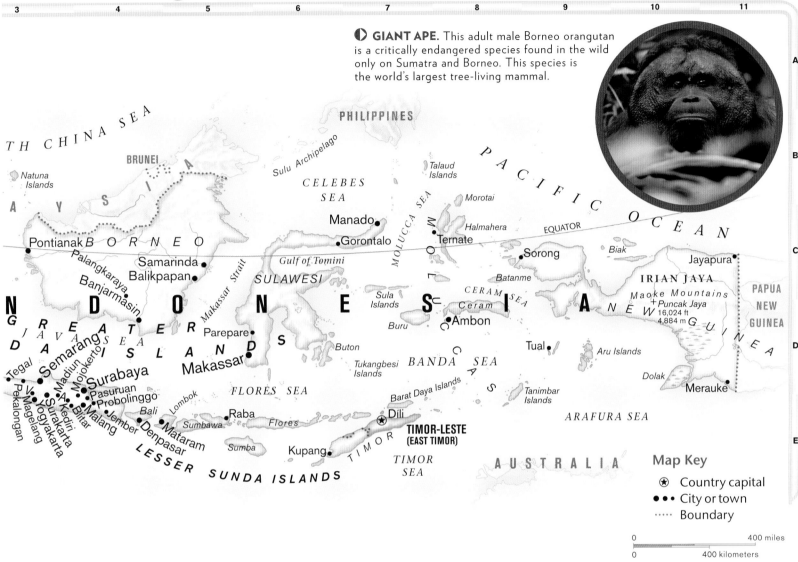

GIANT APE. This adult male Borneo orangutan is a critically endangered species found in the wild only on Sumatra and Borneo. This species is the world's largest tree-living mammal.

PHILIPPINES

TH CHINA SEA

MALAYSIA

BRUNEI

Natuna Islands

Sulu Archipelago

CELEBES SEA

Talaud Islands

Morotai

PACIFIC OCEAN

A
B
C
D
E

Pontianak   BORNEO

Palangkaraya

Samarinda

Balikpapan

Banjarmasin

Manado

Gorontalo

Gulf of Tomini

SULAWESI

EQUATOR

Halmahera

Ternate

MOLUCCA SEA

Sorong

Batanme

Biak

Jayapura

IRIAN JAYA

Maoke Mountains
+ Puncak Jaya
16,024 ft
4,884 m

PAPUA NEW GUINEA

NEW GUINEA

Sula Islands

CERAM SEA

Ceram

Ambon

Buru

INDONESIA

GREATER ISLANDS

JAVA

JAVA SEA

Tegal   Semarang   Madiun   Mojokerto   Kediri
Pekalongan   Magelang   Surakarta   Yogyakarta   Blitar   Malang   Jember
Pasuruan   Probolinggo
Surabaya

Parepare

Makassar

Buton

Tukangbesi Islands

BANDA SEA

Tual

Aru Islands

Dolak

Merauke

Tanimbar Islands

ARAFURA SEA

FLORES SEA

Lombok

Bali   Denpasar   Mataram

Sumbawa   Raba   Flores   Barat Daya Islands

Sumba

Kupang

TIMOR

Dili

TIMOR-LESTE (EAST TIMOR)

TIMOR SEA

AUSTRALIA

LESSER SUNDA ISLANDS

Map Key

⊛ Country capital
••• City or town
····· Boundary

0   400 miles
0   400 kilometers

Two-Point Equidistant Projection

FOLLOWERS OF ISLAM

Country	
Indonesia	204.8*
Pakistan	178.1
India	177.3
Bangladesh	148.6
Egypt	80.0
Nigeria	75.7
Iran	74.8
Turkey	74.7
Algeria	34.8
Morocco	32.4

*Figures are in millions, 2010 data

Islam's origins trace to southwestern Asia, but the religion has spread around the world. The country with the largest Muslim population is Indonesia.

GENETIC STOREHOUSE. Only about 33 percent of Indonesia's Kalimantan Province in eastern Borneo remains covered in rain forest, which is home to many rare species. Forest loss is a result of activities such as logging and road building that are a consequence of the spread of plantation agriculture, especially oil palm cultivation.

THE CONTINENT:
AFRICA

PHYSICAL			POLITICAL	
TOTAL AREA 11,608,000 sq mi (30,065,000 sq km)	**LOWEST POINT** Lake Assal, Djibouti -509 ft (-155 m)	**LARGEST LAKE** Victoria 26,800 sq mi (69,500 sq km)	**POPULATION** 1,215,763,000	**LARGEST COUNTRY** Algeria 919,590 sq mi (2,381,741 sq km)
HIGHEST POINT Kilimanjaro, Tanzania 19,340 ft (5,895 m)	**LONGEST RIVER** Nile 4,400 mi (7,081 km)		**LARGEST METROPOLITAN AREA** Lagos, Nigeria Pop. 13,661,000	**MOST DENSELY POPULATED COUNTRY** Mauritius 1721.3 people per sq mi (664.9 per sq km)

AFRICA

Africa

2 3 4 5 6 7 8

A

EUROPE

Azores

B

MEDITERRANEAN SEA

Strait of Gibraltar

ASIA

Madeira
Islands

MOROCCO

TUNISIA

Suez
Canal

ATLAS MOUNTAINS

Canary
Islands

ALGERIA

LIBYA

EGYPT

Sinai

C

TROPIC OF CANCER

WESTERN
SAHARA
(Morocco)

Ahaggar Mts.

Libyan Desert

Lake
Nasser

RED SEA

CABO
VERDE

MAURITANIA

S A H A R A

Aïr
Massif

Tibesti Mts.

Nile

ERITREA

D

Cape
Verde

Sénégal

M A L I

Niger

NIGER

CHAD

Lake Chad

SUDAN

White Nile

Blue Nile

Lake
Tana

Danakil

Gulf of Aden

Lowest point
in Africa

SENEGAL

GAMBIA

S A H E L

DJIBOUTI

Lake Assal
-509 ft
-155 m

GUINEA-BISSAU

BURKINA FASO

BENIN

NIGERIA

ETHIOPIA

SOMALIA

GUINEA

SIERRA
LEONE

U P P E R   G U I N E A

TOGO

CÔTE
D'IVOIRE
(IVORY COAST)

GHANA

CENTRAL
AFRICAN REPUBLIC

SOUTH
SUDAN

E

LIBERIA

Gulf of Guinea

EQUATORIAL GUINEA

SAO TOME & PRINCIPE

CAMEROON

CONGO

Congo

UGANDA

Lake Turkana
(Lake Rudolf)

KENYA

GREAT RIFT VALLEY

EQUATOR

C O N G O

Virunga Mts.
14,787 ft
4,507 m

Lake
Victoria

ATLANTIC

GABON

L O W E R   G U I N E A

B A S I N

DEMOCRATIC REPUBLIC
OF THE CONGO

RWANDA

BURUNDI

Kilimanjaro
19,340 ft
5,895 m

Highest point
in Africa

F

Cabinda
(Angola)

TANZANIA

Lake Tanganyika

SEYCHELLES

Ascension

KATANGA
PLATEAU

Lake Nyasa
(Lake Malawi)

COMOROS

OCEAN

G

St. Helena

ANGOLA

ZAMBIA

MALAWI

Zambezi

MOZAMBIQUE

Mozambique Channel

MADAGASCAR

INDIAN

Namib Desert

Victoria Falls

ZIMBABWE

MAURITIUS

TROPIC OF CAPRICORN

NAMIBIA

BOTSWANA

KALAHARI
DESERT

Réunion

H

Drakensberg

SWAZILAND

Map Key

— Country boundary

- - - Disputed or
undefined boundary

Orange

SOUTH AFRICA

LESOTHO

OCEAN

0   600 miles

0   600 kilometers

Cape of Good Hope

Cape Agulhas

I

Azimuthal Equidistant Projection

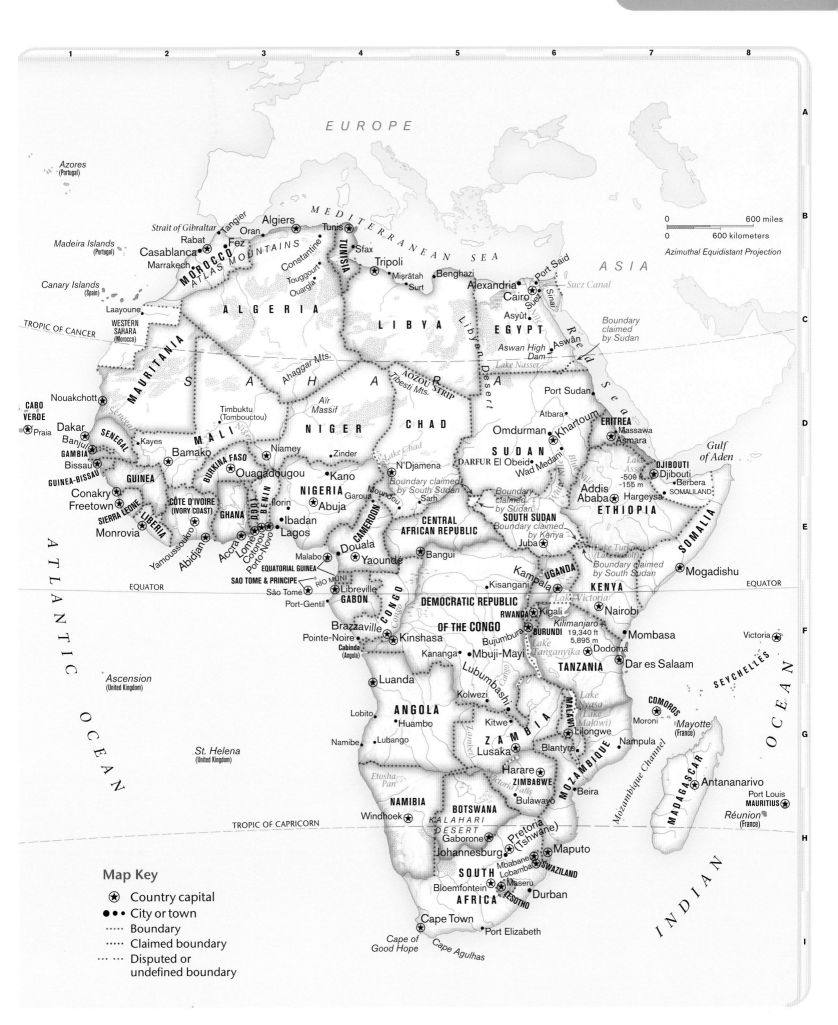

EUROPE

Azores
(Portugal)

MEDITERRANEAN SEA

ASIA

Madeira Islands
(Portugal)

Strait of Gibraltar
Tangier
Algiers ⭐
Tunis ⭐
TUNISIA
Sfax
Tripoli
Port Said
Suez Canal

Rabat ⭐
Oran
Fez
Casablanca
Marrakech
MOROCCO
ATLAS MOUNTAINS
Constantine
Touggourt
Ouargla
Mişrātah
Benghazi
Surt
Alexandria
Cairo ⭐
Suez
Sinai

Canary Islands
(Spain)

Laayoune
WESTERN SAHARA
(Morocco)

TROPIC OF CANCER

ALGERIA
LIBYA
EGYPT
Aswan High Dam
Aswân
Lake Nasser
Boundary claimed by Sudan

MAURITANIA
S A H A R A
Ahaggar Mts.
AOZOU STRIP
Tibesti Mts.
Libyan Desert
Red Sea

CABO VERDE
Nouakchott ⭐
Timbuktu (Tombouctou)
Aïr Massif
NIGER
CHAD
Port Sudan
Atbara

⭐ Praia
Dakar ⭐
Banjul
GAMBIA
Kayes
MALI
Bamako ⭐
Niamey ⭐
Zinder
Lake Chad
N'Djamena ⭐
Omdurman
Khartoum ⭐
ERITREA
Massawa
Asmara ⭐
Gulf of Aden

Bissau
GUINEA-BISSAU
SENEGAL
Senegal
Niger
BURKINA FASO
Ouagadougou ⭐
Kano
SUDAN
DARFUR El Obeid
Wad Medani
DJIBOUTI
Djibouti ⭐
Lake Assal -509 ft -155 m
Berbera
SOMALILAND

GUINEA
Conakry ⭐
Freetown ⭐
SIERRA LEONE
Bissau
Ilorin
NIGERIA
Garoua
Moundou
Sarh
Boundary claimed by South Sudan
Addis Ababa ⭐
Hargeysa
ETHIOPIA

Monrovia ⭐
LIBERIA
CÔTE D'IVOIRE (IVORY COAST)
GHANA
TOGO
BENIN
Abuja ⭐
Ibadan
Lagos
CAMEROON
CENTRAL AFRICAN REPUBLIC
SOUTH SUDAN
Boundary claimed by Kenya
SOMALIA
Mogadishu ⭐

Yamoussoukro ⭐
Abidjan
Accra ⭐
Lomé
Cotonou
Porto-Novo
Malabo ⭐
Douala
Yaoundé ⭐
Bangui ⭐
Juba ⭐
Kampala ⭐
UGANDA
Boundary claimed by South Sudan

EQUATOR
EQUATORIAL GUINEA
SAO TOME & PRINCIPE
RÍO MUNI
Libreville ⭐
Kisangani
KENYA
Lake Turkana (Lake Rudolf)
EQUATOR

São Tomé ⭐
GABON
Port-Gentil
CONGO
Congo
DEMOCRATIC REPUBLIC OF THE CONGO
RWANDA
Kigali ⭐
Lake Victoria
Nairobi ⭐

Brazzaville ⭐
Pointe-Noire
Kinshasa ⭐
Cabinda *(Angola)*
Kananga
Mbuji-Mayi
Bujumbura ⭐
BURUNDI
Kilimanjaro 19,340 ft 5,895 m
Lake Tanganyika
Dodoma ⭐
Mombasa
Victoria ⭐
SEYCHELLES

Ascension
(United Kingdom)

Luanda ⭐
Lubumbashi
TANZANIA
Dar es Salaam

Kolwezi
Zambezi
Kitwe
Lobito
ANGOLA
Huambo
MALAWI
Lilongwe ⭐
COMOROS
Moroni ⭐
Mayotte (France)

St. Helena
(United Kingdom)

Namibe
Lubango
ZAMBIA
Lusaka ⭐
Lake Nyasa (Lake Malawi)
Blantyre
Nampula
Mozambique Channel

A T L A N T I C   O C E A N

Harare ⭐
ZIMBABWE
MOZAMBIQUE
Beira
MADAGASCAR
Antananarivo ⭐

Etosha Pan
Bulawayo
Victoria Falls
Port Louis
MAURITIUS ⭐
Réunion (France)

TROPIC OF CAPRICORN
NAMIBIA
Windhoek ⭐
BOTSWANA
KALAHARI DESERT
Gaborone ⭐
Pretoria (Tshwane) ⭐
Maputo ⭐
I N D I A N   O C E A N

Johannesburg
Mbabane ⭐
Lobamba ⭐
SWAZILAND
Bloemfontein ⭐
Maseru ⭐
LESOTHO
Durban
SOUTH AFRICA

Cape Town ⭐
Port Elizabeth
Cape of Good Hope
Cape Agulhas

Map Key

⭐ Country capital
••• City or town
····· Boundary
····· Claimed boundary
······ Disputed or undefined boundary

0 ___ 600 miles
0 ___ 600 kilometers
Azimuthal Equidistant Projection

Africa

A COMPLEX GIANT

Africa spans nearly as far west to east as it does north to south. The Sahara—the world's largest hot desert—covers Africa's northern third, while to the south lie bands of grassland, tropical rain forest, and more desert. The East African Rift system marks where shifting tectonic plates are splitting off the continent's edge. Africa has a wealth of cultures, speaking some 1,600 languages—more than on any other continent. Though the continent is still largely rural, Africans increasingly migrate to booming cities like Lagos, Cairo, and Johannesburg. Despite rich natural resources, ranging from oil and coal to gemstones and precious metals, Africa is the poorest continent, long plagued by outside interference, corruption, and disease.

CHARGE! Sensing danger, an African elephant charges. The world's largest land mammal, African elephants are at risk due to poaching and loss of habitat.

COLORFUL NEIGHBORHOOD. South Africa's Bo-Kaap once was known as the Malay Quarter because of its early settlers. Dating to the 18th century, this multicultural suburb overlooks Cape Town's city center.

AFRICAN SAVANNA. Zebras graze on the tall grasses of the Serengeti Plain, in eastern Africa. Each year more than 200,000 zebras migrate through the Serengeti, following the seasonal rains.

CRYSTAL WATERS. A snorkeler swims in the clear blue waters off the Seychelles, one of Africa's island countries. Made up of 116 granite and coral islands, it lies about 1,000 miles (1,600 km) east of Kenya.

FREE RIDE. A woman in Kumasi, Ghana, goes about her daily chores with her infant wrapped snugly on her back in a colorful cloth.

THE CONTINENT:
AFRICA

more about
Africa

⬭ **WORSHIPPERS IN THE DESERT.** Muslim faithful gather before the Great Mosque in Mopti, Mali. An earthen structure typical of Muslim architecture in Africa's Sahel, the mosque was built between 1936 and 1943.

◗ **WINDOW ON THE PAST.** Traditional Egyptian sailing vessels called feluccas skim along the Nile River below the ruins at Qubbat al-Hawa. Tombs from ancient Egypt's 6th dynasty are carved into the hillside.

⬭ **MODERN SKYLINE.** Established in 1899 as a railway supply depot, Nairobi, Kenya, is now one of Africa's most modern cities. In Maasai, an indigenous language, the name means "place of cold water."

TALL LOAD. A woman carries a stack of brightly dyed cotton cloth, called wax prints, through a market in Lomé, Togo.

WHERE THE PICTURES ARE

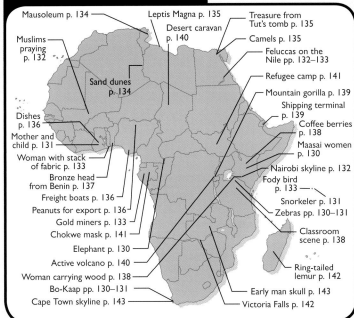

Mausoleum p. 134
Leptis Magna p. 135
Treasure from Tut's tomb p. 135
Muslims praying p. 132
Desert caravan p. 140
Camels p. 135
Sand dunes p. 134
Feluccas on the Nile pp. 132–133
Refugee camp p. 141
Mountain gorilla p. 139
Shipping terminal p. 139
Coffee berries p. 138
Dishes p. 136
Mother and child p. 131
Maasai women p. 130
Woman with stack of fabric p. 133
Nairobi skyline p. 132
Bronze head from Benin p. 137
Fody bird p. 133
Freight boats p. 136
Snorkeler p. 131
Peanuts for export p. 136
Zebras pp. 130–131
Gold miners p. 133
Classroom scene p. 138
Chokwe mask p. 141
Elephant p. 130
Ring-tailed lemur p. 142
Active volcano p. 140
Woman carrying wood p. 138
Early man skull p. 143
Bo-Kaap pp. 130–131
Cape Town skyline p. 143
Victoria Falls p. 142

DIGGING FOR GOLD. Miners dig a pit mine near the edge of the rain forest in Gabon. Oil and mineral extraction is an important part of the country's economy. While searching for traces of gold, however, they expose the fragile soil to erosion.

TROPICAL JEWEL. A ruby red fody perches on a forest branch on Mahé Island in the Seychelles. Native to neighboring Madagascar, the fody eats seeds and insects.

Northern Africa

This region, which is made up of five countries, stretches from the Atlantic Ocean in the west to the Red Sea in the east. To the north the region is bounded by the Mediterranean Sea, while to the south lies the vast dry expanse of the Sahara. The world's longest river—the Nile— winds northward through Egypt, but most of the region is arid—meaning there is too little moisture to support trees or extensive vegetation. Most of the region's population lives in coastal areas or in the fertile valley of the Nile River. In recent years, the region has experienced widespread instability as a result of tensions between conservative Islamic groups and more liberal groups seeking modernization and democratic rule.

THE BASICS

STATS

Largest country
Algeria 919,590 sq mi
(2,381,741 sq km)

Smallest country
Tunisia 63,170 sq mi
(163,610 sq km)

Most populous country
Egypt 97,041,000

Least populous country
Libya 6,653,000

Predominant languages
Arabic, French,
indigenous languages

Predominant religions
Islam, indigenous beliefs

Highest GDP per capita
Algeria $15,000

Lowest GDP capita
Morocco $8,300

Highest life expectancy
Algeria, Libya, Morocco 77 years

Lowest life expectancy
Egypt 73 years

GEO WHIZ

Ibn Battuta, who was born in Tangier, Morocco, in 1304, set off on a pilgrimage to Mecca that turned into a 29-year, 75,000-mile (120,675-km) journey that took him from the Middle East to India, China, the East Indies, and back home.

Egypt's Aswan High Dam, which forms Lake Nasser, produces up to 10 billion kilowatt hours of electricity every year and provides water for farms along the Nile in years of drought.

Kairouan, Tunisia, is considered to be Islam's fourth holiest city after Mecca, Medina, and Jerusalem.

SEA OF SAND. Towering dunes as well as barren, rocky expanses define Earth's largest hot desert—the Sahara, which separates northern Africa from the rest of the continent.

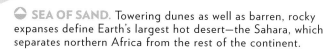

LEADER REMEMBERED. Arab influence in northern Africa is reflected in the dramatic mausoleum of Tunisia's first president, Habib Bourguiba, in the coastal town of Monastir. Bourguiba led Tunisia's fight for independence from French colonial rule. Independence was won in 1956.

◑ **SPIRIT OF THE PAST.** This gold hawk pendant, found in the tomb of King Tut, may represent Horus, one of the oldest Egyptian gods.

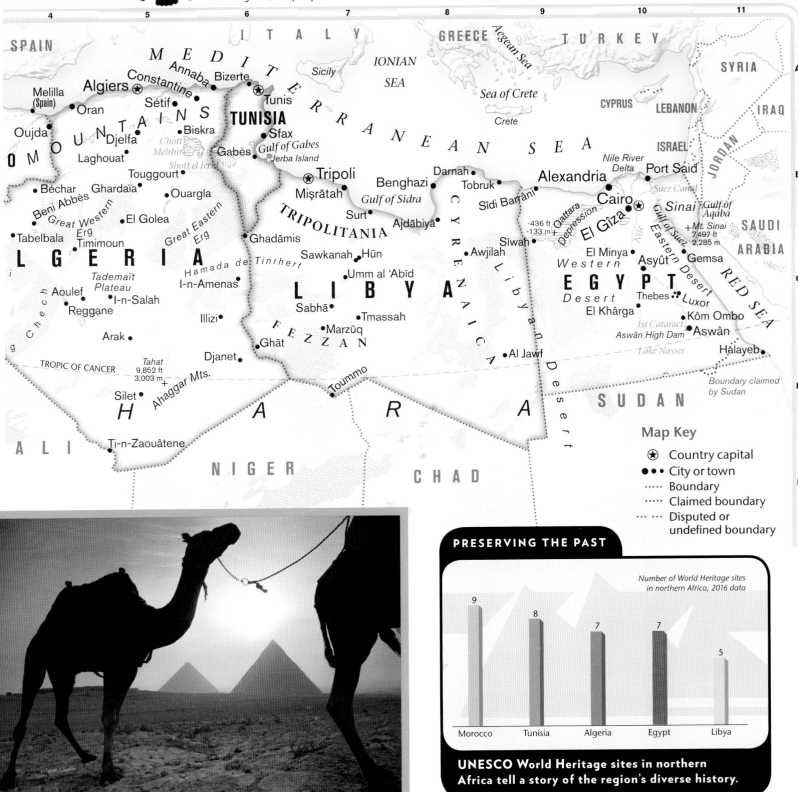

Map Key

- ★ Country capital
- ••• City or town
- ····· Boundary
- ····· Claimed boundary
- ···· Disputed or undefined boundary

PRESERVING THE PAST

Number of World Heritage sites in northern Africa, 2016 data

Morocco	Tunisia	Algeria	Egypt	Libya
9	8	7	7	5

UNESCO World Heritage sites in northern Africa tell a story of the region's diverse history.

◒ **SYMBOLS OF ANCIENT EGYPT.** Camels plod through the desert as the sun sets behind the ancient pyramids of Giza. Built 4,500 years ago, the pyramids were monumental tombs of pharaohs, rulers of ancient Egypt.

◑ **COMPLEX CULTURE.** Leptis Magna, a World Heritage site in Libya, was founded in the seventh century B.C.E. and became a major trade center. Following Roman and later Arab conquests, it fell into ruin.

THE CONTINENT:
AFRICA

THE BASICS

STATS

Largest country
Niger 489,189 sq miles
(1,267,000 sq km)

Smallest country
Cabo Verde 1,557 sq miles
(4,033 sq km)

Most populous country
Nigeria 190,632,000

Least populous country
Cabo Verde 561,000

Predominant languages
French, English, Portuguese, Arabic,
Spanish, indigenous languages

Predominant religions
Islam, Christianity,
indigenous beliefs

Highest GDP per capita
Cabo Verde $6,700

Lowest GDP per capita
Liberia $900

Highest life expectancy
Cabo Verde 72 years

Lowest life expectancy
Guinea-Bissau 51 years

GEO WHIZ

For more than 300 years,
the Slave House on Senegal's
Gorée Island served as a holding
pen for slaves before they were
sent to the Americas and elsewhere. Today, it is a museum
and a memorial.

Nigeria is a major producer
and exporter of oil. Port
Harcourt, in the Niger River
delta, is the center of the
country's oil industry.

Western Africa

Stretching from Cabo Verde
in the west (inset, opposite),
Mauritania in the northwest, and
the barren Sahara in the north,
to Nigeria in the southeast,
16 countries make up western
Africa. Three countries —

⬤ **RIVER TRANSPORT.** Traditional river boats
are an important link in the movement of cargo and
people along the Niger River.

Burkina Faso, Mali, and Niger—are landlocked. The remaining 13
have coastlines along the Atlantic Ocean or the Gulf of Guinea.
Early kingdoms thrived in Mali, Ghana, and Benin, but European
colonization disrupted traditional societies and economies,
and left a legacy of political turmoil. Today, the countries are
independent, but widespread use of French and English reflects
the region's colonial past. Reliance on agriculture plus falling
global oil prices have
left the region with a
struggling economy.

◖ **WAITING FOR SHIPMENT.**
Sacks of peanuts create an artificial
mountain in Kano, Nigeria, where
they wait for transport to Lagos
and then export to world markets.
Nigeria produces more than half of
the region's peanut crop.

◖ **FULL OF COLOR.**
Artistic ceramic plates
brighten an outdoor
marketplace in Kumasi,
Ghana. This country has a
long and rich cultural tradition
of creating pottery for cooking
and for serving food and water.

MASTER ARTISANS. The ancient African kingdom of Benin produced outstanding bronze work. Each piece was created to honor the king.

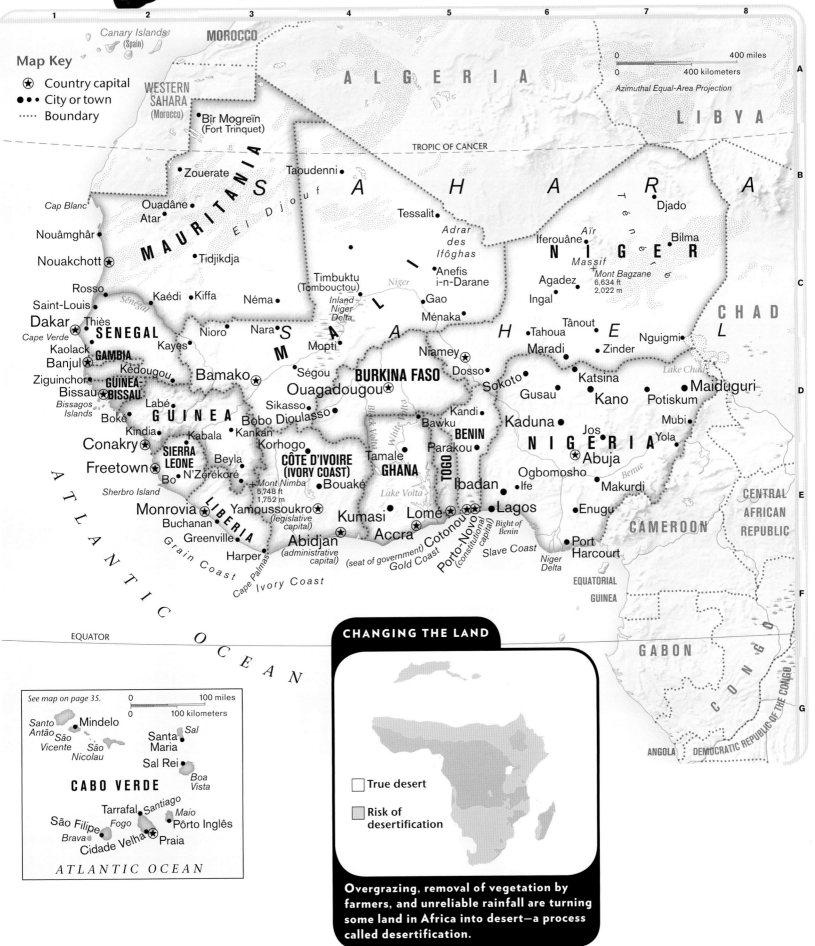

Map Key
- ⊛ Country capital
- ●●● City or town
- ⋯⋯ Boundary

MOROCCO

CANARY ISLANDS (Spain)

WESTERN SAHARA (Morocco)

ALGERIA

LIBYA

0 ___ 400 miles
0 ___ 400 kilometers
Azimuthal Equal-Area Projection

Bîr Mogreïn (Fort Trinquet)

TROPIC OF CANCER

Zouerate
Taoudenni

Cap Blanc
Ouadâne
Atar
Tessalit

MAURITANIA
El Djouf
S A H A R A

Nouâmghâr
Adrar des Ifôghas
Iferouâne
Aïr Massif
Djado

Nouakchott ⊛
Tidjikdja
Bilma

Rosso
Kaédi
Kiffa
Néma
Timbuktu (Tombouctou)
Niger
Anefis
i-n-Darane
Agadez
Mont Bagzane 6,634 ft 2,022 m
N I G E R

Saint-Louis
Inland Niger Delta
Gao
Ingal
Tânout

Dakar ⊛
Thiès
SENEGAL
Nioro
Nara
Mopti
Ménaka
Tahoua

Cape Verde
Kaolack
Kayes
M A L I
Ségou
Niamey ⊛
Maradi
Zinder
Nguigmi

GAMBIA
Banjul
Kédougou
Bamako ⊛
Dosso
Sokoto
Katsina
Lake Chad
CHAD

Ziguinchor
GUINEA-BISSAU
Sikasso
BURKINA FASO
Ouagadougou ⊛
Gusau
Kano
Maiduguri

Bissau ⊛
Labé
Bobo Dioulasso
Kandi
Kaduna
Potiskum
Mubi

Bissagos Islands
Boke
GUINEA
Kankan
Bawku
Parakou
Jos
Yola

Kindia
Kabala
Korhogo
BENIN
NIGERIA
Abuja ⊛

Conakry ⊛
SIERRA LEONE
Beyla
CÔTE D'IVOIRE (IVORY COAST)
Tamale
TOGO
Ogbomosho
Makurdi

Freetown ⊛
Bo
N'Zérékoré
GHANA
Ibadan
Ife
CENTRAL AFRICAN REPUBLIC

Sherbro Island
Mont Nimba 5,748 ft 1,752 m
Bouaké
Lake Volta
Lagos
Enugu

Monrovia
LIBERIA
Yamoussoukro (legislative capital)
Kumasi
Lomé
Cotonou
CAMEROON

Buchanan
Accra
Porto-Novo (constitutional capital)
Bight of Benin
Port Harcourt

Greenville
Abidjan (administrative capital)
(seat of government)
Gold Coast
Slave Coast
Niger Delta
EQUATORIAL GUINEA

Harper
Cape Palmas
Ivory Coast
Grain Coast

ATLANTIC OCEAN

EQUATOR

GABON

CONGO

ANGOLA

DEMOCRATIC REPUBLIC OF THE CONGO

See map on page 35.

0 ___ 100 miles
0 ___ 100 kilometers

Santo Antão
Mindelo
São Vicente
São Nicolau
Santa Maria
Sal
Sal Rei
Boa Vista

CABO VERDE

Tarrafal
Santiago
Maio
São Filipe
Fogo
Pôrto Inglês
Brava
Cidade Velha ⊛
Praia

ATLANTIC OCEAN

CHANGING THE LAND

☐ True desert
☐ Risk of desertification

Overgrazing, removal of vegetation by farmers, and unreliable rainfall are turning some land in Africa into desert—a process called desertification.

THE CONTINENT:
AFRICA

THE BASICS

STATS

Largest country
Tanzania 365,753 sq miles
(947,300 sq km)

Smallest country
Djibouti 8,958 sq miles
(23,200 sq km)

Most populous country
Ethiopia 105,350,000

Least populous country
Djibouti 865,000

Predominant languages
French, Arabic, English, Kiswahili,
indigenous languages

Predominant religions
Christianity, Islam,
indigenous beliefs

Highest GDP per capita
Djibouti, Kenya $3,400

Lowest GDP per capita
Somalia $400

Highest life expectancy
Djibouti 63 years

Lowest life expectancy
Somalia 52 years

GEO WHIZ

As part of a coming-of-age ritual,
each Maasai boy must kill a lion.
The Maasai are a semi-nomadic
people in Kenya and Tanzania.

In 2006, the 3.3-million-year-old
fossilized remains of a child were
found in northern Ethiopia.

Eastern Africa

Eastern Africa's southern countries attract tourists to see big game—lions, elephants, giraffes, cape buffalos, zebras, wildebeests—that live on tropical grasslands called savannas. Some also come to the region to climb its towering volcanic mountains, such as Kilimanjaro and Mount Kenya. Along the western border lie Africa's Great Lakes, a part of the Rift Valley where tectonic forces are gradually separating eastern Africa from the rest of the continent. Religious and ethnic conflicts have plagued the region's northern countries for many years, leading to the political separation of Eritrea from Ethiopia. Civil unrest combined with drought has led to widespread famine, especially in Somalia.

EAGER LEARNERS. Tanzania, a poor country with a literacy rate of only 78 percent, lags in education. Students in this crowded village school compete for the teacher's attention.

FROM FIELD TO CUP. A worker on a coffee estate in Kenya holds freshly harvested coffee berries, which will soon be on their way to world markets. Coffee production was introduced to Kenya in 1900. Today, it directly or indirectly employs more than five million workers.

WOMAN'S WORK. This woman in Kibera, Kenya, carries a heavy load of wood gathered in a nearby forest. Villagers throughout Africa depend on wood as their main source of fuel to cook and heat their homes. This contributes to widespread deforestation.

SOURCE OF THE NILE

Nile River
EQUATOR
DEMOCRATIC
REPUBLIC
OF THE
CONGO
UGANDA
Lake Victoria
KENYA
RWANDA
0   100 miles
0   100 kilometers
BURUNDI
TANZANIA

Lake Victoria is Africa's largest lake. It is also the second largest freshwater lake in the world and a primary source of the Nile River. Pollution and overfishing are endangering the lake's environment.

CRITICALLY ENDANGERED. About half of Earth's roughly 900 wild mountain gorillas live in forests on the slopes of the Virunga Mountains. Poaching, habitat loss, and civil conflict threaten their survival.

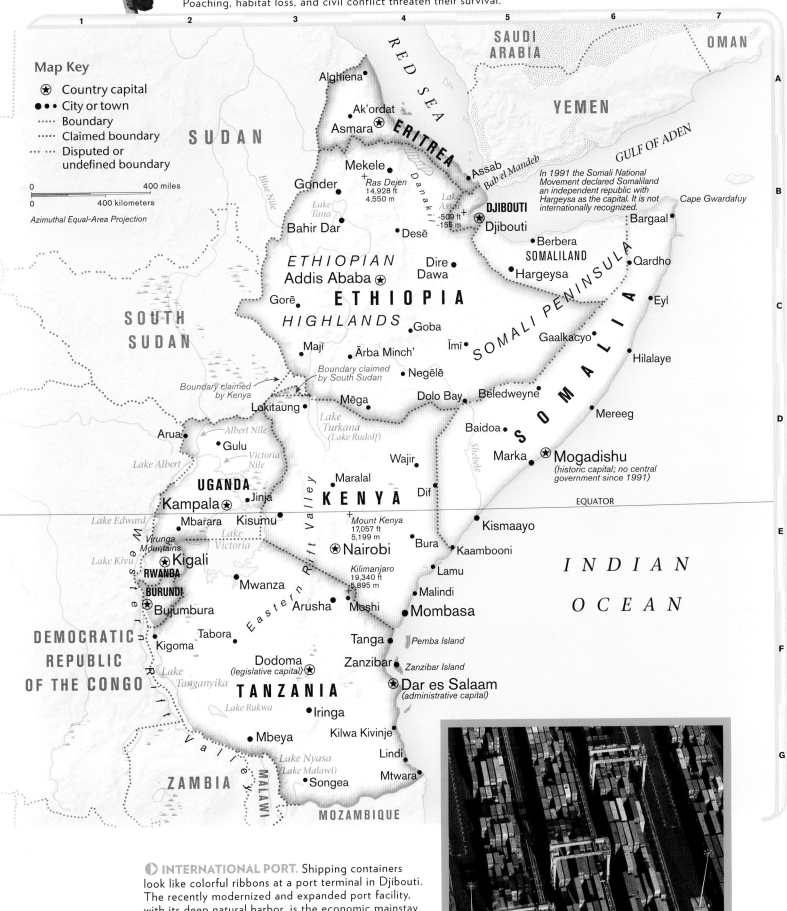

Map Key

★ Country capital
●●● City or town
····· Boundary
····· Claimed boundary
····· Disputed or undefined boundary

0 ————— 400 miles
0 ————— 400 kilometers

Azimuthal Equal-Area Projection

SAUDI ARABIA
OMAN
RED SEA
YEMEN
Alghiena
Ak'ordat
Asmara ⊛ ERITREA
GULF OF ADEN
SUDAN
Mekele
+ Ras Dejen 14,928 ft 4,550 m
Gonder
Danakil
Assab
Bab el Mandeb
Cape Gwardafuy
In 1991 the Somali National Movement declared Somaliland an independent republic with Hargeysa as the capital. It is not internationally recognized.
Blue Nile
Lake Assal -509 ft -155 m
DJIBOUTI
Lake Tana
Djibouti
Bargaal
Bahir Dar
Desē
Berbera
SOMALILAND
Qardho
ETHIOPIAN
Dire Dawa
Hargeysa
Addis Ababa ⊛
SOUTH SUDAN
Gorē
ETHIOPIA
Eyl
HIGHLANDS
Goba
Majī
Īmī
Gaalkacyo
Hilalaye
Ārba Minch'
Boundary claimed by South Sudan
Negēlē
SOMALIA
Boundary claimed by Kenya
Mēga
Dolo Bay
Beledweyne
Mereeg
Lokitaung
Lake Turkana (Lake Rudolf)
Arua
Baidoa
SOMALI PENINSULA
Albert Nile
Shebele
Gulu
Wajir
Marka
Mogadishu ⊛
(historic capital; no central government since 1991)
Lake Albert
Victoria Nile
Maralal
UGANDA
KENYA
Dif
EQUATOR
Kampala ⊛
Jinja
Lake Edward
Mbarara
Kisumu
+ Mount Kenya 17,057 ft 5,199 m
Kismaayo
Virunga Mountains
Lake Victoria
Bura
Lake Kivu
Nairobi ⊛
Kaambooni
INDIAN OCEAN
Kigali ⊛
Kilimanjaro 19,340 ft 5,895 m
Lamu
RWANDA
Mwanza
Malindi
BURUNDI
Moshi
Bujumbura ⊛
Arusha
Mombasa
DEMOCRATIC
Tabora
Tanga
Kigoma
Pemba Island
REPUBLIC
Dodoma (legislative capital) ⊛
Zanzibar
Zanzibar Island
OF THE CONGO
Lake Tanganyika
TANZANIA
Dar es Salaam ⊛
(administrative capital)
Lake Rukwa
Iringa
Eastern Rift Valley
Western Rift Valley
Mbeya
Kilwa Kivinje
Lindi
ZAMBIA
Lake Nyasa (Lake Malawi)
Songea
Mtwara
MALAWI
MOZAMBIQUE

INTERNATIONAL PORT. Shipping containers look like colorful ribbons at a port terminal in Djibouti. The recently modernized and expanded port facility, with its deep natural harbor, is the economic mainstay of this small country in eastern Africa.

THE BASICS

STATS

Largest country
Democratic Republic of the
Congo (DRC)
905,350 sq mi (2,344,858 sq km)

Smallest country
Sao Tome and Principe
372 sq mi (964 sq m)

Most populous country
Democratic Republic of the Congo
83,301,000

Least populous country
Sao Tome and Principe 201,000

Predominant languages
English, French, Arabic,
Portuguese, indigenous languages

Predominant religions
Christianity, Islam,
indigenous beliefs

Highest GDP per capita
Equatorial Guinea $38,600

Lowest GDP per capita
Central African Republic
$700

Highest life expectancy
Sao Tome and Principe 65 years

Lowest life expectancy
Chad 50 years

GEO WHIZ

The Mbuti Pygmies, of the DRC,
yodel as they beat the bush to
drive cat-size antelope into nets.
The hunting technique is more
than a thousand years old.

The two main tributaries of the
Nile join at Khartoum, in Sudan.
Farmers rely on the world's lon-
gest river to water their crops.

Central Africa

The Congo, a major commercial waterway of central Africa, flows through rain forests being cut for timber and palm oil plantations. This places a large area of Earth's biodiversity at risk. To the north, Lake Chad, a large, but shallow lake, fluctuates greatly in size due to high rates of evaporation, unreliable rainfall, and overuse by the 20 million people who live near its shores. Diamonds, copper, and chromium are mined in the Democratic Republic of the Congo (DRC) and the Central African Republic. Coffee is grown in the eastern highlands of the region, and livestock and cotton contribute to the economy of Chad. Religious and ethnic conflicts led to the separation of South Sudan from Sudan in 2011. Ongoing civil unrest and drought have led to widespread famine in South Sudan.

ACTIVE VOLCANO.
Mount Nyiragongo, in the
Virunga Mountains of the DRC,
contains one of the world's
largest lava lakes.

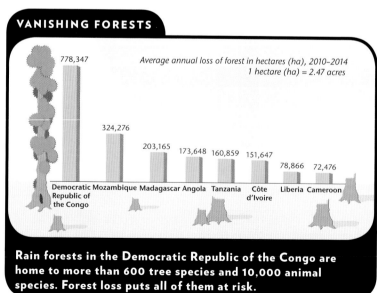

VANISHING FORESTS

Average annual loss of forest in hectares (ha), 2010–2014
1 hectare (ha) = 2.47 acres

Democratic Republic of the Congo	Mozambique	Madagascar	Angola	Tanzania	Côte d'Ivoire	Liberia	Cameroon
778,347	324,276	203,165	173,648	160,859	151,647	78,866	72,476

Rain forests in the Democratic Republic of the Congo are home to more than 600 tree species and 10,000 animal species. Forest loss puts all of them at risk.

DESERT CARAVAN. Legendary Tuareg tribesmen lead their camels across the desert in northern Chad. The camels, loaded with trade goods such as salt, are destined for distant market towns.

CELEBRATING A KING. The Chokwe people of central Africa used masks such as this one to celebrate the inauguration of a new king.

Map Key

⊛ Country capital
•●• City or town
····· Boundary
····· Claimed boundary
····· Disputed or undefined boundary

0   400 miles
0   400 kilometers

Azimuthal Equal-Area Projection

FACING HUNGER. Refugees fleeing civil unrest and hunger in South Sudan wait to receive food at the Khour Al-Waral refugee camp in neighboring Sudan. The camp is home to 50,000 people.

Southern Africa

NATURAL WONDER.
Victoria Falls, third largest
waterfall in the world, is
5,500 feet (1,676 m) wide
and 355 feet (108 m) high.

Ringed by uplands, the region's central basin holds the seasonally lush Okavango Delta and scorching Kalahari Desert. The mighty Zambezi thunders over Victoria Falls on its way to the Indian Ocean, where Madagascar is home to plants and animals found nowhere else in the world. Bantu and San are among the indigenous people who saw their hold on the land give way to Portuguese, Dutch, and British traders and colonists. The region offers a range of mineral resources and a variety of climates and soils that in some places yield bumper crops of grains, grapes, and citrus. Rich deposits of coal, diamonds, and gold have helped make South Africa the continent's economic powerhouse.

STARING EYES.
This ring-tailed lemur rests
in the crook of a forest
tree branch. The ring-tail,
found only in Madagascar,
spends time both on the
ground and in trees. It eats
fruits, leaves, insects, small
birds, and even lizards.

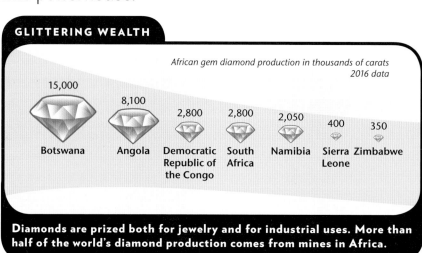

GLITTERING WEALTH

African gem diamond production in thousands of carats
2016 data

15,000	8,100	2,800	2,800	2,050	400	350
Botswana	Angola	Democratic Republic of the Congo	South Africa	Namibia	Sierra Leone	Zimbabwe

**Diamonds are prized both for jewelry and for industrial uses. More than
half of the world's diamond production comes from mines in Africa.**

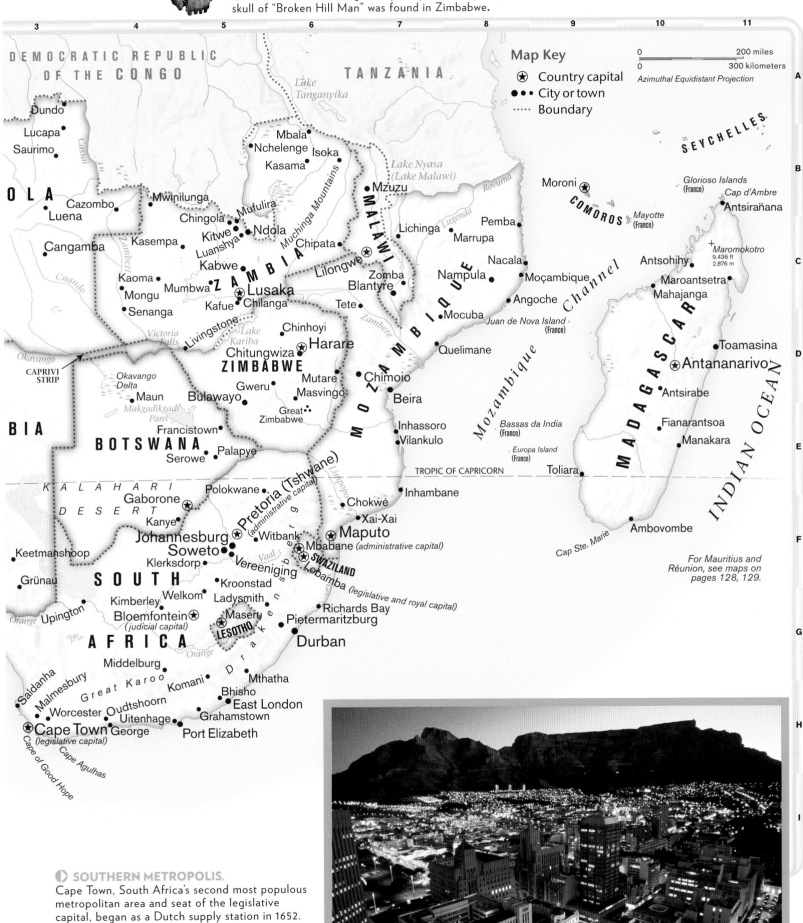

◗ EARLY MAN. Dating back perhaps 70,000 years, this skull of "Broken Hill Man" was found in Zimbabwe.

Map Key

★ Country capital
••• City or town
···· Boundary

0 ————— 200 miles
0 ————— 300 kilometers
Azimuthal Equidistant Projection

DEMOCRATIC REPUBLIC
OF THE CONGO

TANZANIA

Lake Tanganyika

Dundo
Lucapa
Saurimo
Cassai

OLA

Cazombo
Luena
Mwinilunga
Mufulira
Chingola
Kitwe
Ndola
Luanshya
Kabwe
Kasempa
ZAMBIA
Lusaka
Kafue
Chilanga
Mumbwa
Kaoma
Mongu
Senanga

Cangamba
Zambezi
Cuando

Kafue

Mbala
Nchelenge
Isoka
Kasama
Muchinga Mountains

Mzuzu

MALAWI

*Lake Nyasa
(Lake Malawi)*

Lichinga
Lugenda
Rovuma

Pemba
Marrupa

Nacala
Nampula
Moçambique
Angoche
Mocuba

MOZAMBIQUE
Quelimane

SEYCHELLES

Moroni ★

COMOROS
*Mayotte
(France)*

*Glorioso Islands
(France)*
Cap d'Ambre
Antsiranana

Antsohihy
+ *Maromokotro
9,436 ft
2,876 m*
Maroantsetra
Mahajanga

Antananarivo ★
Antsirabe

MADAGASCAR

Chipata
Lilongwe ★
Zomba
Blantyre
Tete

Livingstone
Victoria Falls
Chinhoyi
Harare
Chitungwiza
Lake Kariba
Zambeze

ZIMBABWE
Gweru
Mutare
Masvingo
Great Zimbabwe

Chimoio
Beira

Inhassoro
Vilankulo

Mozambique Channel

*Juan de Nova Island
(France)*

*Bassas da India
(France)*

*Europa Island
(France)*

Toliara

Fianarantsoa
Manakara

TROPIC OF CAPRICORN

INDIAN OCEAN

BIA

Okavango
CAPRIVI
STRIP
Okavango Delta
Maun
Makgadikgadi Pans

BOTSWANA
Francistown
Serowe
Palapye

*KALAHARI
DESERT*

Bulawayo

MOZAMBIQUE

Inhambane
Chokwé
Xai-Xai
Maputo
Mbabane *(administrative capital)*
SWAZILAND
Lobamba *(legislative and royal capital)*

Ambovombe

Cap Ste. Marie

*For Mauritius and
Réunion, see maps on
pages 128, 129.*

Gaborone ★
Kanye
Keetmanshoop
Grünau

Polokwane
Pretoria (Tshwane)
(administrative capital)
Johannesburg
Soweto
Witbank
Klerksdorp
Vereeniging
Vaal

Limpopo

SOUTH

Upington
Orange
Kimberley
Bloemfontein ★
(judicial capital)
Welkom
Kroonstad
Ladysmith
Maseru
LESOTHO
Pietermaritzburg

Richards Bay

AFRICA
Orange
Durban

Middelburg
Komani
Mthatha
Bhisho
East London
Grahamstown

Saldanha
Malmesbury
Worcester
Oudtshoorn
Uitenhage
Great Karoo
George
Port Elizabeth

★ Cape Town
(legislative capital)
Cape Agulhas
Cape of Good Hope

◗ SOUTHERN METROPOLIS.
Cape Town, South Africa's second most populous metropolitan area and seat of the legislative capital, began as a Dutch supply station in 1652. Table Mountain rises in the background.

THE REGION:
AUSTRALIA, NEW ZEALAND & OCEANIA

PHYSICAL

Area and population totals are for the independent countries in the region only.

HIGHEST POINT
Mount Wilhelm, Papua New Guinea
14,793 ft (4,509 m)

LOWEST POINT
Lake Eyre, Australia
-49 ft (-15 m)

LONGEST RIVER
Murray-Darling, Australia
2,310 mi (3,718 km)

LARGEST LAKE
Lake Eyre, Australia
3,430 sq mi (8,884 sq km)

LAND AREA
3,296,000 sq mi
(8,537,000 sq km)

POLITICAL

POPULATION
37,139,000

LARGEST METROPOLITAN AREA
Sydney, Australia
Pop. 4,540,000

LARGEST COUNTRY
Australia
2,988,885 sq mi (7,741,220 sq km)

MOST DENSELY POPULATED COUNTRY
Nauru
1,205.3 people per sq mi (459.1 per sq km)

AUSTRALIA, NEW ZEALAND & OCEANIA

Australia, New Zealand & Oceania

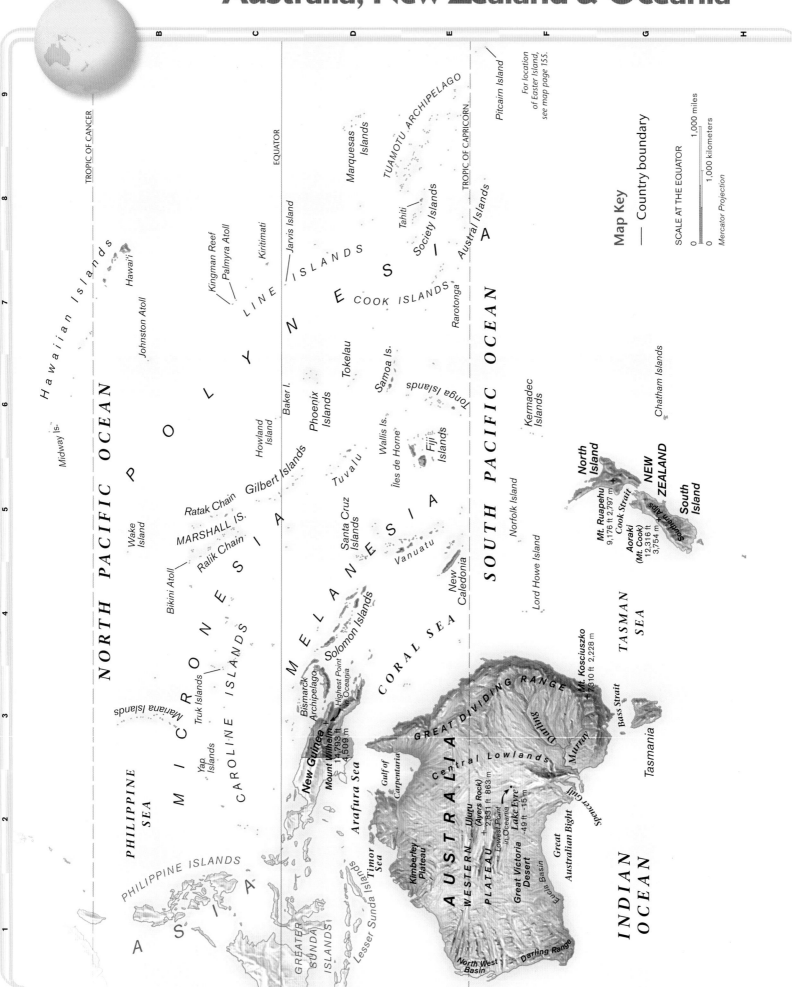

A B C D E F G H

9
8
7
6
5
4
3
2
1

TROPIC OF CANCER

EQUATOR

TROPIC OF CAPRICORN

For location
of Easter Island,
see map page 155.

Pitcairn Island

TUAMOTU ARCHIPELAGO

Marquesas
Islands

Tahiti

Society Islands

Austral Islands

Map Key

— Country boundary

SCALE AT THE EQUATOR

1,000 miles

1,000 kilometers

Mercator Projection

Hawaiian Islands

Hawai'i

Johnston Atoll

Kingman Reef

Palmyra Atoll

Kiritimati

Jarvis Island

LINE ISLANDS

P O L Y N E S I A

COOK ISLANDS

Rarotonga

Midway Is.

NORTH PACIFIC OCEAN

Tokelau

Baker I.

Howland
Island

Phoenix
Islands

Samoa Is.

Tonga Islands

Chatham Islands

SOUTH PACIFIC OCEAN

Wake
Island

Ratak Chain

Gilbert Islands

MARSHALL IS.

Ralik Chain

Bikini Atoll

M I C R O N E S I A

Santa Cruz
Islands

Tuvalu

Wallis Is.

Îles de Horne

Fiji
Islands

Vanuatu

Kermadec
Islands

North
Island

NEW
ZEALAND

Mt. Ruapehu
9,176 ft 2,797 m

Cook Strait

Aoraki
(Mt. Cook)
12,316 ft
3,754 m

South
Island

Southern Alps

Norfolk Island

Lord Howe Island

Mariana Islands

Yap
Islands

Truk Islands

CAROLINE ISLANDS

M E L A N E S I A

Solomon Islands

New
Caledonia

CORAL SEA

TASMAN SEA

PHILIPPINE
SEA

Bismarck
Archipelago

Highest Point
in Oceania

New Guinea

Mount Wilhelm
14,793 ft
4,509 m

Arafura Sea

Gulf of
Carpentaria

GREAT DIVIDING RANGE

Mt. Kosciuszko
7,310 ft 2,228 m

Darling

Murray

Bass Strait

Tasmania

A S I A

PHILIPPINE ISLANDS

GREATER
SUNDA
ISLANDS

Lesser Sunda Islands

Timor
Sea

Kimberley
Plateau

AUSTRALIA

WESTERN
PLATEAU

Uluru
(Ayers Rock)
2,831 ft 863 m

Central Lowlands

Lake Eyre
Lowest Point
in Oceania
-49 ft -15 m

Great Victoria
Desert

Eucla Basin

Great
Australian Bight

Spencer Gulf

INDIAN
OCEAN

North West
Basin

Darling Range

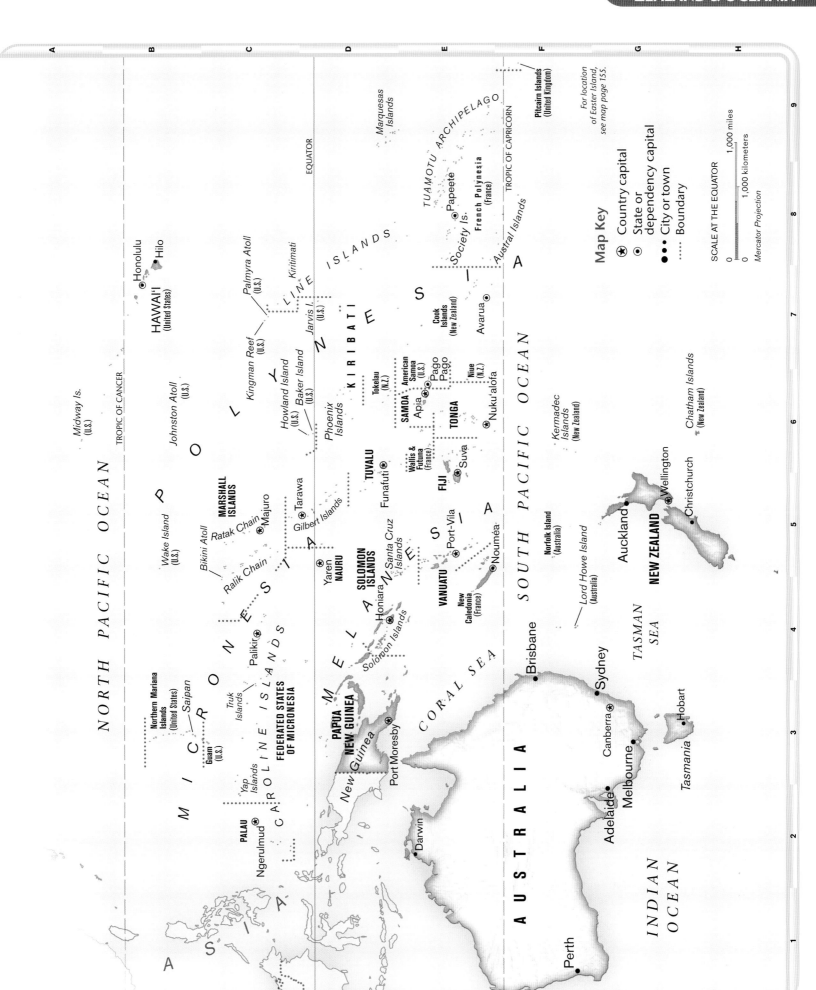

For location of Easter Island, see map page 155.

Map Key

⊛ Country capital
⊙ State or dependency capital
● City or town
••••• Boundary

SCALE AT THE EQUATOR

1,000 miles
1,000 kilometers

Mercator Projection

NORTH PACIFIC OCEAN

SOUTH PACIFIC OCEAN

INDIAN OCEAN

CORAL SEA

TASMAN SEA

EQUATOR

TROPIC OF CANCER

TROPIC OF CAPRICORN

AUSTRALIA

NEW ZEALAND

PAPUA NEW GUINEA

PALAU
Ngerulmud ⊛

FEDERATED STATES OF MICRONESIA
Palikir ⊛

MARSHALL ISLANDS

NAURU
Yaren ⊛

SOLOMON ISLANDS
Honiara ⊛

TUVALU
Funafuti ⊛

KIRIBATI

VANUATU
Port-Vila ⊛

FIJI
Suva ⊛

TONGA
Nuku'alofa ⊛

SAMOA
Apia ⊛

TUVALU

French Polynesia (France)
Papeete ⊙

Cook Islands (New Zealand)
Avarua ⊙

New Caledonia (France)
Nouméa ⊙

American Samoa (U.S.)
Pago Pago ⊙

Niue (N.Z.)

Tokelau (N.Z.)

Wallis & Futuna (France)

HAWAI'I (United States)
Honolulu ⊙
Hilo

MICRONESIA

MELANESIA

POLYNESIA

ASIA

CAROLINE ISLANDS

LINE ISLANDS

TUAMOTU ARCHIPELAGO

Pitcairn Islands (United Kingdom)

Marquesas Islands

Society Is.

Austral Islands

Midway Is. (U.S.)

Wake Island (U.S.)

Johnston Atoll (U.S.)

Palmyra Atoll (U.S.)

Kingman Reef (U.S.)

Howland Island (U.S.)

Baker Island (U.S.)

Jarvis I. (U.S.)

Kiritimati

Phoenix Islands

Bikini Atoll

Ratak Chain

Ralik Chain

Majuro

Tarawa

Gilbert Islands

Santa Cruz Islands

Solomon Islands

Kermadec Islands (New Zealand)

Norfolk Island (Australia)

Lord Howe Island (Australia)

Chatham Islands (New Zealand)

Northern Mariana Islands (United States)
Saipan

Guam (U.S.)

Yap Islands

Truk Islands

New Guinea

Port Moresby

Darwin

Perth

Adelaide

Melbourne

Sydney

Canberra ⊛

Brisbane

Hobart

Tasmania

Auckland

Wellington ⊛

Christchurch

Nauru

Australia,
New Zealand & Oceania

WORLDS APART

⬭ **AUSTRALIAN
TEDDY BEAR.** Koalas,
which are not bears at
all, are native to the
eucalyptus forests of
eastern Australia.

T his vast region includes Australia—the world's smallest continent—New
Zealand, and a fleet of mostly tiny island worlds scattered across the Pacific
Ocean. Apart from Australia, New Zealand, and Papua New Guinea, Oceania's
other 11 independent countries cover about 25,000 square miles (65,000 sq km), an
area only slightly larger than half of New Zealand's North Island. Twenty-one other
island groups are dependencies of the United States, France, Australia, New Zealand,
or the United Kingdom. Long isolation has allowed the growth of diverse marine
communities, such as Australia's Great Barrier Reef, and the evolution of platypuses,
kangaroos, kiwis, and other land animals that live nowhere else on the planet.

◁ **ANCIENT VOYAGERS.**
The Maoris are believed to have sailed
to New Zealand from islands far to the
northeast. Maori warriors traditionally
adorned themselves with elaborate tattoos
to frighten enemies.

PLACE OF LEGENDS. Once part of an ancient seabed, Uluru, also known as Ayers Rock, is sacred to native Aboriginals. This massive sandstone block was exposed by erosion.

TROPICAL HABITAT. Brilliantly colored fish swim among branching corals in the warm waters of the Vatu-i-Ra Channel in the Fiji Islands. The waters around Fiji have some of the richest and most diverse fish populations in the world.

NATIVE COWBOYS. Competition is fierce during a rodeo in Hope Vale, an Aboriginal community on Australia's Cape York Peninsula. Hope Vale is home to several Aboriginal clan groups.

more about
Australia, New Zealand & Oceania

🔴 **A WATER WORLD.** Located just 7 degrees north of the Equator, the islands of the Republic of Palau were a United Nations Trust Territory until 1994, when they gained independence.

🔴 **BIG JUMPER.** The red kangaroo, the largest living marsupial—an animal that carries its young in a pouch—is at home on the dry inland plains of Australia. It can cover 30 feet (9 m) in a single hop.

🔴 **WOOLLY POPULATION.** Sheep outnumber people in Australia and New Zealand. Wool production is an important part of the economies of these two countries.

🔴 **FLYING HIGH.** Prevailing winds lift adventurous tourists in a tandem parasail high above the waters of New Zealand's Bay of Islands. Rising up to 1,200 feet (366 m) above the water, visitors get a bird's-eye view of the islands.

WHERE THE PICTURES ARE

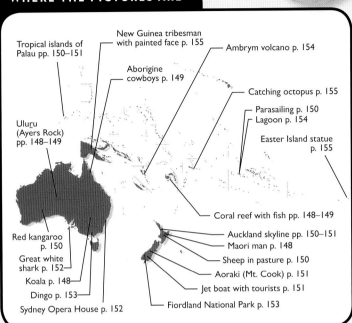

Tropical islands of
Palau pp. 150–151

New Guinea tribesman
with painted face p. 155

Ambrym volcano p. 154

Aborigine
cowboys p. 149

Catching octopus p. 155

Uluru
(Ayers Rock)
pp. 148–149

Parasailing p. 150
Lagoon p. 154

Easter Island statue
p. 155

Coral reef with fish pp. 148–149

Red kangaroo
p. 150

Auckland skyline pp. 150–151
Maori man p. 148

Great white
shark p. 152

Sheep in pasture p. 150

Koala p. 148

Aoraki (Mt. Cook) p. 151

Dingo p. 153

Jet boat with tourists p. 151

Sydney Opera House p. 152

Fiordland National Park p. 153

A WET RIDE. Tourists go for a wild ride in a jet boat
on the roaring waters of New Zealand's Shotover River.

MODERN METROPOLIS.
Modern buildings rise against
a twilight sky in Auckland, on
New Zealand's North Island. It is
home to almost one-third of the
country's population.

SNOWY PEAK. New Zealand's Aoraki (Mount
Cook) rises above the clouds. Legend says the peak is
a frozen Maori warrior.

THE REGION:
AUSTRALIA, NEW ZEALAND & OCEANIA

THE BASICS

STATS

Largest country
Australia 2,998,885 sq mi
(7,741,220 sq km)

Smallest country
New Zealand 103,363 sq mi
(267,710 sq km)

Most populous country
Australia 23,232,000

Least populous country
New Zealand 4,510,000

Predominant languages
English, Maori

Predominant religion
Christianity

Highest GDP per capita
Australia $48,900

Lowest GDP per capita
New Zealand $37,300

Highest life expectancy
Australia 82 years

Lowest life expectancy
New Zealand 81 years

GEO WHIZ

A tree trunk hollowed out by termites is used by Australia's Aboriginals to make a musical instrument called a didgeridoo.

Wellington, in New Zealand, is the southernmost national capital city in the world.

Lake Eyre is Australia's largest lake, but it is very shallow. When filled to capacity, it is not quite 20 feet (6 m) deep.

In September 2010, a magnitude 7.1 earthquake, followed by a 6.3 aftershock in February 2011, caused widespread destruction in Christchurch, on New Zealand's South Island.

Australia & New Zealand

Most people in Australia live along the coast, far from the country's dry interior, known as the Outback. The most populous cities and the best croplands are in the southeast. This "Land Down Under" is increasingly linked by trade to Asia and to 4.5 million "neighbors" in New Zealand. Lying 1,200 miles (1,930 km) across the Tasman Sea, New Zealand is cooler, wetter, and more mountainous than Australia. Geologically active, it has ecosystems ranging from subtropical forests on North Island to snowy peaks on South Island. Both countries enjoy high standards of living and strong agricultural and mining outputs, including wool, wines, gold, coal, and iron ore.

SAILS AT SUNSET.
Reminiscent of a ship in full sail, the Sydney Opera House, in Sydney Harbor, has become a symbol of Australia that is recognized worldwide.

KILLER OF THE DEEP.
Great white sharks inhabit the warm waters off the coast of southern Australia. These marine predators can grow up to 20 feet (6 m) in length.

◑ **DOG OF THE OUTBACK.** The dingo is a wild dog found throughout Australia except Tasmania. Unlike most domestic dogs, the dingo does not bark, although it howls.

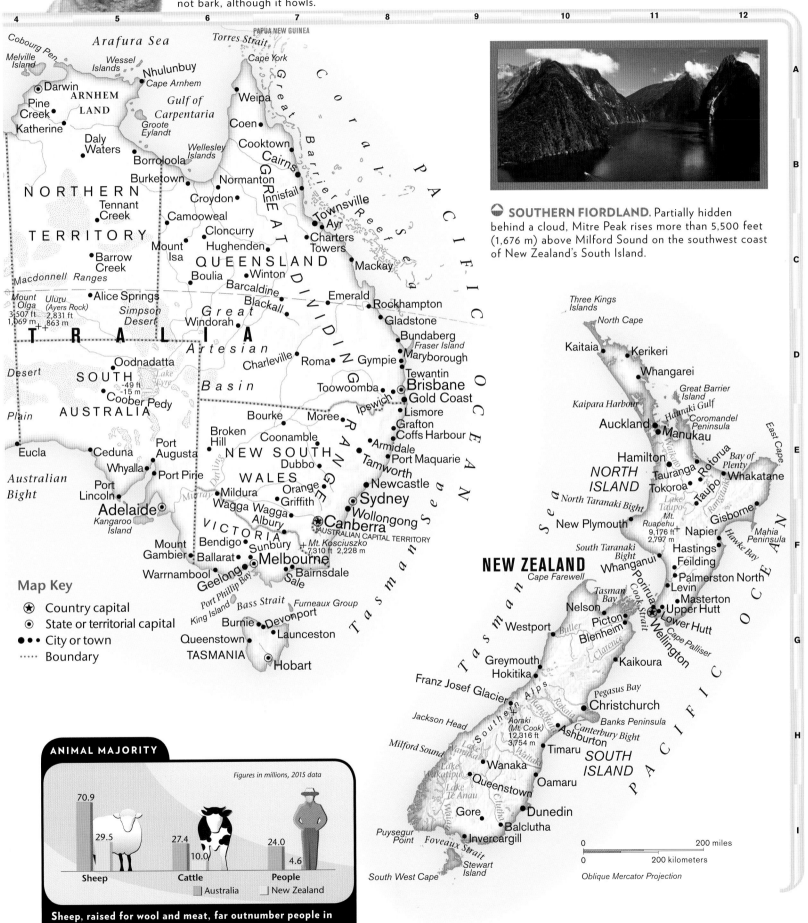

◔ **SOUTHERN FIORDLAND.** Partially hidden behind a cloud, Mitre Peak rises more than 5,500 feet (1,676 m) above Milford Sound on the southwest coast of New Zealand's South Island.

4   5   6   7   8   9   10   11   12

Arafura Sea

Torres Strait
PAPUA NEW GUINEA
Cape York

Cobourg Pen.
Melville Island
Wessel Islands
Nhulunbuy
Cape Arnhem
Darwin
ARNHEM LAND
Pine Creek
Gulf of Carpentaria
Weipa
Coen
Katherine
Daly Waters
Groote Eylandt
Wellesley Islands
Cooktown
Cairns
Borroloola
Innisfail
Burketown
Normanton
Townsville
NORTHERN
Croydon
Ayr
Camooweal
Charters Towers
TERRITORY
Cloncurry
Mackay
Tennant Creek
Hughenden
Mount Isa
QUEENSLAND
Barrow Creek
Boulia
Winton
Macdonnell Ranges
Barcaldine
Emerald
Rockhampton
Mount Olga 3,507 ft 1,069 m
Uluru (Ayers Rock) 2,831 ft 863 m
Alice Springs
Simpson Desert
Great
Blackall
Gladstone
TRALIA
Windorah
Artesian
Bundaberg
Fraser Island
Desert
Oodnadatta
Lake Eyre -49 ft -15 m
Basin
Charleville
Roma
Gympie
Maryborough
SOUTH
Coober Pedy
Tewantin
Plain
AUSTRALIA
Toowoomba
Brisbane
Ipswich
Gold Coast
Eucla
Ceduna
Bourke
Moree
Lismore
Grafton
Coffs Harbour
Australian Bight
Port Augusta
Broken Hill
Coonamble
Armidale
Port Maquarie
Whyalla
Port Pirie
NEW SOUTH
Dubbo
Tamworth
Port Lincoln
WALES
Orange
Newcastle
Adelaide
Mildura
Griffith
Sydney
Kangaroo Island
Wagga Wagga
Wollongong
VICTORIA
Albury
Canberra
AUSTRALIAN CAPITAL TERRITORY
Mount Gambier
Bendigo
Sunbury
Mt. Kosciuszko 7,310 ft 2,228 m
Ballarat
Melbourne
Warrnambool
Geelong
Bairnsdale
Port Phillip Bay
Sale
Bass Strait
Furneaux Group
King Island
Burnie
Devonport
Queenstown
Launceston
TASMANIA
Hobart

Coral Sea
Great Barrier Reef
GREAT DIVIDING RANGE
PACIFIC OCEAN
Tasman Sea
Murray
Darling

Map Key

⊛ Country capital
⊙ State or territorial capital
●●● City or town
····· Boundary

Three Kings Islands
North Cape
Kaitaia
Kerikeri
Whangarei
Great Barrier Island
Kaipara Harbour
Hauraki Gulf
Coromandel Peninsula
Auckland
Manukau
Hamilton
Rotorua
Bay of Plenty
Tauranga
Whakatane
NORTH ISLAND
Tokoroa
Taupo
North Taranaki Bight
Waikato
Lake Taupo
Mt. Ruapehu 9,176 ft 2,797 m
East Cape
New Plymouth
Napier
Gisborne
Mahia Peninsula
South Taranaki Bight
NEW ZEALAND
Hastings
Hawke Bay
Cape Farewell
Whanganui
Feilding
Palmerston North
Levin
Tasman Bay
Masterton
Nelson
Upper Hutt
Westport
Picton
Wellington
Lower Hutt
Blenheim
Cape Palliser
Buller
Greymouth
Kaikoura
Hokitika
Clarence
Franz Josef Glacier
Pegasus Bay
Southern Alps
Christchurch
Jackson Head
Aoraki (Mt. Cook) 12,316 ft 3,754 m
Banks Peninsula
Ashburton
Canterbury Bight
Milford Sound
Timaru
Lake Wanaka
SOUTH ISLAND
Waitaki
Wanaka
Oamaru
Lake Wakatipu
Queenstown
Clutha
Lake Te Anau
Gore
Dunedin
Puysegur Point
Balclutha
Foveaux Strait
Invercargill
South West Cape
Stewart Island

Tasman Sea
PACIFIC OCEAN
Cook Strait
Porirua

0   200 miles
0   200 kilometers
Oblique Mercator Projection

ANIMAL MAJORITY

Figures in millions, 2015 data

	70.9		29.5	27.4	10.0	24.0	4.6

Sheep   Cattle   People

■ Australia   ▌ New Zealand

Sheep, raised for wool and meat, far outnumber people in both Australia and New Zealand. Beef and dairy cattle also surpass human population numbers.

A B C D E F G H I

THE REGION:
AUSTRALIA, NEW ZEALAND & OCEANIA

THE BASICS

STATS

Largest country
Papua New Guinea
178,703 sq mi (462,840 sq km)

Smallest country
Nauru 8 sq mi (21 sq km)

Most populous country
Papua New Guinea 6,910,000

Least populous country
Nauru 10,000

Predominant languages
English, indigenous
languages

Predominant religions
Christianity, indigenous beliefs

Highest GDP per capita
Palau $15,400

Lowest GDP per capita
Kiribati $1,800

Highest life expectancy
Tonga 76 years

Lowest life expectancy
Kiribati 66 years

GEO WHIZ

Five uninhabited islands in the Solomon group have disappeared due to rising sea levels that may be related to climate change, and the inhabited island of Nuatambu has lost more than 50 percent of its land area.

For centuries Fiji's tribal officials would bring out their best utensils—not to serve guests, but to eat them. Cannibalism in Fiji ended when Christianity was adopted in the late 1800s.

The infamous mutiny aboard the British ship H.M.S. *Bounty* took place off Tonga in 1789.

Oceania

Although in its broadest sense Oceania includes Australia and New Zealand, more commonly it refers to some 25,000 islands that make up three large cultural regions in the Pacific Ocean. Melanesia, which extends from Papua New Guinea to Fiji, is closest to Australia. Micronesia lies mostly north of the Equator and includes Palau and the Federated States of Micronesia. New Zealand, Hawai'i, and Rapa Nui (Easter Island) mark the western, northern, and eastern limits of Polynesia, with Tahiti, Samoa, and Tonga near its heart. Oceania's people often face problems of limited living space and freshwater. Plantation agriculture, fishing, tourism, or mining form the economic base for most of the islands in this region.

TROPICAL PARADISE. A reef separates an area of seawater from the ocean, forming a quiet lagoon around the island of Bora Bora in the Society Islands of French Polynesia.

LIVING EARTH. Ambrym volcano, in Vanuatu, is one of the most active volcanoes in Oceania. First observed by Britain's Captain Cook in 1774, Ambrym continues to erupt regularly, adding to the island's black sand beaches.

◑ **UNSOLVED MYSTERY.** Carved from volcanic rock, the giant stone heads, called *moai*, on Rapa Nui (Easter Island) remain a mystery.

◐ **LONG ARMS.** Octopuses live on coral reefs in the warm tropical waters of the South Pacific Ocean. They use the suckers on their tentacles to move around and to catch crustaceans and small fish.

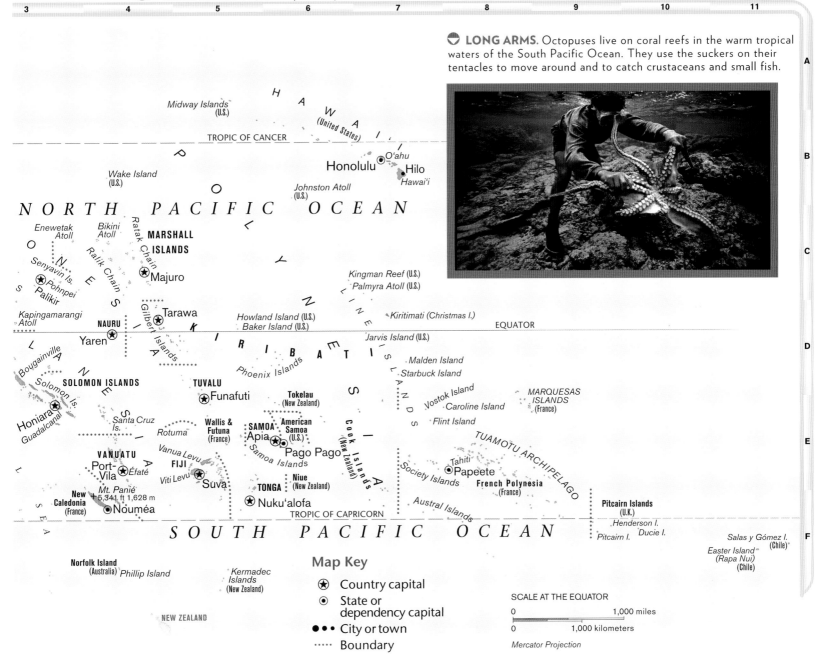

Midway Islands (U.S.)

TROPIC OF CANCER

H A W A I I (United States)

Wake Island (U.S.)

Johnston Atoll (U.S.)

Honolulu ● O'ahu ● Hilo
Hawai'i

N O R T H   P A C I F I C   O C E A N

P O L Y N E S I A

Enewetak Atoll
Bikini Atoll
Ratak Chain
MARSHALL ISLANDS
Ralik Chain
Senyavin Is.
● Pohnpei
Palikir
C A R O L I N E S
Kapingamarangi Atoll
NAURU
Yaren ★
Gilbert Islands

★ Majuro

Tarawa

Howland Island (U.S.)
Baker Island (U.S.)

Kingman Reef (U.S.)
Palmyra Atoll (U.S.)

◆ Kiritimati (Christmas I.)

EQUATOR

Jarvis Island (U.S.)

M I C R O N E S I A

K I R I B A T I

L I N E   I S L A N D S

Malden Island
Starbuck Island

M E L A N E S I A

Bougainville
Solomon Is.
SOLOMON ISLANDS
Honiara ★
Guadalcanal
Santa Cruz Is.

TUVALU
★ Funafuti

Tokelau (New Zealand)

Phoenix Islands

Vostok Island
Caroline Island
Flint Island

MARQUESAS ISLANDS (France)

Rotuma
Wallis & Futuna (France)
SAMOA
Apia ★
American Samoa (U.S.)
● Pago Pago
Samoa Islands

C o o k   I s l a n d s (New Zealand)

P O L Y N E S I A

TUAMOTU ARCHIPELAGO

VANUATU
Port-Vila ★ ● Éfaté
Vanua Levu
FIJI
Viti Levu
★ Suva

TONGA
★ Nuku'alofa

Niue (New Zealand)

Society Islands
Tahiti
● Papeete
French Polynesia (France)

Austral Islands

Pitcairn Islands (U.K.)
● Henderson I.
Pitcairn I. ● Ducie I.

New Caledonia (France)
Mt. Panié + 5,341 ft 1,628 m
◉ Nouméa

TROPIC OF CAPRICORN

S O U T H   P A C I F I C   O C E A N

Salas y Gómez I. (Chile)
Easter Island (Rapa Nui) (Chile)

C O R A L   S E A

Norfolk Island (Australia) Phillip Island

Kermadec Islands (New Zealand)

NEW ZEALAND

Map Key

★ Country capital
◉ State or dependency capital
●●● City or town
····· Boundary

SCALE AT THE EQUATOR

0 ——————— 1,000 miles
0 ——————— 1,000 kilometers

Mercator Projection

◑ **MELANESIAN CUSTOM.** In the Huli culture of Papua New Guinea's Eastern Highlands, men adorn themselves with colorful paints, feathers, and grasses as they prepare to take part in festivals.

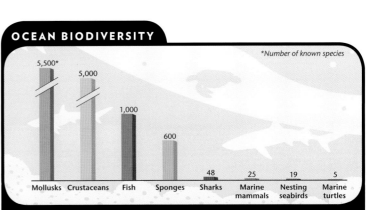

OCEAN BIODIVERSITY

*Number of known species

Mollusks	Crustaceans	Fish	Sponges	Sharks	Marine mammals	Nesting seabirds	Marine turtles
5,500*	5,000	1,000	600	48	25	19	5

The second longest double barrier reef in the world stretches 930 miles (1,500 km) along New Caledonia. The reef is habitat for a diversity of species—some still unclassified.

PHYSICAL

LAND AREA 5,100,000 sq mi (13,209,000 sq km)	**LOWEST POINT** Byrd Glacier (depression) -9,416 ft (-2,870 m)	**AVERAGE PRECIPITATION ON THE POLAR PLATEAU** Less than 2 in (5 cm) per year
HIGHEST POINT Vinson Massif 16,067 ft (4,897 m)	**COLDEST PLACE** Ridge A Annual average temperature -94°F (-70°C)	

POLITICAL

POPULATION There are no indigenous inhabitants, but there are scientists and other staff at both perma- nent and summer-only research stations.	**NUMBER OF INDEPENDENT COUNTRIES** 0	**NUMBER OF COUNTRIES OPERATING YEAR-ROUND RESEARCH STATIONS** 20
	NUMBER OF COUNTRIES CLAIMING LAND 7	**NUMBER OF YEAR-ROUND RESEARCH STATIONS** 40

ANTARCTICA

ANTARCTICA
THE FROZEN SOUTH

Antarctica is the coldest, windiest, and even driest continent. Though its immense ice sheet holds more than 60 percent of Earth's freshwater, its interior averages less than two inches (5 cm) of precipitation per year. Hidden beneath the ice is a continent of valleys, mountains, and lakes, but less than 2 percent of the land actually breaks through the ice cover. Like a finger pointing north toward South America, the Antarctic Peninsula is the most visited region of the continent, but scientists occupy a total of more than 70 permanent and seasonal research stations throughout the continent from which they study this frozen land.

FORMAL DRESS. Black-and-white gentoo penguins live in colonies year-round along the Antarctic Peninsula. These flightless birds dive to more than 300 feet (90 m) to catch fish and krill, their main food source.

DRIFTING RESEARCH. The U.S. Amundsen-Scott research station is located at the geographic South Pole. The station and the ice sheet on which it sits are drifting about 33 feet (10 m) each year.

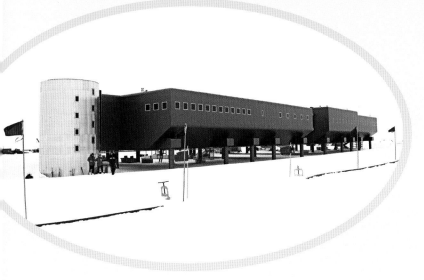

WHERE THE PICTURES ARE

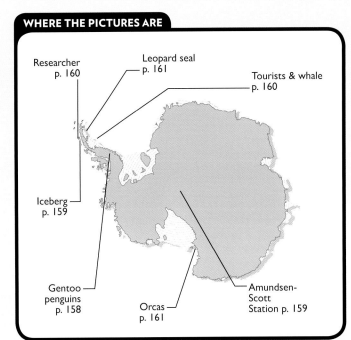

Researcher p. 160

Leopard seal p. 161

Tourists & whale p. 160

Iceberg p. 159

Gentoo penguins p. 158

Orcas p. 161

Amundsen-Scott Station p. 159

BLUE WONDER. An iceberg drifts in the Lemaire Channel near the Antarctic Peninsula. The dense, compressed ice reflects only short wavelengths, giving the ice a blue tint.

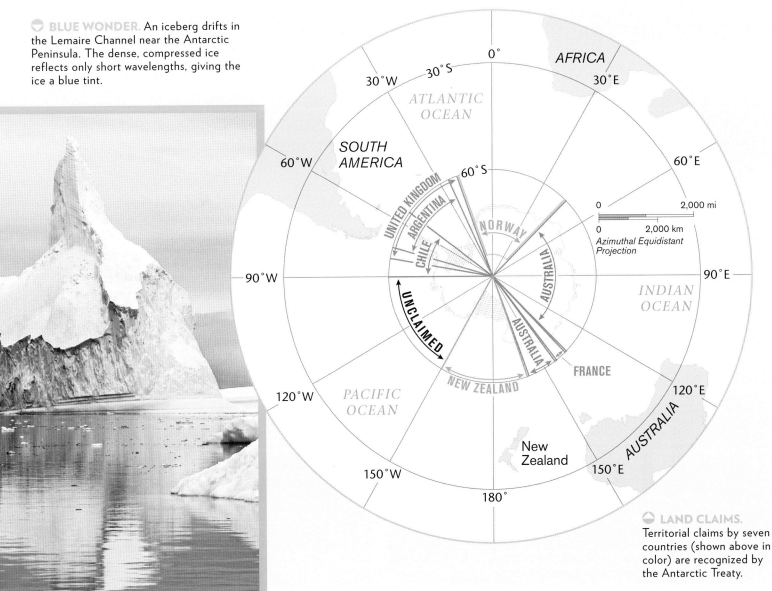

LAND CLAIMS. Territorial claims by seven countries (shown above in color) are recognized by the Antarctic Treaty.

Antarctica

Antarctica is the only continent that has no political boundaries and no economy or permanent population. Seven countries claim portions of the landmass (map, page 159), but according to the Antarctic Treaty, which preserves the continent for peaceful use and scientific study, no country rules.

GEO WHIZ

The Antarctic Convergence, an area where the waters of Earth's four oceans meet the cold Antarctic Circumpolar Current, is one of the planet's richest marine ecosystems.

Krill, a tiny shrimplike creature that thrives in Antarctic waters, is important in the Antarctic food chain. Whales, seals, and penguins are among the creatures that depend on it for survival.

The tiny wingless midge—less than one-quarter inch (6 mm) long—is Antarctica's largest land animal. This insect is able to survive high levels of salt, freezing temperatures, and ultraviolet radiation in the continent's extreme climate.

Mount Erebus, named for a British explorer's ship, is the world's southernmost active volcano.

NATURE STUDY.
A researcher at Palmer Station examines penguin eggs attacked by skuas, birds that feed on penguin eggs.

Under the terms of the Antarctic Treaty, the region beyond 60° south latitude is set aside for peaceful scientific study and research. Antarctica was first visited by Europeans in 1821, but there has never been a permanent human population. Today, more than 4,000 scientists live at research stations during the southern summer (October to March) studying climate history that is preserved in the ice sheets that cover the continent and observing the effects of current climate change on plant and animal life. During the cold, dark southern winter, the research population drops to only a little over 1,000. In addition to scientists, almost 30,000 tourists visit Antarctica during the southern summer, mainly along the Antarctic Peninsula, where they view wildlife such as seals, whales, penguins, and other birds.

South Orkney Islands

South Shetland Islands

Joinville Island

Palmer Station (United States)

Antarc

Bellingshausen Sea

Average number of daylight hours per month, Palmer Station (64°46'S; 64°03'W), 2017 data

JAN	19.42
FEB	15.78
MAR	12.51
APR	9.10
MAY	5.85
JUN	3.69
JUL	4.97
AUG	8.00
SEP	11.34
OCT	14.67
NOV	18.36
DEC	21.14

Because of its very high southern latitude, Antarctica experiences extreme fluctuations in the length of daylight hours. At the South Pole (90° S) there are months of total darkness.

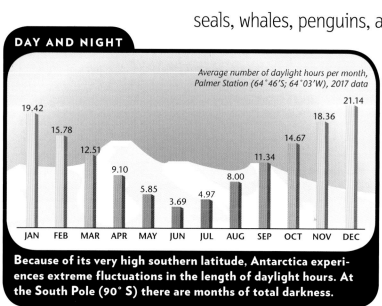

STANDING GUARD. Leopard seals' preferred food is penguins, but they also eat other species of seals and have even been known to attack humans.

ATLANTIC OCEAN

Fimbul Ice Shelf

Cape Norvegia

ANTARCTIC CIRCLE

Riiser-Larsen Peninsula

Lützow-Holm Bay

INDIAN OCEAN

0   500 miles
0   500 kilometers
Azimuthal Equidistant Projection

Riiser-Larsen Ice Shelf

Queen Maud Land

Enderby Land

Weddell Sea

Larsen C iceberg detached July 12, 2017

Coats Land

Cape Darnley

Larsen Ice Shelf

+ *Mt. Jackson 10,446 ft 3,184 m*

Filchner Ice Shelf

Berkner Island

Amery Ice Shelf

Prydz Bay

tic Peninsula

Alexander Island

Ronne Ice Shelf

Pensacola Mountains

Coldest place in the world

RIDGE A

American Highland

West Ice Shelf

POLAR PLATEAU

EAST

Ellsworth Land

Vinson Massif + 16,067 ft 4,897 m

+ *Highest point in Antarctica*

Ellsworth Mts.

WEST

ANTARCTICA

★ South Pole
■ Amundsen-Scott Station (United States)

ANTARCTICA

Thurston Island

ANTARCTICA

Marie Byrd Land

■ Vostok Station (Russia)

Wilkes Land

Shackleton Ice Shelf

Amundsen Sea

Getz Ice Shelf

Ross Ice Shelf

Byrd Glacier -9,416 ft -2,870 m

← *Lowest point in Antarctica*

Roosevelt Island

Cape Poinsett

PACIFIC OCEAN

Ross Sea

Mt. Erebus 12,448 ft 3,794 m +

Ross I.

Cape Crozier

McMurdo Sound

Victoria Land

Porpoise Bay

Map Key
★ Pole
■ Research station

Mt. Minto 13,665 ft 4,165 m +

Cape Adare

ANTARCTIC CIRCLE

★ South Magnetic Pole

SOUTHERN EXPLORATION. Adventurous tourists, riding in a Zodiac, get a close-up look at a humpback whale diving under the waters of the Weddell Sea. These motorized inflatable boats enable passengers to travel from their expedition ship, anchored in deep water, to the shores of the Antarctic Peninsula.

COLD SWIM. A mother orca and her calf come up for air in the icy waters of McMurdo Sound. Orcas live in social groups called pods and work together to catch a meal of fish, seals, or sea lions.

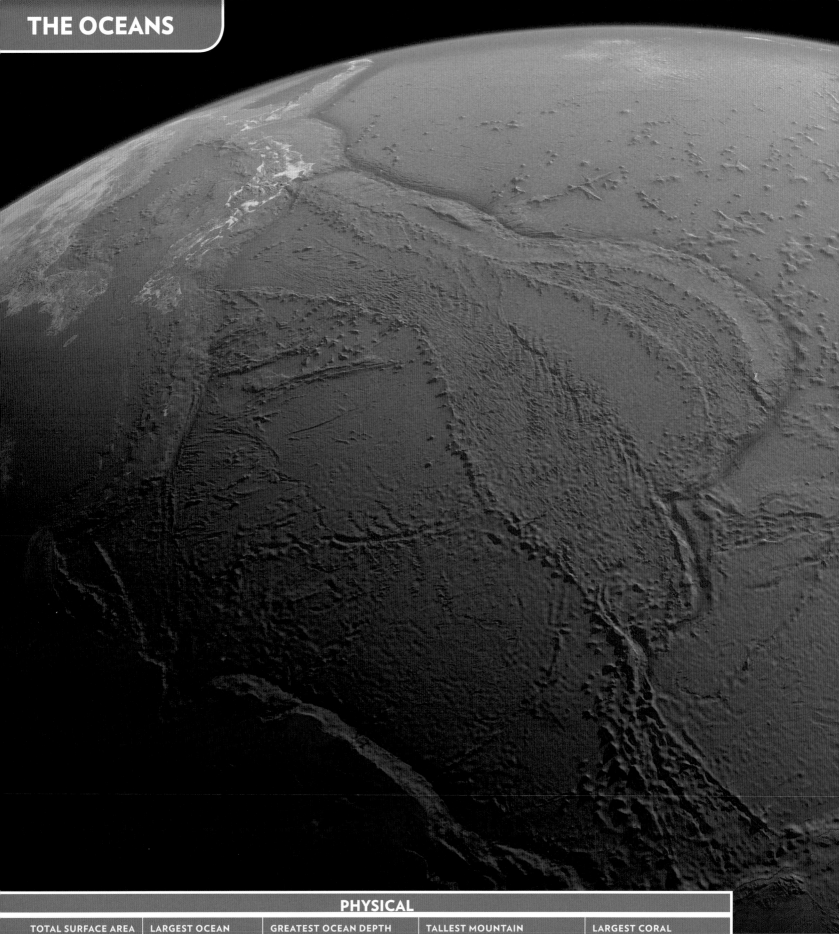

THE OCEANS

PHYSICAL

TOTAL SURFACE AREA	LARGEST OCEAN	GREATEST OCEAN DEPTH	TALLEST MOUNTAIN (SEAFLOOR TO SUMMIT)	LARGEST CORAL REEF ECOSYSTEM
139,434,000 sq mi (361,132,000 sq km)	Pacific 69,000,000 sq mi (178,800,000 sq km)	Challenger Deep, Pacific Ocean -36,037 ft (-10,984 m)	Mauna Kea, Hawai'i, U.S.A. 32,696 ft (9,966 m)	Great Barrier Reef, Australia 134,000 sq mi (348,300 sq km)
PERCENT OF EARTH'S SURFACE 71%	SMALLEST OCEAN Arctic 5,600,000 sq mi (14,700,000 sq km)	LONGEST MOUNTAIN RANGE Mid-Ocean Ridge 37,000 mi (60,000 km)	GREATEST TIDAL RANGE Bay of Fundy, Canada's Atlantic Coast 53 ft (16 m)	

THE OCEANS

Investigating the Oceans

The map at right shows that more than 70 percent of Earth's surface is underwater, mainly covered by four great oceans. There is growing support for recognizing a fifth ocean, called the Southern Ocean, in the area from Antarctica to 60° S latitude. The oceans are really inter-connected bodies of water that together form one global ocean.

The ocean floor is as varied as the surface of the continents, but mapping the oceans is challenging. Past explorers cut their way through jungles of the Amazon and conquered icy heights of the Himalaya, but explorers could not march across the floor of the Pacific Ocean, which in places descends to more than 36,000 feet (10,984 m) below the surface of the water.

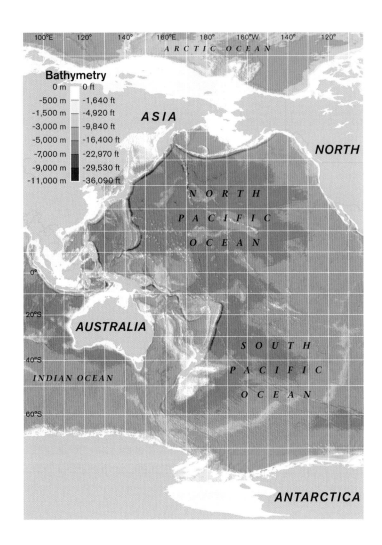

Bathymetry

0 m	0 ft
-500 m	-1,640 ft
-1,500 m	-4,920 ft
-3,000 m	-9,840 ft
-5,000 m	-16,400 ft
-7,000 m	-22,970 ft
-9,000 m	-29,530 ft
-11,000 m	-36,090 ft

⬤ **UNDERWATER LANDSCAPE.** The landscape of the ocean floor is varied and constantly changing. A continental edge that slopes gently beneath the water is called a continental shelf (1). Mountain ranges, called mid-ocean ridges (2), rise where ocean plates are spreading and magma flows out to create new land. Elsewhere, plates plunge into trenches (3) more than six miles (10 km) deep. In addition, magma, rising through vents called hot spots, pushes through ocean plates, creating seamounts (4) and volcanoes (5).

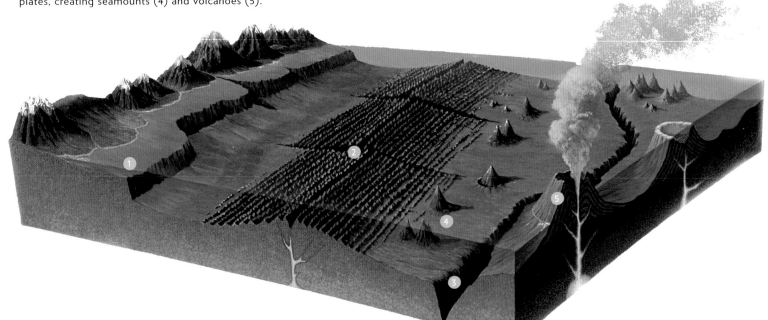

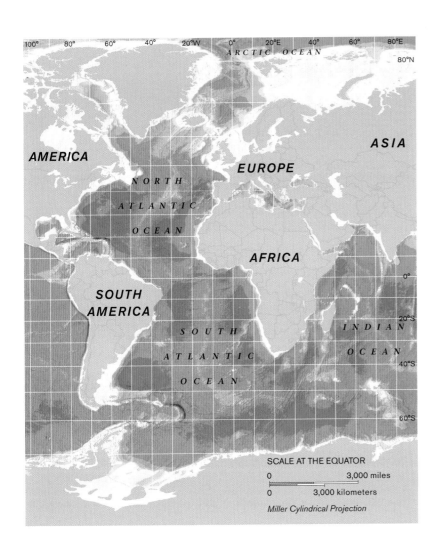

SCALE AT THE EQUATOR

0   3,000 miles

0   3,000 kilometers

Miller Cylindrical Projection

⬤ **FROM OCEAN TO SATELLITE.** In the 1990s, scientists developed the Argo Float to collect data from below the ocean surface. Argo Floats sink to a preset depth, often thousands of feet, where they gather data, such as temperature and salt content. At regular intervals, the floats rise to the surface (above) and transmit the data collected to a satellite. Then the cycle starts over again.

◖ **SEEING WITH YOUR EARS.**
Special instruments, such as this acoustic buoy, use sound waves bounced off the ocean floor to record variations in water temperature. This technique, called Acoustic Thermometry of Ocean Climate (ATOC), may someday help monitor long-term climate changes.

⬤ **EYE ON THE OCEAN.** Satellites orbiting high above Earth's surface record digital images of ocean colors, sea surface temperatures, and salinity levels. These can be used to identify and follow plant and animal activity as well as changes in the ocean environment.

THE OCEANS

THE BASICS

STATS

Surface area
69,000,000 sq mi
(178,800,000 sq km)

Percent of Earth's water area
49.5%

Greatest depth
Challenger Deep
(in the Mariana Trench)
-36,037 ft (-10,984 m)

Tides
Highest: 30 ft (9 m)
near Korean peninsula
Lowest: 1 ft (0.3 m)
near Midway Islands

GEO WHIZ

**The Pacific Ocean has more
islands—tens of thousands of
them—than any other ocean.**

**The ocean's name comes
from the Latin *Mare Pacificum*,
meaning "peaceful sea," but
earthquakes and volcanic activity
along the Ring of Fire generate
powerful waves called tsunamis,
which cause death and destruction when they slam ashore.**

**With the greatest area of tropical
waters, the Pacific is also home
to the largest number of coral
reefs, including Earth's longest:
Australia's Great Barrier Reef.**

**Only about 1,000 Hawaiian
monk seals remain in the wild.
Most live in protected waters of
the Hawaiian archipelago.**

Pacific Ocean

IN THE MIDST OF DANGER.
A false-clown anemonefish swims
among the tentacles of a sea
anemone off the coast of the
Philippines, in the western Pacific.
This colorful fish is immune to the
anemone's paralyzing sting.

The Pacific Ocean, largest of Earth's oceans, is more than 15 times larger than the United States and covers more than 30 percent of Earth's surface. The margins of the Pacific are often called the Ring of Fire because many active volcanoes and earthquakes occur where the ocean plate is moving under the edges of continental plates. The south-western Pacific is dotted with many islands. Also in the western Pacific, Challenger Deep in the Mariana Trench plunges to 36,037 ft (10,984 m) below sea level. Most of the world's fish catch comes from the Pacific, and oil and gas reserves in the Pacific are an important energy source.

CIRCLE OF LIFE. Atolls, such as this one near Okinawa, Japan, are ocean landforms created by tiny marine animals called corals. These creatures live in warm tropical waters. The circular shapes of atolls often mark the coastlines of sunken volcanic islands.

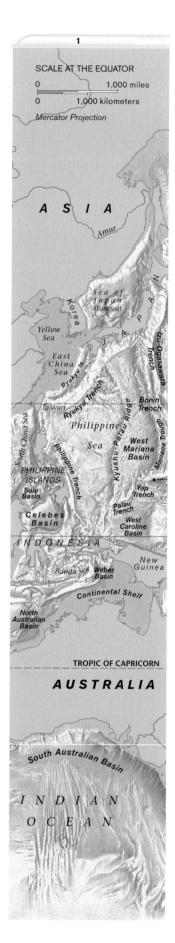

SCALE AT THE EQUATOR
0   1,000 miles
0   1,000 kilometers
Mercator Projection

ASIA

TROPIC OF CAPRICORN

AUSTRALIA

INDIAN OCEAN

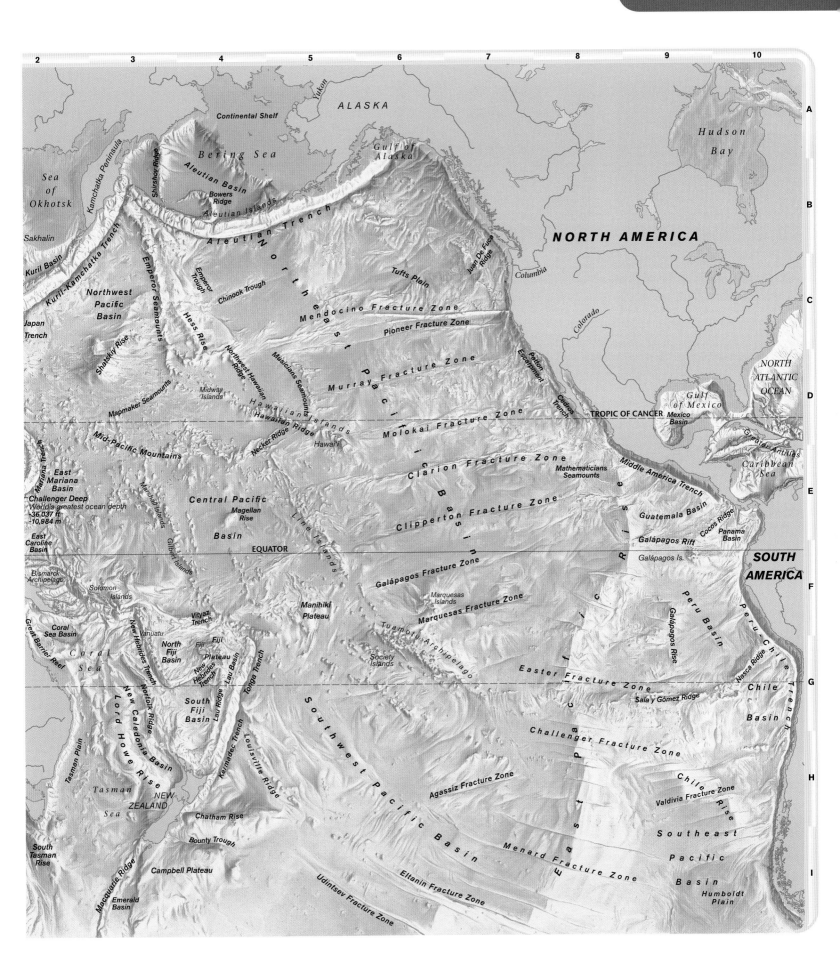

2   3   4   5   6   7   8   9   10

A
B
C
D
E
F
G
H
I

ALASKA

Yukon

Continental Shelf

Bering Sea

Hudson Bay

Kamchatka Peninsula

Aleutian Basin

Shirshov Ridge

Bowers Ridge

Aleutian Islands

Gulf of Alaska

Sea of Okhotsk

Sakhalin

Aleutian Trench

NORTH AMERICA

Kuril Basin

Kuril-Kamchatka Trench

Emperor Trough

North

Tufts Plain

Juan De Fuca Ridge

Columbia

Japan Trench

Northwest Pacific Basin

Emperor Seamounts

Hess Rise

Chinook Trough

Mendocino Fracture Zone

Pioneer Fracture Zone

Colorado

Shatskiy Rise

Northwest Hawaiian Ridge

Musicians Seamounts

Murray Fracture Zone

Patton Escarpment

NORTH ATLANTIC OCEAN

Mapmaker Seamounts

Midway Islands

Hawaiian Islands

Cedros Trench

TROPIC OF CANCER   Mexico Basin

Gulf of Mexico

Mid-Pacific Mountains

Hawaiian Ridge

Necker Ridge

Hawai'i

Molokai Fracture Zone

Greater Antilles

Mariana Trench

Central Pacific

Magellan Rise

Line Islands

Clarion Fracture Zone

Mathematicians Seamounts

Middle America Trench

Caribbean Sea

East Mariana Basin

Marshall Islands

Clipperton Fracture Zone

Guatemala Basin

Cocos Ridge

Challenger Deep
World's greatest ocean depth
-36,037 ft
-10,984 m

Basin

EQUATOR

Galápagos Rift

Panama Basin

East Caroline Basin

Gilbert Islands

Galápagos Is.

SOUTH AMERICA

Bismarck Archipelago

Solomon Islands

Galápagos Fracture Zone

Marquesas Islands

Marquesas Fracture Zone

Galápagos Rise

Peru Basin

Great Sea Basin

Vanuatu

Vityaz Trench

Manihiki Plateau

Tuamotu Archipelago

Peru-Chile Trench

Coral Sea Basin

New Hebrides Trench

North Fiji Basin

Fiji

Fiji Plateau

Society Islands

Easter Fracture Zone

Nazca Ridge

Coral Sea

New Hebrides Trench

New Hebrides Trench

Lau Basin

Tonga Trench

Sala y Gómez Ridge

Chile Basin

Great Barrier Reef

Norfolk Ridge

South Fiji Basin

Lau Ridge

Southwest Pacific Basin

Challenger Fracture Zone

New Caledonia Basin

Kermadec Trench

Louisville Ridge

Chile Rise

Tasman Plain

Lord Howe Rise

Tasman Sea

NEW ZEALAND

Agassiz Fracture Zone

Valdivia Fracture Zone

Chatham Rise

Southeast

South Tasman Rise

Bounty Trough

Menard Fracture Zone

Pacific

Campbell Plateau

Basin

Macquarie Ridge

Emerald Basin

Udintsev Fracture Zone

Eltanin Fracture Zone

Humboldt Plain

Atlantic Ocean

THE BASICS

STATS

Surface area
35,400,000 sq mi
(91,700,000 sq km)

Percent of Earth's water area
25.4%

Greatest depth
Puerto Rico Trench
-28,232 ft (-8,605 m)

Tides
Highest: 53 ft (16 m)
Bay of Fundy, Canada
Lowest: 1.5 ft (0.5 m)
Gulf of Mexico and
Mediterranean Sea

GEO WHIZ

In 2005, the Atlantic Ocean
experienced a record-setting 27
named tropical storms, including
14 hurricanes. Three hurricanes
(Katrina, Rita, and Wilma)
reached category 5 level, with
sustained winds of at least
155 miles an hour (249 km/h).

The Atlantic Ocean is about half
the size of the Pacific and growing. As molten rock from Earth's
interior escapes where spreading
occurs along the Mid-Atlantic
Ridge, new ocean floor forms.

Each year, the amount of water
that flows into the Atlantic
Ocean from the Amazon River,
in South America, is equal to
20 percent of Earth's available
freshwater.

⚪ **CAMOUFLAGE ON ICE.** A young
harp seal, called a pup, rests on the ice
in Canada's Gulf of St. Lawrence. Pups
are cared for by their mothers for only
12 days. After that, they must survive
on their own.

Among Earth's great oceans, the
Atlantic is second only to the Pacific in
size. The floor of the Atlantic is split by
the Mid-Atlantic Ridge, which is part of
the Mid-Ocean Ridge—the longest
mountain chain on Earth. The Atlantic
poses many hazards to human activity.
Tropical storms called hurricanes form
in the warm tropical waters off the west
coast of Africa and move across the ocean to bombard the islands
of the Caribbean and coastal areas of North America with damaging
winds, waves, and rain in the late summer and fall. In the cold waters
of the North Atlantic, sea ice and icebergs pose risks to shipping,
especially during winter and spring.

The Atlantic has rich deposits of oil and natural gas, but drilling
has raised concerns about pollution. In addition, the Atlantic has
important marine fisheries, but overfishing has put some species
at risk. Sea lanes between Europe and the Americas are among the
most heavily trafficked in the world.

◗ **HIDDEN DANGER.**
Icebergs (right) are huge
blocks of ice that break away,
or calve, from the edges of
glaciers. They pose a danger
to ships because only about 10
percent of their bulk is visible
above the waterline. A tragic
disaster associated with an
iceberg was the 1912 sinking
of the R.M.S. *Titanic,* whose
ghostly ruins lie below the
waters of the North Atlantic
Ocean (far right).

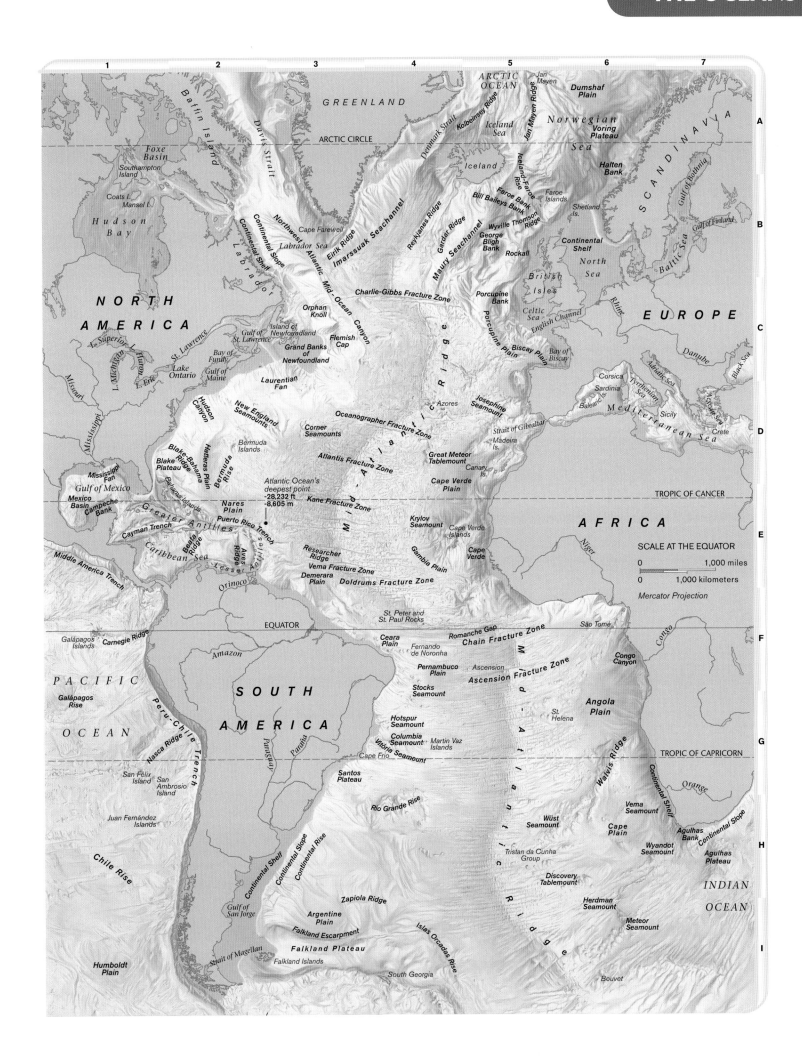

1 **2** **3** **4** **5** **6** **7**

ARCTIC
OCEAN

GREENLAND

Jan Mayen

Dumshaf
Plain

Norwegian
Voring
Plateau

SCANDINAVIA

ARCTIC CIRCLE

Denmark Strait

Kolbeinsey Ridge

Iceland
Sea

Jan Mayen Ridge

Sea

Gulf of Bothnia

Foxe
Basin

Davis Strait

Iceland

Halten
Bank

Southampton
Island

Baffin Island

Iceland-Faroe
Rise

Faroe Bank

Faroe
Islands

Shetland
Is.

Coats I.
Mansel I.

Continental Shelf

Cape Farewell

Eirik Ridge

Reykjanes Ridge

Gardar Ridge

Maury Seachannel

Bill Baileys Bank

Wyville Thomson
Ridge

George
Bligh
Bank

Rockall

Continental
Shelf

North
Sea

Gulf of Finland

Baltic Sea

HUDSON
BAY

Continental Slope

Labrador Sea

Labrador

Atlantic Mid-Ocean Canyon

Imarssuak Seachannel

Charlie-Gibbs Fracture Zone

Porcupine
Bank

British
Isles

Rhine

NORTH
AMERICA

Orphan
Knoll

Flemish
Cap

Mid-Atlantic Ridge

Porcupine Plain

Celtic
Sea

English Channel

EUROPE

L. Superior L. Huron

St. Lawrence

Gulf of
St. Lawrence

Island of
Newfoundland

Biscay Plain

Bay of
Biscay

Danube

Black Sea

Missouri

L. Michigan

Lake
Erie

Lake
Ontario

Bay of
Fundy

Gulf of
Maine

Grand Banks
of Newfoundland

Azores

Josephine
Seamount

Corsica

Sardinia

Adriatic Sea

Tyrrhenian
Sea

Laurentian
Fan

Oceanographer Fracture Zone

Strait of Gibraltar

Madeira
Is.

Balearic Is.

Sicily

Mediterranean Sea

Crete

Mississippi

Hudson
Canyon

New England
Seamounts

Corner
Seamounts

Great Meteor
Tablemount

Canary
Is.

Blake-Bahama
Ridge

Bermuda
Islands

Atlantis Fracture Zone

Blake
Plateau

Hatteras Plain

Bermuda
Rise

Cape Verde
Plain

TROPIC OF CANCER

Mississippi
Fan

Atlantic Ocean's
deepest point
-28,232 ft
-8,605 m

Kane Fracture Zone

AFRICA

Gulf of Mexico

Bahama Islands

Nares
Plain

Mexico
Basin

Campeche
Bank

Greater Antilles

Puerto Rico Trench

Krylov
Seamount

Cape Verde
Islands

Niger

SCALE AT THE EQUATOR

Cayman Trench

Beata
Ridge

Aves
Ridge

Researcher
Ridge

Gambia Plain

Cape
Verde

0   1,000 miles

Middle America Trench

Lesser Antilles

Caribbean Sea

Vema Fracture Zone

0   1,000 kilometers

Orinoco

Demerara
Plain

Doldrums Fracture Zone

Mercator Projection

EQUATOR

St. Peter and
St. Paul Rocks

Galápagos
Islands

Carnegie Ridge

Amazon

Ceara
Plain

Fernando
de Noronha

Romanche Gap

Chain Fracture Zone

São Tomé

Congo

PACIFIC

Galápagos
Rise

Pernambuco
Plain

Ascension

Mid-Atlantic Ridge

Ascension Fracture Zone

Congo
Canyon

OCEAN

SOUTH
AMERICA

Stocks
Seamount

Angola
Plain

Peru-Chile Trench

Paraguay

Paraná

Hotspur
Seamount

St.
Helena

San Félix
Island

Nasca Ridge

San
Ambrosio
Island

Columbia
Seamount

Martin Vaz
Islands

Vitória Seamount

Cape Frio

TROPIC OF CAPRICORN

Orange

Continental Shelf

Juan Fernández
Islands

Santos
Plateau

Vema
Seamount

Agulhas
Bank

Continental Slope

Rio Grande Rise

Wüst
Seamount

Cape
Plain

Wyandot
Seamount

Agulhas
Plateau

Chile Rise

Continental Shelf

Continental Slope

Continental Rise

Tristan da Cunha
Group

INDIAN
OCEAN

Gulf of
San Jorge

Zapiola Ridge

Discovery
Tablemount

Herdman
Seamount

Humboldt
Plain

Argentine
Plain

Falkland Escarpment

Islas Orcadas Rise

Mid-Atlantic Ridge

Meteor
Seamount

Strait of Magellan

Falkland Plateau

Falkland Islands

South Georgia

Bouvet

A
B
C
D
E
F
G
H
I

THE BASICS

STATS

Surface area
29,400,000 sq mi
(76,200,000 sq km)

Percent of Earth's water area
21%

Greatest depth
Java Trench
-23,376 ft (-7,125 m)

Tides
Highest: 36 ft (11 m)
Lowest: 2 ft (0.6 m)
Both along Australia's west coast

GEO WHIZ

Some of the world's largest breeding grounds for humpback whales are in the Indian Ocean, the Arabian Sea, and off the east coast of Africa.

The Bay of Bengal is sometimes called Cyclone Alley because of the large number of tropical storms that occur there each year between May and November.

Sailors from what is now Indonesia used seasonal winds called monsoons to reach Africa's east coast. They arrived on the continent long before Europeans did.

A December 2004 earthquake caused a tsunami that killed more than 225,000 people in countries bordering the Indian Ocean. Waves reached as high as 49 feet (15 m).

Indian Ocean

The Indian Ocean stretches from Africa's east coast to the southern coast of Asia and the western coast of Australia. It is the third largest of Earth's great oceans. Changing air pressure systems over its warm waters trigger South Asia's famous monsoon climate—a weather pattern in which winds reverse directions seasonally. The Bay of Bengal, an arm of the Indian Ocean, experiences devastating tropical storms, similar to hurricanes, but called cyclones in this region. Islands along the eastern edge of the Indian Ocean plate experience earthquakes that sometimes cause destructive ocean waves called tsunamis.

The Arabian Sea, Persian Gulf, and Red Sea, extensions of the Indian Ocean, are important sources of oil and natural gas and account for more than half of Earth's offshore oil production. Sea routes of the Indian Ocean connect the Middle East to the rest of the world, carrying vital energy resources on huge tanker ships.

◖ **LIVING FOSSIL.**
A coelacanth swims in the warm waters of the western Indian Ocean off the Comoro Islands. Once thought to have become extinct 65 million years ago along with the dinosaurs, a living coelacanth was discovered in 1938.

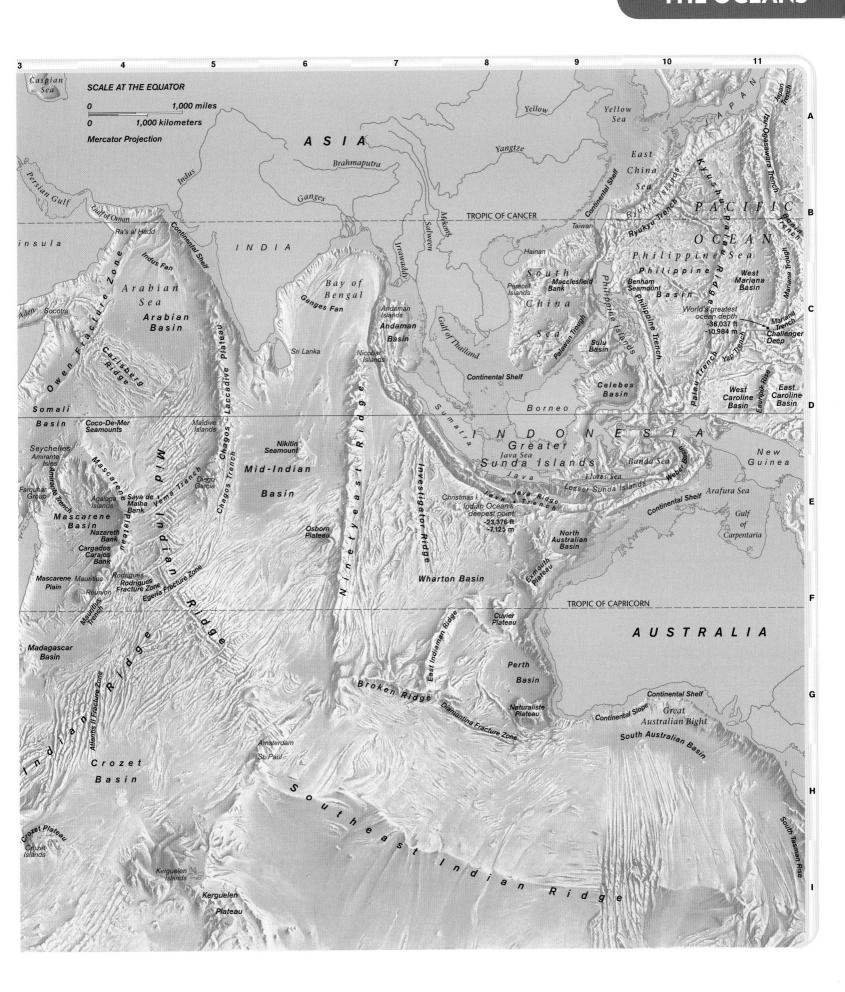

3 4 5 6 7 8 9 10 11

Caspian Sea

SCALE AT THE EQUATOR

0 ——— 1,000 miles
0 ——— 1,000 kilometers
Mercator Projection

A S I A

Brahmaputra

Yellow

Yellow Sea

Yangtze

East China Sea

Indus

Ganges

Mekong

TROPIC OF CANCER

Salween

J A P A N

Izu-Ogasawara Trench

Japan Trench

Persian Gulf

Gulf of Oman

Ra's al Hadd

Continental Shelf

I N D I A

Irrawaddy

Taiwan

Kyushu-Palau Ridge

Ryukyu Islands

Ryukyu Trench

P A C I F I C

Bonin Trench

insula

Indus Fan

Hainan

O C E A N

Aden

Socotra

Arabian Sea

Bay of Bengal

Ganges Fan

Andaman Islands

Paracel Islands

Macclesfield Bank

South

Philippine Sea

Benham Seamount

Philippine Basin

West Mariana Basin

Marianas Trough

Arabian Basin

Carlsberg Ridge

Laccadive Plateau

Sri Lanka

Andaman Basin

Gulf of Thailand

China

Philippine Islands

Philippine Trench

World's greatest ocean depth
–36,037 ft
–10,984 m

Mariana Trench
Challenger Deep

Owen Fracture Zone

Nicobar Islands

Sea

Palawan Trough

Sulu Basin

Yap Trench

Palau Trench

Somali

Coco-De-Mer Seamounts

Maldive Islands

Nikitin Seamount

Ninetyeast Ridge

Sumatra

Celebes Basin

West Caroline Basin

Eauripik Rise

East Caroline Basin

Basin

Seychelles
Amirante Isles

Chagos Trench

Mid-Indian

I N D O N E S I A

Greater

Banda Sea

New Guinea

Farquhar Group

Mascarene Plateau

Amirante Trench

Agalega Islands

Saya de Malha Bank

Diego Garcia

Basin

Sunda Islands

Java

Flores Sea

Weber Basin

Mascarene Basin

Nazareth Bank

Osborn Plateau

Investigator Ridge

Christmas I.

Java Ridge

Lesser Sunda Islands

Continental Shelf

Arafura Sea

Cargados Carajos Bank

Indian Ocean's deepest point
–23,376 ft
–7,125 m

Java Trench

Gulf of Carpentaria

Mascarene Plain

Mauritius

Rodrigues

Reunion

Rodrigues Fracture Zone

Egeria Fracture Zone

Wharton Basin

North Australian Basin

Exmouth Plateau

Mauritius Trench

TROPIC OF CAPRICORN

Madagascar Basin

Cuvier Plateau

A U S T R A L I A

East Indiaman Ridge

Perth Basin

Broken Ridge

Diamantina Fracture Zone

Naturaliste Plateau

Continental Shelf

Continental Slope

Great Australian Bight

South Australian Basin

Amsterdam

St. Paul

South Tasman Rise

Crozet Basin

Crozet Plateau

Crozet Islands

Kerguelen Islands

Kerguelen Plateau

S o u t h e a s t   I n d i a n   R i d g e

Mid-Indian Ridge

Vema Trench

Atlantis II Fracture Zone

Indian Ridge

A B C D E F G H I

THE OCEANS

THE BASICS

STATS

Surface area
5,600,000 sq mi
(14,700,000 sq km)

Percent of Earth's water area
4.1%

Greatest depth
Molloy Deep: -18,599 ft
(-5,669 m)

Tides
Less than a 1-ft (0.3-m) variation
throughout the ocean

GEO WHIZ

Satellite monitoring of Arctic
sea ice since the late 1970s shows
that the extent of the sea ice is
declining at a rate of 13.3 percent
every 10 years—possibly as a
result of climate change.

The geographic North Pole lies
roughly in the middle of the
Arctic Ocean under 13,000 feet
(3,962 m) of water.

In 1958, a submarine named the
U.S.S. *Nautilus* cruised beneath
the frozen surface of the Arctic
Ocean, proving that the enormous ice sheet rests on water,
not land.

Arctic Ocean

The Arctic Ocean lies mostly north
of the Arctic Circle, bounded by North
America, Europe, and Asia. Unlike the
other oceans, the Arctic is subject to
persistent cold throughout the year.
Also, because of its very high latitude,
the Arctic experiences winters of per-
petual night and summers of continual
daylight. Except for coastal margins, the
Arctic Ocean is covered by permanent
drifting pack ice that averages almost
10 feet (3 m) in thickness. Some scientists are concerned that the polar ice
may be melting due to climate change,
putting at risk the habitat of polar bears
and other arctic animals.

◐ **ARCTIC RESEARCH.** Scientists wearing cold
weather survival suits prepare to measure salt content,
nutrients, and plant and animal life in ice and meltwater.
They also record data related to climate change, such as
the shrinking of polar sea ice.

◑ **FREE RIDE.**
A baby polar bear
catches a ride as its
mother crosses the
frozen landscape of
Canada's Arctic. Polar
bear populations are
showing signs of stress
as sea ice shrinks.

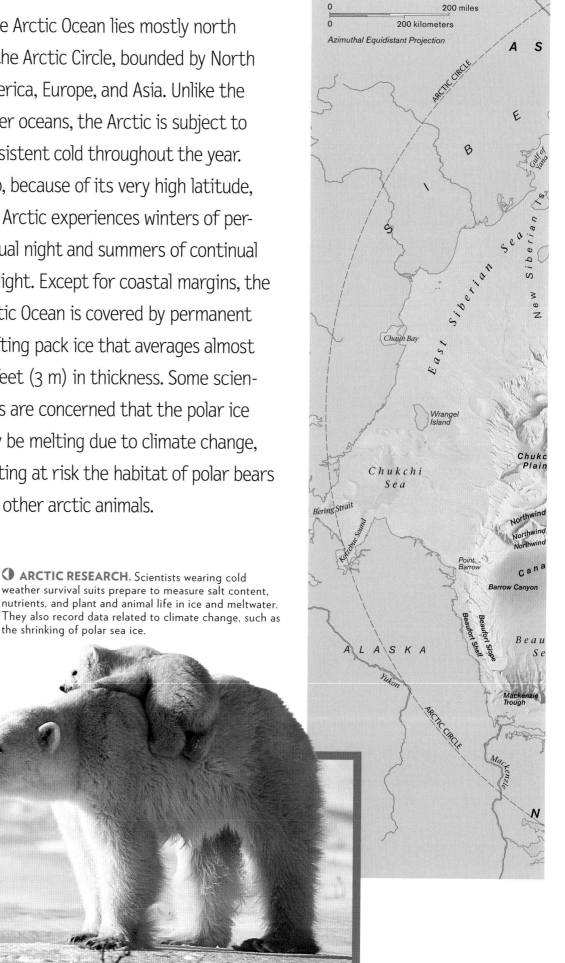

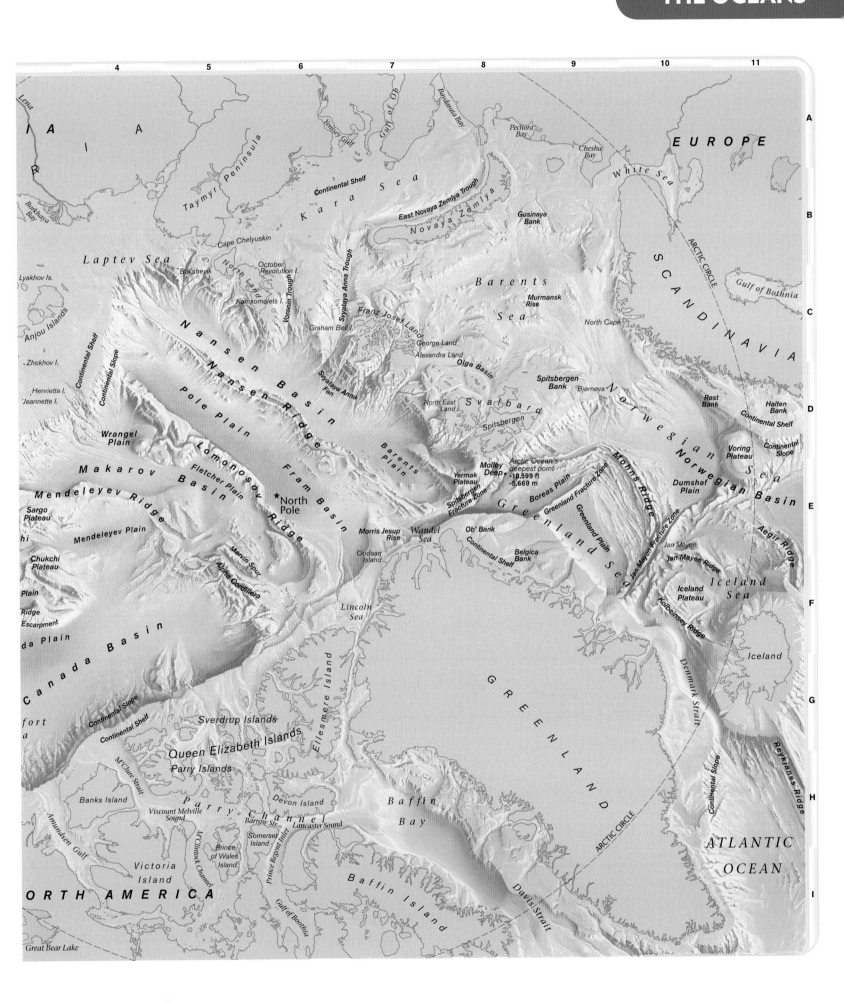

A
B
C
D
E
F
G
H
I

4   5   6   7   8   9   10   11

Lena

I A

A

R

Borkhaya
Bay

Lyakhov Is.

Anjou Islands

Zhokhov I.

Henrietta I.
Jeannette I.

hi

Sargo
Plateau

Chukchi
Plateau

Plain

Ridge

Escarpment

da Plain

fort
a

Laptev Sea

Taymyr Peninsula

North Land

Bol'shevik

October
Revolution I.

Komsomolets I.

Cape Chelyuskin

Voronin Trough

Continental Shelf

Kara Sea

Yenisey Gulf

Gulf of Ob

Boydarata Bay

EUROPE

White Sea

ARCTIC CIRCLE

SCANDINAVIA

Pechora
Bay

Chesha
Bay

East Novaya Zemlya Trough

Novaya Zemlya

Gusinaya
Bank

Gulf of Bothnia

Barents

Sea

Murmansk
Rise

North Cape

Graham Bell I.

Svyataya Anna Trough

Franz Josef Land

George Land

Alexandra Land

Olga Basin

Spitsbergen
Bank

Bjørnøya

Røst
Bank

Halten
Bank

Continental Shelf

Continental
Slope

Continental Shelf

Continental Slope

Nansen Basin

Nansen Ridge

Nansen Basin

Pole Plain

Lomonosov Ridge

Fletcher Plain

Pole Plain

Fram Basin

North Pole

Wrangel
Plain

Makarov
Basin

Mendeleyev Ridge

Mendeleyev Plain

Marvin Spur

Alpha Cordillera

Svyataya Anna
Fan

North East
Land

Svalbard

Spitsbergen

Barents
Plain

Yermak
Plateau

Spitsbergen
Fracture Zone

Molloy
Deep

Arctic Ocean's
deepest point
-18,599 ft
-5,669 m

Greenland Sea

Boreas Plain

Greenland Fracture Zone

Greenland Plain

Morris
Ridge

Voring
Plateau

Dumshaf
Plain

Norwegian

Norwegian Sea

Norwegian Basin

Aegir Ridge

Morris Jesup
Rise

Oodaaq
Island

Wandel
Sea

Ob' Bank

Continental
Shelf

Belgica
Bank

Jan Mayen Fracture Zone

Jan Mayen

Jan Mayen Ridge

Iceland
Plateau

Iceland
Sea

Kolbeinsey Ridge

Iceland

Lincoln
Sea

Canada Basin

Continental Slope

Continental Shelf

Sverdrup Islands

Queen Elizabeth Islands

Parry Islands

Ellesmere Island

GREENLAND

Denmark Strait

M'Clure Strait

Banks Island

Viscount Melville
Sound

Parry Channel

Barrow Str.

Lancaster Sound

Devon Island

Somerset
Island

Prince
of Wales
Island

M'Clintock Channel

Prince Regent Inlet

Gulf of Boothia

Baffin
Bay

Baffin Island

Davis Strait

ATLANTIC

OCEAN

Reykjanes Ridge

Continental Slope

Amundsen Gulf

Victoria
Island

NORTH AMERICA

Great Bear Lake

ARCTIC CIRCLE

FLAGS & FACTS

These flags and factoids represent the world's 195 independent countries—those with national governments that are recognized as having the highest legal authority over the land and people within their boundaries. Data are based on the CIA's 2017 *World Factbook*. The flags shown are national flags recognized by the United Nations. Area figures include land and inland water bodies. Languages are those most commonly spoken within a country or official languages, which are marked with an asterisk (*). Only the most commonly practiced religions are listed. All GDP per capita figures are in U.S. dollars and are adjusted to reflect purchasing power parity (PPP).

NORTH AMERICA

Antigua and Barbuda
Area: 171 sq mi
(443 sq km)
Population: 95,000
Percent urban: 23%
Capital: St. John's
Language: English*, Creole
Religion: Christianity
GDP per capita: $25,200
Life expectancy: 77 years

Bahamas
Area: 5,359 sq mi
(13,880 sq km)
Population: 330,000
Percent urban: 83%
Capital: Nassau
Language: English*
Religion: Christianity
GDP per capita: $24,600
Life expectancy: 72 years

Barbados
Area: 166 sq mi
(430 sq km)
Population: 292,000
Percent urban: 31.4%
Capital: Bridgetown
Language: English*, Creole
Religion: Christianity
GDP per capita: $17,100
Life expectancy: 75 years

Belize
Area: 8,867 sq mi
(22,966 sq km)
Population: 360,000
Percent urban: 43.7%
Capital: Belmopan
Language: English*, Spanish, Creole, Mayan
Religion: Christianity
GDP per capita: $8,200
Life expectancy: 69 years

Canada
Area: 3,855,081 sq mi
(9,984,670 sq km)
Population: 35,624,000
Percent urban: 82.2%
Capital: Ottawa
Language: English*, French*
Religion: Christianity
GDP per capita: $46,400
Life expectancy: 82 years

Costa Rica
Area: 19,730 sq mi
(51,100 sq km)
Population: 4,930,000
Percent urban: 78.5%
Capital: San José
Language: Spanish*, English
Religion: Christianity
GDP per capita: $16,400
Life expectancy: 79 years

Cuba
Area: 42,803 sq mi
(110,860 sq km)
Population: 11,147,000
Percent urban: 77.3%
Capital: Havana
Language: Spanish*
Religion: Christianity
GDP per capita: $11,900
Life expectancy: 79 years

Dominica
Area: 290 sq mi
(751 sq km)
Population: 74,000
Percent urban: 70.1%
Capital: Roseau
Languages: English*, Creole
Religion: Christianity
GDP per capita: $11,300
Life expectancy: 77 years

Dominican Republic
Area: 18,791 sq mi
(48,670 sq km)
Population: 10,734,000
Percent urban: 80.6%
Capital: Santo Domingo
Language: Spanish*
Religion: Christianity
GDP per capita: $16,000
Life expectancy: 78 years

El Salvador
Area: 8,124 sq mi
(21,041 sq km)
Population: 6,172,000
Percent urban: 67.6%
Capital: San Salvador
Language: Spanish*
Religion: Christianity
GDP per capita: $8,900
Life expectancy: 75 years

Grenada
Area: 133 sq mi
(344 sq km)
Population: 112,000
Percent urban: 35.7%
Capital: St. George's
Language: English*, Creole
Religion: Christianity
GDP per capita: $14,100
Life expectancy: 74 years

Guatemala
Area: 42,042 sq mi
(108,889 sq km)
Population: 15,461,000
Percent urban: 52.5%
Capital: Guatemala City
Language: Spanish*, indigenous languages
Religion: Christianity, indigenous beliefs
GDP per capita: $7,900
Life expectancy: 72 years

Haiti
Area: 10,714 sq mi
(27,750 sq km)
Population: 10,647,000
Percent urban: 60.9%
Capital: Port-au-Prince
Language: French*, Creole*
Religion: Christianity, indigenous beliefs
GDP per capita: $1,800
Life expectancy: 64 years

Honduras
Area: 43,278 sq mi
(112,090 sq km)
Population: 9,039,000
Percent urban: 55.9%
Capital: Tegucigalpa
Language: Spanish*, indigenous languages
Religion: Christianity
GDP per capita: $5,300
Life expectancy: 71 years

Jamaica
Area: 4,244 sq mi
(10,991 sq km)
Population: 2,991,000
Percent urban: 55.3%
Capital: Kingston
Language: English*, Creole
Religion: Christianity
GDP per capita: $9,000
Life expectancy: 74 years

Mexico
Area: 758,445 sq mi
(1,964,375 sq km)
Population: 124,575,000
Percent urban: 79.8%
Capital: Mexico City
Language: Spanish
Religion: Christianity
GDP per capita: $18,900
Life expectancy: 76 years

Nicaragua
Area: 50,336 sq mi
(130,370 sq km)
Population: 6,026,000
Percent urban: 59.4%
Capital: Managua
Language: Spanish*
Religion: Christianity
GDP per capita: $5,500
Life expectancy: 73 years

Panama
Area: 29,120 sq mi
(75,420 sq km)
Population: 3,753,000
Percent urban: 67.2%
Capital: Panama City
Language: Spanish*, indigenous languages
Religion: Christianity
GDP per capita: $23,000
Life expectancy: 79 years

St. Kitts and Nevis
Area: 101 sq mi
(261 sq km)
Population: 53,000
Percent urban: 32.3%
Capital: Basseterre
Language: English*
Religion: Christianity
GDP per capita: $26,100
Life expectancy: 76 years

St. Lucia
Area: 238 sq mi
(616 sq km)
Population: 165,000
Percent urban: 18.6%
Capital: Castries
Language: English*, Creole
Religion: Christianity
GDP per capita: $11,800
Life expectancy: 78 years

St. Vincent and the Grenadines
Area: 150 sq mi
(389 sq km)
Population: 102,000
Percent urban: 51.2%
Capital: Kingstown
Language: English*, Creole
Religion: Christianity
GDP per capita: $11,300
Life expectancy: 75 years

Trinidad and Tobago
Area: 1,980 sq mi
(5,128 sq km)
Population: 1,218,000
Percent urban: 8.3%
Capital: Port of Spain
Language: English*, Creole
Religion: Christianity, Hinduism
GDP per capita: $31,900
Life expectancy: 73 years

United States
Area: 3,794,079 sq mi
(9,826,675 sq km)
Population: 326,626,000
Percent urban: 82%
Capital: Washington, D.C.
Language: English, Spanish
Religion: Christianity
GDP per capita: $57,400
Life expectancy: 80 years

SOUTH AMERICA

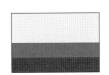

Argentina
Area: 1,073,512 sq mi
(2,780,400 sq km)
Population: 44,293,000
Percent urban: 92%
Capital: Buenos Aires
Language: Spanish*, English, Italian, German, French
Religion: Christianity
GDP per capita: $20,000
Life expectancy: 77 years

Bolivia
Area: 424,162 sq mi
(1,098,581 sq km)
Population: 11,138,000
Percent urban: 69.3%
Capital: La Paz (administrative), Sucre (constitutional)
Language: Spanish*, Quechua*, Aymara*, other indigenous languages*
Religion: Christianity
GDP per capita: $7,200
Life expectancy: 69 years

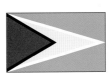

Brazil
Area: 3,287,594 sq mi
(8,514,877 sq km)
Population: 207,353,000
Percent urban: 86.2%
Capital: Brasília
Language: Portuguese*
Religion: Christianity
GDP per capita: $15,200
Life expectancy: 74 years

Chile
Area: 291,931 sq mi
(756,102 sq km)
Population: 17,789,000
Percent urban: 89.9%
Capital: Santiago
Language: Spanish*, English
Religion: Christianity
GDP per capita: $24,100
Life expectancy: 79 years

Colombia
Area: 439,733 sq mi
(1,138,910 sq km)
Population: 47,699,000
Percent urban: 77%
Capital: Bogotá
Language: Spanish*
Religion: Christianity
GDP per capita: $14,100
Life expectancy: 76 years

Ecuador
Area: 109,483 sq mi
(283,561 sq km)
Population: 16,291,000
Percent urban: 64.2%
Capital: Quito
Language: Spanish*, indigenous languages
Religion: Christianity
GDP per capita: $11,100
Life expectancy: 77 years

Guyana
Area: 83,000 sq mi
(214,969 sq km)
Population: 738,000
Percent urban: 28.8%
Capital: Georgetown
Language: English*, Creole
Religion: Christianity, Hinduism
GDP per capita: $7,900
Life expectancy: 68 years

Paraguay
Area: 157,047 sq mi
(406,752 sq km)
Population: 6,944,000
Percent urban: 60.2%
Capital: Asunción
Language: Spanish*, Guaraní*
Religion: Christianity
GDP per capita: $9,400
Life expectancy: 77 years

Peru
Area: 496,222 sq mi
(1,285,216 sq km)
Population: 31,037,000
Percent urban: 79.2%
Capital: Lima
Language: Spanish*, Quechua*, Aymara*
Religion: Christianity
GDP per capita: $12,900
Life expectancy: 74 years

Suriname
Area: 63,251 sq mi
(163,820 sq km)
Population: 592,000
Percent urban: 66%
Capital: Paramaribo
Language: Dutch*, Sranan, English
Religion: Christianity, Hinduism, Islam
GDP per capita: $14,000
Life expectancy: 72 years

Uruguay
Area: 68,037 sq mi
(176,215 sq km)
Population: 3,360,000
Percent urban: 95.6%
Capital: Montevideo
Language: Spanish*
Religion: Christianity
GDP per capita: $21,500
Life expectancy: 77 years

Venezuela
Area: 352,143 sq mi
(912,050 sq km)
Population: 31,304,000
Percent urban: 89.1%
Capital: Caracas
Language: Spanish*, indigenous languages
Religion: Christianity
GDP per capita: $13,800
Life expectancy: 76 years

EUROPE

Albania
Area: 11,100 sq mi
(28,748 sq km)
Population: 3,048,000
Percent urban: 59.3%
Capital: Tirana
Language: Albanian*
Religion: Islam, Christianity
GDP per capita: $11,800
Life expectancy: 78 years

Andorra
Area: 181 sq mi
(468 sq km)
Population: 86,000
Percent urban: 84.1%
Capital: Andorra la Vella
Language: Catalan*, French, Spanish, Portuguese
Religion: Christianity
GDP per capita: $49,900
Life expectancy: 83 years

Austria
Area: 32,383 sq mi
(83,871 sq km)
Population: 8,754,000
Percent urban: 66.1%
Capital: Vienna
Language: German*
Religion: Christianity
GDP per capita: $48,000
Life expectancy: 82 years

FLAGS & FACTS

Belarus
Area: 80,154 sq mi
(207,600 sq km)
Population: 9,550,000
Percent urban: 77.4%
Capital: Minsk
Language: Russian*, Belarusian*
Religion: Christianity
GDP per capita: $18,000
Life expectancy: 73 years

Belgium
Area: 11,787 sq mi
(30,528 sq km)
Population: 11,491,000
Percent urban: 97.9%
Capital: Brussels
Language: Dutch*, French*, German*
Religion: Christianity
GDP per capita: $45,000
Life expectancy: 81 years

Bosnia and Herzegovina
Area: 19,767 sq mi
(51,197 sq km)
Population: 3,856,000
Percent urban: 40.1%
Capital: Sarajevo
Language: Bosnian*, Serbian*,
Croatian*
Religion: Islam, Christianity
GDP per capita: $11,000
Life expectancy: 77 years

Bulgaria
Area: 42,810 sq mi
(110,879 sq km)
Population: 7,102,000
Percent urban: 74.6%
Capital: Sofia
Language: Bulgarian*
Religion: Christianity
GDP per capita: $20,300
Life expectancy: 75 years

Croatia
Area: 21,851 sq mi
(56,594 sq km)
Population: 4,292,000
Percent urban: 59.6%
Capital: Zagreb
Language: Croatian*
Religion: Christianity
GDP per capita: $22,800
Life expectancy: 76 years

Cyprus
Area: 3,572 sq mi
(9,251 sq km)
Population: 1,222,000
Percent urban: 66.8%
Capital: Nicosia
Language: Greek*, Turkish*
Religion: Christianity, Islam
GDP per capita: $35,000
Life expectancy: 79 years

Czechia (Czech Republic)
Area: 30,451 sq mi
(78,867 sq km)
Population: 10,675,000
Percent urban: 73%
Capital: Prague
Language: Czech*
Religion: Christianity
GDP per capita: $33,200
Life expectancy: 79 years

Denmark
Area: 16,639 sq mi
(43,094 sq km)
Population: 5,606,000
Percent urban: 88%
Capital: Copenhagen
Language: Danish, English
Religion: Christianity
GDP per capita: $48,000
Life expectancy: 79 years

Estonia
Area: 17,463 sq mi
(45,228 sq km)
Population: 1,252,000
Percent urban: 67.4%
Capital: Tallinn
Language: Estonian*, Russian
Religion: Christianity
GDP per capita: $29,300
Life expectancy: 77 years

Finland
Area: 130,558 sq mi
(338,145 sq km)
Population: 5,518,000
Percent urban: 84.5%
Capital: Helsinki
Language: Finnish*, Swedish*
Religion: Christianity
GDP per capita: $42,200
Life expectancy: 81 years

France
Area: 248,572 sq mi
(643,801 sq km)
Population: 67,106,000
Percent urban: 80%
Capital: Paris
Language: French*
Religion: Christianity
GDP per capita: $42,300
Life expectancy: 82 years

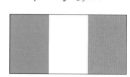

Germany
Area: 137,846 sq mi
(357,022 sq km)
Population: 80,594,000
Percent urban: 75.7%
Capital: Berlin
Language: German*
Religion: Christianity
GDP per capita: $48,100
Life expectancy: 81 years

Greece
Area: 50,949 sq mi
(131,957 sq km)
Population: 10,768,000
Percent urban: 78.6%
Capital: Athens
Language: Greek*
Religion: Christianity
GDP per capita: $26,700
Life expectancy: 81 years

Hungary
Area: 35,918 sq mi
(93,028 sq km)
Population: 9,851,000
Percent urban: 72.1%
Capital: Budapest
Language: Hungarian*, English,
German
Religion: Christianity
GDP per capita: $27,500
Life expectancy: 76 years

Iceland
Area: 39,768 sq mi
(103,000 sq km)
Population: 340,000
Percent urban: 94.3%
Capital: Reykjavik
Language: Icelandic, English,
Nordic languages
Religion: Christianity
GDP per capita: $49,200
Life expectancy: 83 years

Ireland
Area: 27,132 sq mi
(70,273 sq km)
Population: 5,011,000
Percent urban: 63.8%
Capital: Dublin
Language: English*, Irish (Gaelic)*
Religion: Christianity
GDP per capita: $69,200
Life expectancy: 81 years

Italy
Area: 116,347 sq mi
(301,340 sq km)
Population: 62,138,000
Percent urban: 69.3%
Capital: Rome
Language: Italian*
Religion: Christianity
GDP per capita: $36,800
Life expectancy: 82 years

Kosovo
Area: 4,203 sq mi
(10,887 sq km)
Population: 1,895,000
Percent urban: NA
Capital: Pristina
Language: Albanian*, Serbian*
Religion: Islam
GDP per capita: $9,600
Life expectancy: NA

Latvia
Area: 24,938 sq mi
(64,589 sq km)
Population: 1,945,000
Percent urban: 67.4%
Capital: Riga
Language: Latvian*, Russian
Religion: Christianity
GDP per capita: $25,700
Life expectancy: 75 years

Liechtenstein
Area: 62 sq mi
(160 sq km)
Population: 38,000
Percent urban: 14.3%
Capital: Vaduz
Language: German*
Religion: Christianity
GDP per capita: $139,100
Life expectancy: 82 years

Lithuania
Area: 25,212 sq mi
(65,300 sq km)
Population: 2,824,000
Percent urban: 66.5%
Capital: Vilnius
Language: Lithuanian*
Religion: Christianity
GDP per capita: $30,000
Life expectancy: 75 years

Luxembourg
Area: 998 sq mi
(2,586 sq km)
Population: 594,000
Percent urban: 90.7%
Capital: Luxembourg
Language: Luxembourgish*, French*,
German*
Religion: Christianity
GDP per capita: $104,000
Life expectancy: 82 years

Macedonia
Area: 9,928 sq mi
(25,713 sq km)
Population: 2,104,000
Percent urban: 57.3%
Capital: Skopje
Language: Macedonian*, Albanian*
Religion: Christianity, Islam
GDP per capita: $14,600
Life expectancy: 76 years

Malta
Area: 122 sq mi
(316 sq km)
Population: 416,000
Percent urban: 95.6%
Capital: Valletta
Language: Maltese*, English*
Religion: Christianity
GDP per capita: $39,900
Life expectancy: 80 years

Moldova
Area: 13,070 sq mi
(33,851 sq km)
Population: 3,474,000
Percent urban: 45.2%
Capital: Chisinau
Language: Romanian (Moldovan)*,
Russian
Religion: Christianity
GDP per capita: $5,300
Life expectancy: 71 years

Monaco
Area: 0.8 sq mi
(2.0 sq km)
Population: 31,000
Percent urban: 100%
Capital: Monaco
Language: French*, English, Italian,
Monégasque
Religion: Christianity
GDP per capita: $115,700
Life expectancy: 90 years

Montenegro
Area: 5,333 sq mi
(13,812 sq km)
Population: 643,000
Percent urban: 64.4%
Capital: Podgorica
Language: Serbian, Montenegrin*
Religion: Christianity, Islam
GDP per capita: $16,600
Life expectancy: NA

Netherlands
Area: 16,040 sq mi
(41,543 sq km)
Population: 17,085,000
Percent urban: 91.5%
Capital: Amsterdam
Language: Dutch*
Religion: Christianity
GDP per capita: $51,000
Life expectancy: 81 years

Norway
Area: 125,020 sq mi
(323,802 sq km)
Population: 5,320,000
Percent urban: 81%
Capital: Oslo
Language: Norwegian*, Sami
Religion: Christianity
GDP per capita: $69,200
Life expectancy: 82 years

Poland
Area: 120,728 sq mi
(312,685 sq km)
Population: 38,476,000
Percent urban: 60.5%
Capital: Warsaw
Language: Polish*
Religion: Christianity
GDP per capita: $27,800
Life expectancy: 78 years

Portugal
Area: 35,556 sq mi
(92,090 sq km)
Population: 10,840,000
Percent urban: 64.6%
Capital: Lisbon
Language: Portuguese*,
Mirandese*
Religion: Christianity
GDP per capita: $28,900
Life expectancy: 79 years

Romania
Area: 92,043 sq mi
(238,391 sq km)
Population: 21,530,000
Percent urban: 54.9%
Capital: Bucharest
Language: Romanian*
Religion: Christianity
GDP per capita: $22,300
Life expectancy: 75 years

Russia
Area: 6,601,631 sq mi
(17,098,242 sq km)
Population: 142,258,000
Percent urban: 74.2%
Capital: Moscow
Language: Russian*
Religion: Christianity, Islam
GDP per capita: $26,500
Life expectancy: 71 years

San Marino
Area: 24 sq mi
(61 sq km)
Population: 34,000
Percent urban: 94.2%
Capital: San Marino
Language: Italian
Religion: Christianity
GDP per capita: $59,500
Life expectancy: 83 years

Serbia
Area: 29,913 sq mi
(77,474 sq km)
Population: 7,111,000
Percent urban: 55.8%
Capital: Belgrade
Language: Serbian*
Religion: Christianity
GDP per capita: $14,500
Life expectancy: 76 years

Slovakia
Area: 18,932 sq mi
(49,035 km)
Population: 5,446,000
Percent urban: 53.4%
Capital: Bratislava
Language: Slovak*
Religion: Christianity
GDP per capita: $31,300
Life expectancy: 77 years

Slovenia
Area: 7,827 sq mi
(20,273 sq km)
Population: 1,972,000
Percent urban: 49.6%
Capital: Ljubljana
Language: Slovenian*
Religion: Christianity
GDP per capita: $32,100
Life expectancy: 78 years

Spain
Area: 195,123 sq mi
(505,370 sq km)
Population: 48,958,000
Percent urban: 80%
Capital: Madrid
Language: Spanish*, Catalan,
Galician, Basque
Religion: Christianity
GDP per capita: $36,400
Life expectancy: 82 years

Sweden
Area: 173,859 sq mi
(450,295 sq km)
Population: 9,960,000
Percent urban: 83.1%
Capital: Stockholm
Language: Swedish*
Religion: Christianity
GDP per capita: $49,800
Life expectancy: 82 years

Switzerland
Area: 15,937 sq mi
(41,277 sq km)
Population: 8,236,000
Percent urban: 74.1%
Capital: Bern
Language: German*, French*,
Italian*, Romansch*
Religion: Christianity
GDP per capita: $59,600
Life expectancy: 83 years

FLAGS & FACTS

Ukraine
Area: 233,031 sq mi
(603,550 sq km)
Population: 44,034,000
Percent urban: 70.1%
Capital: Kiev
Language: Ukrainian*, Russian
Religion: Christianity
GDP per capita: $8,300
Life expectancy: 72 years

Armenia
Area: 11,484 sq mi
(29,743 sq km)
Population: 3,045,000
Percent urban: 62.5%
Capital: Yerevan
Language: Armenian*
Religion: Christianity
GDP per capita: $8,600
Life expectancy: 75 years

Bhutan
Area: 14,824 sq mi
(38,394 sq km)
Population: 758,000
Percent urban: 40.1%
Capital: Thimphu
Language: Sharchhopka, Dzongkha*,
Lhotshamkha
Religion: Buddhism, Hinduism
GDP per capita: $8,200
Life expectancy: 70 years

Georgia
Area: 26,911 sq mi
(69,700 sq km)
Population: 4,926,000
Percent urban: 54%
Capital: Tbilisi
Language: Georgian*
Religion: Christianity, Islam
GDP per capita: $10,000
Life expectancy: 76 years

Iraq
Area: 169,234 sq mi
(438,317 sq km)
Population: 39,192,000
Percent urban: 69.7%
Capital: Baghdad
Language: Arabic*, Kurdish*
Religion: Islam
GDP per capita: $17,900
Life expectancy: 75 years

United Kingdom
Area: 94,058 sq mi
(243,610 sq km)
Population: 64,769,000
Percent urban: 83.1%
Capital: London
Language: English, regional
languages
Religion: Christianity
GDP per capita: $42,500
Life expectancy: 81 years

Azerbaijan
Area: 33,436 sq mi
(86,600 sq km)
Population: 9,961,000
Percent urban: 55.2%
Capital: Baku
Language: Azerbaijani*
Religion: Islam
GDP per capita: $17,400
Life expectancy: 73 years

Brunei
Area: 2,226 sq mi
(5,765 sq km)
Population: 444,000
Percent urban: 77.8%
Capital: Bandar Seri Begawan
Language: Malay*, English
Religion: Islam
GDP per capita: $76,900
Life expectancy: 77 years

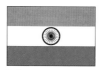

India
Area: 1,269,212 sq mi
(3,287,263 sq km)
Population: 1,281,936,000
Percent urban: 33.5%
Capital: New Delhi
Language: Hindi*, English*, state
languages
Religion: Hinduism, Islam
GDP per capita: $6,600
Life expectancy: 69 years

Israel
Area: 8,019 sq mi
(20,770 sq km)
Population: 8,300,000
Percent urban: 92.3%
Capital: Jerusalem
Language: Hebrew*, Arabic, English
Religion: Judaism, Islam
GDP per capita: $35,200
Life expectancy: 82 years

Vatican City (Holy See)
Area: 0.2 sq mi
(0.4 sq km)
Population: 1,000
Percent urban: 100%
Capital: Vatican City
Language: Italian, Latin, French
Religion: Christianity
GDP per capita: NA
Life expectancy: NA

Bahrain
Area: 293 sq mi
(760 sq km)
Population: 1,411,000
Percent urban: 88.9%
Capital: Manama
Language: Arabic*, English
Religion: Islam, Christianity
GDP per capita: $50,700
Life expectancy: 79 years

Cambodia
Area: 69,898 sq mi
(181,035 sq km)
Population: 16,204,000
Percent urban: 21.2%
Capital: Phnom Penh
Language: Khmer*
Religion: Buddhism
GDP per capita: $3,700
Life expectancy: 65 years

Indonesia
Area: 735,354 sq mi
(1,904,569 sq km)
Population: 260,581,000
Percent urban: 55.2%
Capital: Jakarta
Language: Indonesian*, indigenous
languages
Religion: Islam, Christianity
GDP per capita: $11,700
Life expectancy: 73 years

Japan
Area: 145,913 sq mi
(377,915 sq km)
Population: 126,451,000
Percent urban: 94.3%
Capital: Tokyo
Language: Japanese
Religion: Shintoism, Buddhism
GDP per capita: $41,300
Life expectancy: 85 years

ASIA

Afghanistan
Area: 251,826 sq mi
(652,230 sq km)
Population: 34,125,000
Percent urban: 27.6%
Capital: Kabul
Language: Dari*, Pashto*, Turkic
languages
Religion: Islam
GDP per capita: $1,900
Life expectancy: 51 years

Bangladesh
Area: 55,598 sq mi
(143,998 sq km)
Population: 157,827,000
Percent urban: 35.8%
Capital: Dhaka
Language: Bengali*
Religion: Islam, Hinduism
GDP per capita: $3,900
Life expectancy: 73 years

China
Area: 3,705,386 sq mi
(9,596,960 sq km)
Population: 1,379,303,000
Percent urban: 57.9%
Capital: Beijing
Language: Mandarin*
Religion: Officially atheist;
Buddhism, Christianity,
indigenous beliefs
GDP per capita: $15,400
Life expectancy: 76 years

Iran
Area: 636,368 sq mi
(1,648,195 sq km)
Population: 82,022,000
Percent urban: 74.4%
Capital: Tehran
Language: Persian (Farsi)*
Religion: Islam
GDP per capita: $18,100
Life expectancy: 71 years

Jordan
Area: 34,495 sq mi
(89,342 sq km)
Population: 10,248,000
Percent urban: 84.1%
Capital: Amman
Language: Arabic*, English
Religion: Islam
GDP per capita: $12,300
Life expectancy: 75 years

Kazakhstan
Area: 1,052,084 sq mi
(2,724,900 sq km)
Population: 18,557,000
Percent urban: 53.2%
Capital: Astana
Language: Kazakh*, Russian*
Religion: Islam, Christianity
GDP per capita: $25,100
Life expectancy: 71 years

Kuwait
Area: 6,880 sq mi
(17,818 sq km)
Population: 2,875,000
Percent urban: 98.4%
Capital: Kuwait City
Language: Arabic*, English
Religion: Islam, Christianity
GDP per capita: $71,900
Life expectancy: 78 years

Kyrgyzstan
Area: 77,201 sq mi
(199,951 sq km)
Population: 5,789,000
Percent urban: 36%
Capital: Bishkek
Language: Kyrgyz*, Uzbek, Russian*
Religion: Islam, Christianity
GDP per capita: $3,500
Life expectancy: 71 years

Laos
Area: 91,428 sq mi
(236,800 sq km)
Population: 7,127,000
Percent urban: 40.7%
Capital: Vientiane
Language: Lao*, French, indigenous
languages
Religion: Buddhism
GDP per capita: $5,700
Life expectancy: 64 years

Lebanon
Area: 4,015 sq mi
(10,400 sq km)
Population: 6,230,000
Percent urban: 88%
Capital: Beirut
Language: Arabic*, French, English
Religion: Islam, Christianity
GDP per capita: $18,500
Life expectancy: 78 years

Malaysia
Area: 127,354 sq mi
(329,847 sq km)
Population: 31,382,000
Percent urban: 76%
Capital: Kuala Lumpur
Language: Malaysian*, English
Religion: Islam, Buddhism,
Christianity
GDP per capita: $27,300
Life expectancy: 75 years

Maldives
Area: 115 sq mi
(298 sq km)
Population: 393,000
Percent urban: 47.5%
Capital: Male
Language: Dhivehi*, English
Religion: Islam
GDP per capita: $15,500
Life expectancy: 76 years

Mongolia
Area: 603,905 sq mi
(1,564,116 sq km)
Population: 3,068,000
Percent urban: 73.6%
Capital: Ulaanbaatar
Language: Mongolian*
Religion: Buddhism
GDP per capita: $12,300
Life expectancy: 70 years

Myanmar (Burma)
Area: 261,227 sq mi
(676,578 sq km)
Population: 55,124,000
Percent urban: 35.2%
Capital: Nay Pyi Taw
(administrative), Yangon (Rangoon)
(legislative)
Language: Burmese*
Religion: Buddhism, Christianity,
Islam
GDP per capita: $5,800
Life expectancy: 67 years

Nepal
Area: 56,827 sq mi
(147,181 sq km)
Population: 29,384,000
Percent urban: 19.4%
Capital: Kathmandu
Language: Nepali*, Maithali
Religion: Hinduism, Buddhism
GDP per capita: $2,500
Life expectancy: 71 years

North Korea
Area: 46,540 sq mi
(120,538 sq km)
Population: 25,248,000
Percent urban: 61.2%
Capital: Pyongyang
Language: Korean
Religion: Mainly atheist; Buddhism,
Confucianism, indigenous beliefs
GDP per capita: $1,700
Life expectancy: 70 years

Oman
Area: 119,498 sq mi
(309,500 sq km)
Population: 3,424,000
Percent urban: 78.5%
Capital: Muscat
Language: Arabic*, English
Religion: Islam
GDP per capita: $46,700
Life expectancy: 76 years

Pakistan
Area: 307,372 sq mi
(796,095 sq km)
Population: 204,925,000
Percent urban: 39.7%
Capital: Islamabad
Language: Punjabi, Sindhi, Saraiki,
Pashto, Urdu*, English*
Religion: Islam
GDP per capita: $5,100
Life expectancy: 68 years

Philippines
Area: 115,830 sq mi
(300,000 sq km)
Population: 104,256,000
Percent urban: 44.2%
Capital: Manila
Language: Filipino (Tagalog)*,
English*, indigenous languages
Religion: Christianity
GDP per capita: $7,700
Life expectancy: 69 years

Qatar
Area: 4,473 sq mi
(11,586 sq km)
Population: 2,314,000
Percent urban: 99.4%
Capital: Doha
Language: Arabic*, English
Religion: Islam, Christianity,
Hinduism
GDP per capita: $127,700
Life expectancy: 79 years

Saudi Arabia
Area: 829,995 sq mi
(2,149,690 sq km)
Population: 28,572,000
Percent urban: 83.5%
Capital: Riyadh
Language: Arabic*
Religion: Islam
GDP per capita: $55,200
Life expectancy: 75 years

Singapore
Area: 269 sq mi
(697 sq km)
Population: 5,889,000
Percent urban: 100%
Capital: Singapore
Language: Mandarin*, English*,
Malay*, Tamil*
Religion: Buddhism, Islam, Taoism,
Christianity
GDP per capita: $87,900
Life expectancy: 85 years

South Korea
Area: 38,502 sq mi
(99,720 sq km)
Population: 51,181,000
Percent urban: 82.7%
Capital: Seoul
Language: Korean, English
Religion: Christianity, Buddhism
GDP per capita: $37,700
Life expectancy: 82 years

Sri Lanka
Area: 25,332 sq mi
(65,610 sq km)
Population: 22,409,000
Percent urban: 18.5%
Capital: Colombo (administrative),
Sri Jayewardenepura Kotta
(legislative)
Language: Sinhala*, Tamil*, English
Religion: Buddhism, Hinduism,
Islam, Christianity
GDP per capita: $12,300
Life expectancy: 77 years

Syria
Area: 71,498 sq mi
(185,180 sq km)
Population: 18,029,000
Percent urban: 58.5%
Capital: Damascus
Language: Arabic*, Kurdish, English,
French
Religion: Islam, Christianity
GDP per capita: $2,900
Life expectancy: 75 years

FLAGS & FACTS

Tajikistan
Area: 55,251 sq mi
(143,100 sq km)
Population: 8,469,000
Percent urban: 27%
Capital: Dushanbe
Language: Tajik*, Russian
Religion: Islam
GDP per capita: $3,000
Life expectancy: 68 years

Thailand
Area: 198,116 sq mi
(513,120 sq km)
Population: 68,414,000
Percent urban: 52.7%
Capital: Bangkok
Language: Thai*
Religion: Buddhism
GDP per capita: $16,900
Life expectancy: 75 years

Timor-Leste (East Timor)
Area: 5,743 sq mi
(14,874 sq km)
Population: 1,291,000
Percent urban: 34%
Capital: Dili
Language: Tetum*, Portuguese*,
Indonesian, English
Religion: Christianity
GDP per capita: $4,200
Life expectancy: 68 years

Turkey
Area: 302,533 sq mi
(783,562 sq km)
Population: 80,845,000
Percent urban: 74.4%
Capital: Ankara
Language: Turkish*, Kurdish
Religion: Islam
GDP per capita: $24,900
Life expectancy: 75 years

Turkmenistan
Area: 188,455 sq mi
(488,100 sq km)
Population: 5,351,000
Percent urban: 50.8%
Capital: Ashgabat
Language: Turkmen*, Russian
Religion: Islam, Christianity
GDP per capita: $17,500
Life expectancy: 70 years

United Arab Emirates
Area: 32,278 sq mi
(83,600 sq km)
Population: 6,072,000
Percent urban: 86.1%
Capital: Abu Dhabi
Language: Arabic*, Persian, English
Religion: Islam, Christianity
GDP per capita: $67,900
Life expectancy: 78 years

Uzbekistan
Area: 172,741 sq mi
(447,400 sq km)
Population: 29,749,000
Percent urban: 36.6%
Capital: Tashkent
Language: Uzbek*, Russian
Religion: Islam, Christianity
GDP per capita: $6,600
Life expectancy: 74 years

Vietnam
Area: 127,880 sq mi
(331,210 sq km)
Population: 96,160,000
Percent urban: 34.9%
Capital: Hanoi
Language: Vietnamese*, English
Religion: Buddhism, Christianity
GDP per capita: $6,400
Life expectancy: 73 years

Yemen
Area: 203,848 sq mi
(527,968 sq km)
Population: 28,037,000
Percent urban: 35.8%
Capital: Sanaa
Language: Arabic*
Religion: Islam
GDP per capita: $2,400
Life expectancy: 66 years

AFRICA

Algeria
Area: 919,590 sq mi
(2,381,741 sq km)
Population: 40,969,000
Percent urban: 71.9%
Capital: Algiers
Language: Arabic*, French, Berber*
Religion: Islam
GDP per capita: $15,000
Life expectancy: 77 years

Angola
Area: 481,351 sq mi
(1,246,700 sq km)
Population: 29,310,000
Percent urban: 45.6%
Capital: Luanda
Language: Portuguese*, Bantu,
other indigenous languages
Religion: Christianity
GDP per capita: $6,800
Life expectancy: 56 years

Benin
Area: 43,483 sq mi
(112,622 sq km)
Population: 11,039,000
Percent urban: 44.8%
Capital: Porto-Novo (constitutional),
Cotonou (seat of government)
Language: French*, Fon, Yoruba
Religion: Christianity, Islam,
indigenous beliefs
GDP per capita: $2,100
Life expectancy: 62 years

Botswana
Area: 224,606 sq mi
(581,730 sq km)
Population: 2,215,000
Percent urban: 58%
Capital: Gaborone
Language: Setswana, English*
Religion: Christianity
GDP per capita: $17,000
Life expectancy: 55 years

Burkina Faso
Area: 105,869 sq mi
(274,200 sq km)
Population: 20,108,000
Percent urban: 31.5%
Capital: Ouagadougou
Language: French*, indigenous
languages
Religion: Islam, Christianity
GDP per capita: $1,800
Life expectancy: 56 years

Burundi
Area: 10,745 sq mi
(27,830 sq km)
Population: 11,467,000
Percent urban: 12.7%
Capital: Bujumbura
Language: Kirundi*, French*,
English*
Religion: Christianity
GDP per capita: $800
Life expectancy: 61 years

Cabo Verde
Area: 1,557 sq mi
(4,033 sq km)
Population: 561,000
Percent urban: 66.8%
Capital: Praia
Language: Portuguese*, Creole
Religion: Christianity
GDP per capita: $6,700
Life expectancy: 72 years

Cameroon
Area: 183,567 sq mi
(475,440 sq km)
Population: 24,995,000
Percent urban: 55.5%
Capital: Yaoundé
Language: English*, French*,
indigenous languages
Religion: Christianity, Islam
GDP per capita: $3,200
Life expectancy: 59 years

Central African Republic
Area: 240,534 sq mi
(622,984 sq km)
Population: 5,625,000
Percent urban: 40.6%
Capital: Bangui
Language: French*, Sangho
Religion: Christianity, indigenous
beliefs, Islam
GDP per capita: $700
Life expectancy: 52 years

Chad
Area: 495,752 sq mi
(1,284,000 sq km)
Population: 12,076,000
Percent urban: 22.8%
Capital: N'Djamena
Language: French*, Arabic*,
indigenous languages
Religion: Islam, Christianity
GDP per capita: $2,400
Life expectancy: 50 years

Comoros
Area: 863 sq mi
(2,235 sq km)
Population: 808,000
Percent urban: 28.5%
Capital: Moroni
Language: Arabic*, French*,
Shikomoro*
Religion: Islam
GDP per capita: $1,500
Life expectancy: 64 years

Congo
Area: 132,046 sq mi
(342,000 sq km)
Population: 4,955,000
Percent urban: 66.2%
Capital: Brazzaville
Language: French*, Lingala,
Monokutuba, other indigenous
languages
Religion: Christianity, indigenous
beliefs
GDP per capita: $6,700
Life expectancy: 59 years

**Congo, Democratic
Republic of the**
Area: 905,350 sq mi
(2,344,858 sq km)
Population: 83,301,000
Percent urban: 43.5%
Capital: Kinshasa
Language: French*, Lingala, other
indigenous languages
Religion: Christianity, indigenous
beliefs, Islam
GDP per capita: $800
Life expectancy: 57 years

Côte d'Ivoire (Ivory Coast)
Area: 124,503 sq mi
(322,463 sq km)
Population: 24,185,000
Percent urban: 55.5%
Capitals: Abidjan (administrative),
Yamoussoukro (legislative)
Language: French*, Dioula, other
indigenous languages
Religion: Islam, Christianity
GDP per capita: $3,600
Life expectancy: 59 years

Djibouti
Area: 8,958 sq mi
(23,200 sq km)
Population: 865,000
Percent urban: 77.5%
Capital: Djibouti
Language: French*, Arabic*, Somali,
Afar
Religion: Islam
GDP per capita: $3,400
Life expectancy: 63 years

Egypt
Area: 386,660 sq mi
(1,001,450 sq km)
Population: 97,041,000
Percent urban: 43.3%
Capital: Cairo
Language: Arabic*, English, French
Religion: Islam, Christianity
GDP per capita: $12,600
Life expectancy: 73 years

Equatorial Guinea
Area: 10,830 sq mi
(28,051 sq km)
Population: 778,000
Percent urban: 40.3%
Capital: Malabo
Language: Spanish*, French*,
Portuguese*, indigenous languages
Religion: Christianity, indigenous
beliefs
GDP per capita: $38,600
Life expectancy: 64 years

Eritrea
Area: 45,405 sq mi
(117,600 sq km)
Population: 5,919,000
Percent urban: 23.6%
Capital: Asmara
Language: Tigrinya*, Arabic*,
English*, indigenous languages
Religion: Islam, Christianity
GDP per capita: $1,400
Life expectancy: 65 years

Ethiopia
Area: 426,370 sq mi
(1,104,300 sq km)
Population: 105,350,000
Percent urban: 20.4%
Capital: Addis Ababa
Language: Oromo, Amharic*, Somali,
Tigrinya, Afar
Religion: Christianity, Islam
GDP per capita: $1,900
Life expectancy: 62 years

Gabon
Area: 103,346 sq mi
(267,667 sq km)
Population: 1,772,000
Percent urban: 87.6%
Capital: Libreville
Language: French*, indigenous
languages
Religion: Christianity
GDP per capita: $19,100
Life expectancy: 52 years

Gambia
Area: 4,361 sq mi
(11,295 sq km)
Population: 2,051,000
Percent urban: 60.8%
Capital: Banjul
Language: English*, indigenous
languages
Religion: Islam
GDP per capita: $1,700
Life expectancy: 65 years

Ghana
Area: 92,098 sq mi
(238,533 sq km)
Population: 27,500,000
Percent urban: 55.3%
Capital: Accra
Language: Assanta, Ewe, Fante,
English*
Religion: Christianity, Islam
GDP per capita: $4,400
Life expectancy: 67 years

Guinea
Area: 94,925 sq mi
(245,857 sq km)
Population: 12,414,000
Percent urban: 38.2%
Capital: Conakry
Language: French*, indigenous
languages
Religion: Islam
GDP per capita: $1,300
Life expectancy: 61 years

Guinea-Bissau
Area: 13,948 sq mi
(36,125 sq km)
Population: 1,792,000
Percent urban: 50.8%
Capital: Bissau
Language: Creole, Portuguese*
Religion: Islam, Christianity,
animism
GDP per capita: $1,700
Life expectancy: 51 years

Kenya
Area: 224,080 sq mi
(580,367 sq km)
Population: 47,616,000
Percent urban: 26.5%
Capital: Nairobi
Language: English*, Kiswahili*,
indigenous languages
Religion: Christianity, Islam
GDP per capita: $3,400
Life expectancy: 64 years

Lesotho
Area: 11,720 sq mi
(30,355 sq km)
Population: 1,958,000
Percent urban: 28.4%
Capital: Maseru
Language: Sesotho*, English*
Religion: Christianity, indigenous
beliefs
GDP per capita: $3,600
Life expectancy: 53 years

Liberia
Area: 43,000 sq mi
(111,369 sq km)
Population: 4,689,000
Percent urban: 50.5%
Capital: Monrovia
Language: English*, indigenous
languages
Religion: Christianity, Islam
GDP per capita: $900
Life expectancy: 59 years

Libya
Area: 679,358 sq mi
(1,759,540 sq km)
Population: 6,653,000
Percent urban: 79%
Capital: Tripoli
Language: Arabic*, Italian, English
Religion: Islam
GDP per capita: $8,700
Life expectancy: 77 years

Madagascar
Area: 226,657 sq mi
(587,041 sq km)
Population: 25,054,000
Percent urban: 36.4%
Capital: Antananarivo
Language: French*, Malagasy*
Religion: Christianity, indigenous
beliefs, Islam
GDP per capita: $1,500
Life expectancy: 66 years

Malawi
Area: 45,747 sq mi
(118,484 sq km)
Population: 19,196,000
Percent urban: 16.6%
Capital: Lilongwe
Language: English*, Chichewa, other
indigenous languages
Religion: Christianity, Islam
GDP per capita: $1,100
Life expectancy: 61 years

Mali
Area: 478,838 sq mi
(1,240,192 sq km)
Population: 17,885,000
Percent urban: 41.4%
Capital: Bamako
Language: French*, Bambara, other
indigenous languages
Religion: Islam
GDP per capita: $2,300
Life expectancy: 56 years

FLAGS & FACTS

Mauritania
Area: 397,953 sq mi
(1,030,700 sq km)
Population: 3,759,000
Percent urban: 61%
Capital: Nouakchott
Language: Arabic*, indigenous
languages
Religion: Islam
GDP per capita: $4,300
Life expectancy: 63 years

Mauritius
Area: 788 sq mi
(2,040 sq km)
Population: 1,356,000
Percent urban: 39.4%
Capital: Port Louis
Language: Creole, English*
Religion: Hinduism, Christianity,
Islam
GDP per capita: $20,400
Life expectancy: 76 years

Morocco
Area: 172,413 sq mi
(446,550 sq km)
Population: 33,987,000
Percent urban: 61.2%
Capital: Rabat
Language: Arabic*, Tamazight*,
French
Religion: Islam
GDP per capita: $8,300
Life expectancy: 77 years

Mozambique
Area: 308,641 sq mi
(799,380 sq km)
Population: 26,574,000
Percent urban: 32.8%
Capital: Maputo
Language: Emakhuwa, Portuguese*,
Xichangana, other indigenous
languages
Religion: Christianity, Islam
GDP per capita: $1,200
Life expectancy: 53 years

Namibia
Area: 318,259 sq mi
(824,292 sq km)
Population: 2,485,000
Percent urban: 48.6%
Capital: Windhoek
Language: Indigenous languages,
Afrikaans, English*
Religion: Christianity, indigenous
beliefs
GDP per capita: $11,300
Life expectancy: 64 years

Niger
Area: 489,189 sq mi
(1,267,000 sq km)
Population: 19,245,000
Percent urban: 19.3%
Capital: Niamey
Language: French*, indigenous
languages
Religion: Islam, indigenous beliefs,
Christianity
GDP per capita: $1,100
Life expectancy: 56 years

Nigeria
Area: 356,667 sq mi
(923,768 sq km)
Population: 190,632,000
Percent urban: 49.4%
Capital: Abuja
Language: English*, indigenous
languages
Religion: Islam, Christianity,
indigenous beliefs
GDP per capita: $5,900
Life expectancy: 53 years

Rwanda
Area: 10,169 sq mi
(26,338 sq km)
Population: 11,901,000
Percent urban: 30.7%
Capital: Kigali
Language: Kinyarwanda*, Kiswahili,
French*, English*
Religion: Christianity
GDP per capita: $2,000
Life expectancy: 60 years

Sao Tome and Principe
Area: 372 sq mi
(964 sq km)
Population: 201,000
Percent urban: 66.2%
Capital: São Tomé
Language: Portuguese*, Forro
Religion: Christianity
GDP per capita: $3,100
Life expectancy: 65 years

Senegal
Area: 75,954 sq mi
(196,722 sq km)
Population: 14,669,000
Percent urban: 44.4%
Capital: Dakar
Language: French*, Wolof, other
indigenous languages
Religion: Islam
GDP per capita: $2,600
Life expectancy: 62 years

Seychelles
Area: 176 sq mi
(455 sq km)
Population: 94,000
Percent urban: 54.5%
Capital: Victoria
Language: Creole*, English*,
French*
Religion: Christianity
GDP per capita: $27,600
Life expectancy: 75 years

Sierra Leone
Area: 27,699 sq mi
(71,740 sq km)
Population: 6,163,000
Percent urban: 40.7%
Capital: Freetown
Language: English*, Mende, Temne,
Krio
Religion: Islam, indigenous beliefs,
Christianity
GDP per capita: $1,700
Life expectancy: 58 years

Somalia
Area: 246,199 sq mi
(637,657 sq km)
Population: 11,031,000
Percent urban: 40.5%
Capital: Mogadishu
Language: Somali*, Arabic*, Italian,
English
Religion: Islam
GDP per capita: $400
Life expectancy: 52 years

South Africa
Area: 470,691 sq mi
(1,219,090 sq km)
Population: 54,842,000
Percent urban: 65.8%
Capital: Pretoria (Tshwane)
(administrative), Cape Town
(legislative), Bloemfontein (judicial)
Language: IsiZulu*, IsiXhosa*, other
indigenous languages*, Afrikaans*,
English*
Religion: Christianity
GDP per capita: $13,200
Life expectancy: 63 years

South Sudan
Area: 248,775 sq mi
(644,329 sq km)
Population: 13,026,000
Percent urban: 19.3%
Capital: Juba
Language: English*, Arabic,
indigenous languages
Religion: Animism, Christianity
GDP per capita: $1,700
Life expectancy: NA

Sudan
Area: 718,719 sq mi
(1,861,484 sq km)
Population: 37,346,000
Percent urban: 34.2%
Capital: Khartoum
Language: Arabic*, English*
Religion: Islam
GDP per capita: $4,400
Life expectancy: 64 years

Swaziland
Area: 6,704 sq mi
(17,364 sq km)
Population: 1,467,000
Percent urban: 21.3%
Capital: Mbabane (administrative),
Lobamba (legislative and royal)
Language: English*, siSwati*
Religion: Christianity
GDP per capita: $9,800
Life expectancy: 52 years

Tanzania
Area: 365,753 sq mi
(947,300 sq km)
Population: 53,951,000
Percent urban: 33%
Capital: Dar es Salaam
(administrative), Dodoma (legislative)
Language: Kiswahili*, English*,
indigenous languages
Religion: Christianity, Islam
GDP per capita: $3,100
Life expectancy: 62 years

Togo
Area: 21,925 sq mi
(56,785 sq km)
Population: 7,965,000
Percent urban: 41%
Capital: Lomé
Language: French*, Ewe, Mina,
Kabye, Dagomba
Religion: Indigenous beliefs,
Christianity, Islam
GDP per capita: $1,600
Life expectancy: 65 years

Tunisia
Area: 63,170 sq mi
(163,610 sq km)
Population: 11,404,000
Percent urban: 67.3%
Capital: Tunis
Language: Arabic*, French, Berber
Religion: Islam
GDP per capita: $11,600
Life expectancy: 76 years

Uganda
Area: 93,065 sq mi
(241,038 sq km)
Population: 39,570,000
Percent urban: 16.8%
Capital: Kampala
Language: English*, Swahili*, Ganda
(Luganda)
Religion: Christianity, Islam
GDP per capita: $2,100
Life expectancy: 55 years

Zambia
Area: 290,586 sq mi
(752,618 sq km)
Population: 15,972,000
Percent urban: 41.8%
Capital: Lusaka
Language: Bembe, Nyanja, Tonga,
other indigenous languages,
English*
Religion: Christianity
GDP per capita: $3,900
Life expectancy: 53 years

Zimbabwe
Area: 150,871 sq mi
(390,757 sq km)
Population: 13,805,000
Percent urban: 32.2%
Capital: Harare
Language: Shona*, Ndebele*, English*,
indigenous languages*
Religion: Christianity, indigenous
beliefs
GDP per capita: $2,000
Life expectancy: 58 years

AUSTRALIA, NEW ZEALAND & OCEANIA

Australia
Area: 2,988,885 sq mi
(7,741,220 sq km)
Population: 23,232,000
Percent urban: 89.7%
Capital: Canberra
Language: English
Religion: Christianity
GDP per capita: $48,900
Life expectancy: 82 years

Fiji
Area: 7,056 sq mi
(18,274 sq km)
Population: 921,000
Percent urban: 54.5%
Capital: Suva
Language: English*, Fijian*, Hindi
Religion: Christianity, Hinduism
GDP per capita: $9,300
Life expectancy: 73 years

Kiribati
Area: 313 sq mi
(811 sq km)
Population: 108,000
Percent urban: 44.6%
Capital: Tarawa
Language: I-Kiribati, English*
Religion: Christianity
GDP per capita: $1,800
Life expectancy: 66 years

Marshall Islands
Area: 70 sq mi
(181 sq km)
Population: 75,000
Percent urban: 73.2%
Capital: Majuro
Language: Marshallese*, English*
Religion: Christianity
GDP per capita: $3,300
Life expectancy: 73 years

Micronesia, Federated States of
Area: 271 sq mi
(702 sq km)
Population: 104,000
Percent urban: 22.5%
Capital: Palikir
Language: English*, indigenous
languages
Religion: Christianity
GDP per capita: $3,200
Life expectancy: 73 years

Nauru
Area: 8 sq mi
(21 sq km)
Population: 10,000
Percent urban: 100%
Capital: Yaren
Language: Nauruan*, English
Religion: Christianity
GDP per capita: $11,600
Life expectancy: 67 years

New Zealand
Area: 103,363 sq mi
(267,710 sq km)
Population: 4,510,000
Percent urban: 86.4%
Capital: Wellington
Language: English*, Maori*
Religion: Christianity
GDP per capita: $37,300
Life expectancy: 81 years

Palau
Area: 177 sq mi
(459 sq km)
Population: 21,000
Percent urban: 88.2%
Capital: Ngerulmud
Language: Palauan*, English*,
Filipino
Religion: Christianity
GDP per capita: $15,400
Life expectancy: 73 years

Papua New Guinea
Area: 178,703 sq mi
(462,840 sq km)
Population: 6,910,000
Percent urban: 13.1%
Capital: Port Moresby
Language: Tok Pisin*, English*, Hiri
Motu*, other indigenous languages
Religion: Christianity
GDP per capita: $3,500
Life expectancy: 67 years

Samoa
Area: 1,093 sq mi
(2,831 sq km)
Population: 200,000
Percent urban: 18.8%
Capital: Apia
Language: Samoan*, English
Religion: Christianity
GDP per capita: $5,500
Life expectancy: 74 years

Solomon Islands
Area: 11,157 sq mi
(28,896 sq km)
Population: 648,000
Percent urban: 23.2%
Capital: Honiara
Language: Melanesian pidgin,
English*, indigenous languages
Religion: Christianity
GDP per capita: $2,000
Life expectancy: 75 years

Tonga
Area: 288 sq mi
(747 sq km)
Population: 106,000
Percent urban: 23.9%
Capital: Nuku'alofa
Language: Tongan*, English*
Religion: Christianity
GDP per capita: $5,400
Life expectancy: 76 years

Tuvalu
Area: 10 sq mi
(26 sq km)
Population: 11,000
Percent urban: 61.5%
Capital: Funafuti
Language: Tuvaluan*, English*
Religion: Christianity
GDP per capita: $3,500
Life expectancy: 67 years

Vanuatu
Area: 4,706 sq mi
(12,189 sq km)
Population: 283,000
Percent urban: 26.8%
Capital: Port-Vila
Language: Bislama*, English*,
French*, indigenous languages
Religion: Christianity
GDP per capita: $2,600
Life expectancy: 73 years

Glossary

acid rain precipitation containing acid droplets resulting from the mixture of moisture in the air with carbon dioxide, nitrogen oxide, sulfur dioxide, and hydrocarbons released by factories and motor vehicles

archipelago group or chain of islands

atheist person or group that does not believe in any deity

basin area of land that is lower at the center than at the rim

bathymetry measurement of depth at various places in the ocean or other body of water

bay body of water, usually smaller than a gulf, that is partially surrounded by land

biomass total volume of organic material in a certain area or ecosystem that can be used as a renewable energy source (a biofuel)

border area along each side of the boundary that separates one country from another

boundary most commonly, a line that has been established by people to mark the limit of one political unit, such as a country or state, and the beginning of another; geographical features such as mountains sometimes act as boundaries.

caloric supply measure of the amount of food available to a particular person, household, or community

canal human-made waterway that is used by ships or to carry water for irrigation

canyon deep, narrow valley that has steep sides

carat unit of weight for precious stones equal to 200 milligrams

cliff very steep rock face, usually along a coast or on the side of a mountain

climate change change in typical climate patterns, including temperature or precipitation; may result from natural cycles or from human activities such as use of fossil fuels

continent one of the seven main landmasses on Earth's surface

continental climate interior areas found only in the Northern Hemisphere north of mild climate regions; summer to winter temperature extremes

country territory with a government that is the highest legal authority over the land and people within its boundaries

Creole language formed from a mixture of different languages, such as French and an indigenous language

delta lowland formed by silt, sand, and gravel deposited by a river at its mouth

desert hot or cold region that receives 10 inches (25 cm) or less of rain or other forms of precipitation a year

desertification spread of desertlike conditions in semiarid regions that is the result of human pressures, such as overgrazing, removal of natural vegetation, and cultivation of land, as well as climatic changes

divide elevated boundary line separating river systems from which rivers flow in different directions

dry climate areas experiencing low annual precipitation and day to night temperature extremes

earthquake sudden movement or shaking of Earth's crust, often resulting in damage on the surface

elevation distance above sea level, usually measured in feet or meters

escarpment cliff that separates two nearly flat land areas that lie at different elevations

fault break in Earth's crust along which movement up, down, or sideways occurs

fjord/fiord long narrow coastal inlet associated with past glaciation, as in Norway and Chile

fork place where a river splits into two smaller streams

geographic pole 90° N or 90° S latitude; location of the ends of Earth's axis

glacier large, slow-moving mass of ice

greenhouse gases gases, such as carbon dioxide and methane, that contribute to atmospheric warming

gross domestic product (GDP) per capita total value of goods and services produced by a country's economy in a year divided by the country's total population; figures in this atlas are in U.S. dollars and based on **purchasing power parity (PPP),** an economic calculation for comparing the value of different currencies that takes into account the cost of living in each country.

gulf portion of the ocean that cuts into the land; usually larger than a bay

harbor body of water, sheltered by natural or artificial barriers, that is deep enough for ships

hemisphere half a sphere; Earth can be divided into Northern and Southern Hemispheres, or Eastern and Western Hemispheres.

highland climate areas associated with mountains where elevation is the main factor in determining temperature and precipitation

highlands an elevated area or the more mountainous region of a country

hybrid car a car that is powered by gasoline and electricity

ice cap thick layer of ice and snow covering less than 19,300 square miles (50,000 sq km)

ice sheet thick layer of ice and snow covering more than 19,300 square miles (50,000 sq km)

indigenous naturally occurring in a particular area or region, as with people, languages, or religions

inlet narrow opening in the land that is filled with water flowing from an ocean, a lake, or a river

island landmass, smaller than a continent, that is completely surrounded by water

lagoon shallow body of water that is open to the sea but also protected from it by a reef or sandbar

lake body of water that is surrounded by land; large lakes are sometimes called seas.

landform physical feature shaped by tectonic activity, weathering, and erosion; Earth's four major kinds are plains, mountains, plateaus, and hills.

landmass large area of Earth's crust that lies above sea level, such as a continent

large-scale map map, such as a street map, that shows a small area in great detail

Latin America cultural region generally considered to include Mexico, Central America, South America, and the West Indies; Spanish and Portuguese are the principal languages.

latitude measurement in degrees north or south of 0° (Equator) to 90°

leeward side away from or sheltered from the wind

life expectancy average number of years a person can expect to live

lingua franca language not native to the local population that is used as a common or commercial language

longitude measurement in degrees east or west from 0° (prime meridian) to 180°

magma molten rock in Earth's mantle

magnetic pole point at which the axis of Earth's magnetic field intersects Earth's surface; compass needles align with Earth's magnetic field so that one end points to the north magnetic pole, the other to the south magnetic pole.

mesa eroded plateau, broader than it is high, found in arid or semiarid regions

metropolitan area a city and its surrounding suburbs or communities

Middle East term commonly used for the countries of southwestern Asia, but which can also include northern Africa from Morocco to Egypt

molten liquefied by heat; melted

mountain landform, higher than a hill, that rises at least 1,000 feet (300 m) above the surrounding land and is wider at its base than at its top, or peak; a series of mountains is called a range.

nation people who share a common culture or sense of history; often used as another word for "country," although people within a country may be of many cultures

ocean the large body of salt water that surrounds the continents and covers more than two-thirds of Earth's surface

pack ice large blocks of ice that form on the surface of the sea, pushed together by wind and currents

peninsula extension of land that is surrounded by water on three sides

pidgin simplified form of speech that allows speakers of different languages to communicate

plain large area of relatively flat land that is often covered with grasses

plantation agriculture type of commercial agriculture specializing in one or two crops, such as coffee or bananas

plate tectonics theory that Earth's crust is broken into large sections, or plates, that slowly move over the mantle (diagram, p. 16)

plateau relatively flat area, larger than a mesa, that rises above the surrounding landscape

poaching illegal killing or taking of animals from their natural habitats

polar climate area north of the Arctic Circle and south of the Antarctic Circle where temperatures remain cold year-round and precipitation is low

population density in a country, the average number of people living on each square mile or square kilometer of land (calculated by dividing population by land area)

Prairie Provinces popular name for the Canadian provinces of Manitoba, Saskatchewan, and Alberta

prime meridian imaginary line that runs through Greenwich, England, and is accepted as the line of 0° longitude

projection process of representing the round Earth on a flat surface, such as a map

Glossary

rain shadow dry region on the leeward side of a mountain range

reef offshore ridge made of coral, rocks, or sand; a reef that lies parallel to a coastline and is separated from it by a lagoon is called a barrier reef.

renewable resources resources that are replenished naturally, but the supply of which can be endangered by over-use and pollution

revolution movement of Earth in its orbit around the sun (365 days/1 year)

rotation movement of Earth on its axis (24 hours/1 day)

rural relating to an area outside a city and its surrounding suburbs with low population density and an agricultural economy

Sahel semiarid grassland in Africa along the Sahara's southern border

savanna tropical grassland with scattered trees

scale on a map, a means of explaining the relationship between distances on the map and actual distances on Earth's surface

sea ocean or a partially enclosed body of salt water that is connected to the ocean; completely enclosed bodies of salt water, such as the Dead Sea, are really lakes.

sea level average surface level of Earth's oceans from which the height of land areas can be measured

Silk Road ancient trade route stretching from China to the Mediterranean

slot canyon very narrow, deep canyon formed by water and wind erosion

small-scale map map, such as a country map, that shows a large area without much detail

sound long, broad inlet of the ocean that lies parallel to the coast and often separates an island and the mainland

Soviet Union shortened name for the Union of Soviet Socialist Republics (U.S.S.R.), a former Communist republic (1920–1991) in eastern Europe and northern and central Asia, made up of 15 republics, of which Russia was the largest

staple chief food of a people's diet

steppe Slavic word referring to relatively flat, mostly treeless temperate grasslands that stretch across much of the central parts of Europe and Asia

strait narrow passage of water that connects two larger bodies of water

Sunbelt U.S. region made up of southern and western states that are experiencing major population in-migration and economic growth

territory land that is under the jurisdiction of a country but is not a state or a province

topography features, such as mountains and valleys, that are evident on Earth's surface

tornado violently rotating column of air associated with thunderstorms

transshipment movement of goods or containers to one location before moving on, often by a different form of transportation, to a final destination

tributary stream that flows into a larger river

tropical cyclone large weather system that forms over warm tropical water; with sustained winds of at least 74 miles an hour (119 km/h), it is called a hurricane in the Atlantic Ocean and eastern Pacific; a cyclone in the Bay of Bengal, Indian Ocean, and South Pacific, and a typhoon in the western Pacific.

tropics region lying within $23^{1}/2°$ north and south of the Equator that experiences warm temperatures year-round

tsunami very large ocean wave caused by an earthquake or other powerful underwater disturbance, such as a volcanic eruption

urban relating to a city and its densely populated surrounding area with a non-agricultural economy

valley long depression, usually created by a river, that is bordered by higher land

virgin forest forest made up of trees that have never been cut down by humans

volcano opening in Earth's crust through which molten rock erupts; a volcano that has not erupted in the past 10,000 years but is expected to erupt again is said to be dormant.

wat Buddhist monastery or temple in southeastern Asia

windward side or direction that faces the wind

Geo Facts & Figures

PLANET EARTH

Mass:
6,584,800,000,000,000,000,000 tons
(5,973,600,000,000,000,000,000
metric tons)
Distance around the Equator: 24,902 mi
(40,075 km)
Area: 196,940,000 sq mi
(510,072,000 sq km)
Land area: 57,506,000 sq mi
(148,940,000 sq km)
Water area: 139,434,000 sq mi
(361,132,000 sq km))

The Continents
Asia: 17,208,000 sq mi
(44,570,000 sq km)
Africa: 11,608,000 sq mi
(30,065,000 sq km)
North America: 9,449,000 sq mi
(24,474,000 sq km)
South America: 6,880,000 sq mi
(17,819,000 sq km)
Antarctica: 5,100,000 sq mi
(13,209,000 sq km)
Europe: 3,841,000 sq mi
(9,947,000 sq km)
Australia: 2,989,000 sq mi
(7,741,000 sq km)

Highest Mountain on Each Continent
Everest, Asia: 29,035 ft (8,850 m)
Aconcagua, South America: 22,831 ft
(6,959 m)
Denali (McKinley), North America:
20,210 ft (6,194 m)
Kilimanjaro, Africa: 19,340 ft
(5,895 m)
El'brus, Europe: 18,510 ft (5,642 m)
Vinson Massif, Antarctica: 16,067 ft
(4,897 m)
Kosciuszko, Australia: 7,310 ft
(2,228 m)

Lowest Point on Each Continent
Byrd Glacier (depression), Antarctica:
−9,416 ft (−2,870 m)
Dead Sea, Asia: −1,388 ft (−423 m)
Lake Assal, Africa: −509 ft (−155 m)
Laguna del Carbón, South America:
−344 ft (−105 m)
Death Valley, North America:
−282 ft (−86 m)
Caspian Sea, Europe: −92 ft (−28 m)
Lake Eyre, Australia: −49 ft (−15 m)

Longest Rivers
Nile, Africa: 4,400 mi (7,081 km)
Amazon, South America: 4,150 mi
(6,679 km)
Yangtze (Chang), Asia: 3,880 mi
(6,244 km)
Mississippi-Missouri, North America:
3,780 mi (6,083 km)
Yenisey-Angara, Asia: 3,610 mi
(5,536 km)
Yellow (Huang), Asia: 3,590 mi (5,778 km)
Ob-Irtysh, Asia: 3,430 mi (5,520 km)
Amur, Asia: 3,420 mi (5,504 km)
Lena, Asia: 3,200 mi (5,150 km)
Congo, Africa: 3,180 mi (5,118 km)

Largest Islands
Greenland: 836,000 sq mi
(2,166,000 sq km)
New Guinea: 306,000 sq mi
(792,500 sq km)
Borneo: 280,100 sq mi (725,500 sq km)
Madagascar: 226,600 sq mi
(587,000 sq km)
Baffin: 196,000 sq mi (507,500 sq km)
Sumatra: 165,000 sq mi
(427,300 sq km)
Honshu: 87,800 sq mi (227,400 sq km)
Great Britain: 84,200 sq mi
(218,100 sq km)
Victoria: 83,900 sq mi (217,300 sq km)
Ellesmere: 75,800 sq mi
(196,200 sq km)

Oceans
Pacific: 69,000,000 sq mi
(178,800,000 sq km)
Atlantic: 35,400,000 sq mi
(91,700,000 sq km)
Indian: 29,400,000 sq mi
(76,200,000 sq km)
Arctic: 5,600,000 sq mi
(14,700,000 sq km)

Largest Seas (by area)
Coral: 1,615,500 sq mi
(4,184,000 sq km)
South China: 1,388,400 sq mi
(3,596,000 sq km)
Caribbean: 1,094,200 sq mi
(2,834,000 sq km)
Bering: 973,000 sq mi
(2,520,000 sq km)
Mediterranean: 953,300 sq mi
(2,469,000 sq km)
Okhotsk: 627,400 sq mi
(1,625,000 sq km)
Gulf of Mexico: 591,500 sq mi
(1,532,000 sq km)
Norwegian: 550,200 sq mi
(1,425,000 sq km)
Greenland: 447,100 sq mi
(1,158,000 sq km)
Japan (East Sea): 389,200 sq mi
(1,008,000 sq km)

Largest Lakes (by area)
Caspian Sea, Europe-Asia: 143,200 sq mi
(371,000 sq km)
Superior, North America: 31,700 sq mi
(82,100 sq km)
Victoria, Africa: 26,800 sq mi
(69,500 sq km)
Huron, North America: 23,000 sq mi
(59,600 sq km)
Michigan, North America: 22,300 sq mi
(57,800 sq km)
Tanganyika, Africa: 12,600 sq mi
(32,600 sq km)
Baikal, Asia: 12,200 sq mi
(31,500 sq km)

BACK OF THE BOOK

Geo Facts & Figures

Largest Lakes (cont'd)
Great Bear, North America: 12,100 sq mi
   (31,300 sq km)
Malawi (Nyasa), Africa: 11,200 sq mi
   (28,900 sq km)
Great Slave, North America: 11,000 sq mi
   (28,600 sq km)

GEOGRAPHIC EXTREMES

Highest Mountain
Everest, China/Nepal:
   29,035 ft (8,850 m)

Deepest Point in the Ocean
Challenger Deep, Mariana Trench, Pacific:
   -36,037 ft (-10,984 m)

Hottest Place
Dalol, Danakil Depression, Ethiopia:
   annual average temperature 93°F
   (34°C)

Coldest Place
Ridge A, Antarctica:
   annual average temperature -94°F
   (-70°C)

Wettest Place
Mawsynram, Meghalaya, India: annual
   average rainfall 467 in (1,187 cm)

Driest Place
Arica, Atacama Desert, Chile: barely
   measurable rainfall

Largest Hot Desert
Sahara, Africa: 3,475,000 sq mi
   (9,000,000 sq km)

Largest Cold Desert
Antarctica: 5,100,000 sq mi
   (13,209,000 sq km)

PEOPLE

Most Populous Continent
Asia   4,405,052,000

Least Populous Continent
Antarctica   no permanent population
Australia   23,232,000

Population Density by Continent (highest to lowest)
Asia   256.0 people/sq mi
    98.8 people /sq km
Europe   178.1 people/sq mi
    68.7 people /sq km
Africa   104.7 people/sq mi
    40.4 people /sq km
North America   67.7 people/sq mi
    26.1 people /sq km
South America   60.8 people/sq mi
    23.5 people /sq km
Austr/NZ/Oceania 11.5 people/sq mi
    4.4 people /sq km

Most Populous Country
China   1,379,303,000

Least Populous Country
Vatican City   1,000

Most Densely Populated Countries
Monaco   30,645.0 people/sq mi
    (15,322.5 people/sq km)
Singapore   21,891.9 people/sq mi
    (8,449.0 people/sq km)
Bahrain   4,815.5 people/sq mi
    (1,856.5 people/sq km)
Maldives   3,414.9 people/sq mi
    (1,317.8 people/sq km)
Malta   3,412.6 people/sq mi
    (1,317.5 people/sq km)
Bangladesh   2,838.7 people/sq mi
    (1,096.0 people/sq km)
Barbados   1,761.1 people/sq mi
    (679.9 people/sq km)

Mauritius   1,721.3 people/sq mi
    (664.9 people/sq km)
Lebanon   1,551.6 people/sq mi
    (599.0 people/sq km)
San Marino   1,397.4 people/sq mi
    (549.8 people/sq km)

Least Densely Populated Countries
Mongolia   5.1 people/sq mi
    (2.0 people/sq km)
Australia   7.8 people/sq mi
    (3.0 people/sq km)
Namibia   7.8 people/sq mi
    (3.0 people/sq km)
Iceland   8.5 people/sq mi
    (3.3 people/sq km)
Guyana   8.9 people/sq mi
    (3.4 people/sq km)
Canada   9.2 people/sq mi
    (3.6 people/sq km)
Mauritania   9.4 people/sq mi
    (3.6 people/sq km)
Suriname   9.4 people/sq mi
    (3.6 people/sq km)
Libya   9.8 people/sq mi
    (3.8 people/sq km)
Botswana   10.0 people/sq mi
    (3.8 people/sq km)

Most Populous Metropolitan Areas
Tokyo, Japan	38,140,000
Delhi, India	26,454,000
Shanghai, China	24,484,000
Mumbai (Bombay), India	21,357,000
São Paulo, Brazil	21,297,000
Beijing, China	21,240,000
Mexico City, Mexico	21,157,000
Osaka, Japan	20,337,000
Cairo, Egypt	19,128,000
New York, U.S.A.	18,604,000

Countries With the Highest Population Growth Rate

South Sudan	3.83%
Angola	3.52%
Malawi	3.31%
Burundi	3.25%
Uganda	3.20%
Niger	3.19%
Mali	3.02%
Burkina Faso	3.00%
Zambia	2.93%
Ethiopia	2.85%

Countries With the Lowest Population Growth Rate

Lebanon	-1.1%
Latvia	-1.08%
Lithuania	-1.08%
Moldova	-1.05%
Bulgaria	-0.61%
Estonia	-0.57%
Federated States of Micronesia	-0.52%
Croatia	-0.5%
Serbia	-0.46%
Ukraine	-0.41%

Countries With the Highest Life Expectancy

Monaco	90 years
Japan	85 years
Singapore	85 years
Iceland	83 years
San Marino	83 years
Switzerland	83 years
Australia	82 years
Austria	82 years
Canada	82 years
France	82 years
Israel	82 years
Italy	82 years
Liechtenstein	82 years
Luxembourg	82 years
Norway	82 years
South Korea	82 years
Spain	82 years
Sweden	82 years

Countries With the Lowest Life Expectancy

Chad	50 years
Afghanistan	51 years
Guinea-Bissau	51 years
Central African Republic	52 years
Gabon	52 years
Somalia	52 years
Swaziland	52 years
Lesotho	53 years
Mozambique	53 years
Nigeria	53 years
Zambia	53 years

Countries With the Highest Percent Urban Population

Monaco	100%
Nauru	100%
Singapore	100%
Vatican City	100%
Qatar	99.4%
Kuwait	98.4%
Belgium	97.9%
Malta	95.6%
Uruguay	95.6%
Iceland	94.3%
Japan	94.3%
San Marino	94.2%

Countries With the Lowest Percent Urban Population

Trinidad & Tobago	8.3%
Burundi	12.7%
Papua New Guinea	13.1%
Liechtenstein	14.3%
Malawi	16.6%
Uganda	16.8%
Sri Lanka	18.5%
St. Lucia	18.6%
Samoa	18.8%
Niger	19.3%
South Sudan	19.3%
Nepal	19.4%

Countries With the Highest Gross Domestic Product per Person (PPP)

Liechtenstein	$139,100
Qatar	$127,700
Monaco	$115,700
Luxembourg	$104,000
Singapore	$87,900
Brunei	$76,900
Kuwait	$71,900
Ireland	$69,200
Norway	$69,200
United Arab Emirates	$67,900

Countries With the Lowest Gross Domestic Product per Person (PPP)

Somalia	$400
Central African Republic	$700
Burundi	$800
Dem. Rep. of the Congo	$800
Liberia	$900
Malawi	$1,100
Niger	$1,100
Mozambique	$1,200
Guinea	$1,300
Eritrea	$1,400

Outside Websites

With an adult's help, check out these websites for more information about various topics discussed in this atlas.

Antarctica
www.coolantarctica.com

Biomes
www.blueplanetbiomes.org

Climate change
climate.nasa.gov

Climates
www.worldclimate.com

Countries of the world (statistics)
www.cia.gov/library/publications/
resources/the-world-factbook

Endangered species
www.iucnredlist.org

Extreme facts about the world
www.extremescience.com

Flags of the world
www.crwflags.com/fotw/flags

Languages: "Say Hello"
www.ipl.org/div/hello

Mapping the world
www.google.com/earth

National anthems
www.nationalanthems.info

Natural disasters
Earthquakes: earthquake.usgs.gov/
earthquakes
Hurricanes: www.nhc.noaa.gov
Tsunamis: www.tsunami.noaa.gov
Volcanoes: volcanoes.usgs.gov/
index.html

Population
Population clock: www.census.gov/
popclock
World population: www.prb.org/pdf17/
2017_World_Population.pdf

Religions of the world
www.adherents.com

Solar system
solarsystem.nasa.gov/planets

Time
Time around the world: www.world
timeserver.com
Time zones: worldtimezone.com

Weather around the world
weather.com

World Heritage sites
whc.unesco.org/en/list

Abbreviations

°E	degrees East	L.	Lake	N.Z.	New Zealand
°N	degrees North	LA.	Louisiana	OKLA.	Oklahoma
°S	degrees South	LIECH.	Liechtenstein	OREG.	Oregon
°W	degrees West	LUX.	Luxembourg	P.E.I.	Prince Edward Island
°C	degrees Celsius	m	meters	p.	page
°F	degrees Fahrenheit	MASS.	Massachusetts	pp.	pages
AFGHAN.	Afghanistan	MD.	Maryland	PA.	Pennsylvania
ALA.	Alabama	ME.	Maine	Pen.	Peninsula
ARK.	Arkansas	mi	miles	R.I.	Rhode Island
B.&H.	Bosnia and Herzegovina	MICH.	Michigan	Rep.	Republic
BELG.	Belgium	MINN.	Minnesota	S	South
COLO.	Colorado	MISS.	Mississippi	S. DAK.	South Dakota
CONN.	Connecticut	MO.	Missouri	S.C.	South Carolina
D.C.	District of Columbia	MONT.	Montana	sq km	square kilometers
DEL.	Delaware	MONT.	Montenegro	sq mi	square miles
DEM.	Democratic	Mt.	Mount, Mountain	St., Ste.	Saint, Sainte
E	East	Mts.	Mountains	Str.	Strait
FLA.	Florida	N	North	SWITZ.	Switzerland
ft	feet	N. DAK.	North Dakota	TENN.	Tennessee
GA.	Georgia	N. MEX.	New Mexico	U.A.E.	United Arab Emirates
GDP	Gross Domestic Product	N.B.	New Brunswick	U.K.	United Kingdom
I.	Island	N.C.	North Carolina	U.S./U.S.A.	United States
ILL.	Illinois	N.H.	New Hampshire	VA.	Virginia
IND.	Indiana	N.J.	New Jersey	VT.	Vermont
Is.	Islands	N.P.	National Park	W	West
KANS.	Kansas	N.Y.	New York	W. VA.	West Virginia
km	kilometers	NEBR.	Nebraska	WASH.	Washington
KY.	Kentucky	NETH.	Netherlands	WIS.	Wisconsin
KYRG.	Kyrgyzstan	NEV.	Nevada	WYO.	Wyoming

Index

Map references are in boldface **(50)** *type. Letters and numbers following in lightface* (D12) *locate the place-names using the map grid. (Refer to page 7 for more details.)*

Ionian Sea — Laccadive Sea

Potiskum — San José del Guaviare

Map Data Sources

8 (Find Your House) SkylineGlobe. www.skylineglobe.com; 17 (Tectonic Features), USGS Earthquake Hazards Program and USGS National Earthquake Information Center (NEIC). earthquake.usgs.gov; Smithsonian Institution, Global Volcanism Program. volcano.si.edu; USGS and the International Association of Volcanology and Chemistry of the Earth's Interior. vulcan.wr.usgs.gov; 22 (Climatic Zones), © H.J. de Blij, P.O. Muller, and John Wiley & Sons, Inc.; 25 (Land and Ocean Temperature Averages), NOAA National Centers for Environmental Information, State of the Climate: Global Climate Report for July 2017. Published online August 2017. www.ncdc.noaa.gov/sotc/global/201707; 26 (Vegetation Zones), *Biodiversity*. NG Maps for *National Geographic* magazine (February 1999); 28 (Human Footprint), Venter, O., E.W. Sanderson, A. Magrach, J.R. Allan, J. Beher, K.R. Jones, H.P. Possingham, W.F. Laurance, P. Wood, B.M. Fekete, M.A. Levy, and J.E.M. Watson. "Sixteen years of change in the global terrestrial human footprint and implications for biodiversity conservation." *Nature Communications* 2016. doi:10.1038/ncomms12558; Watson, J.E.M., D.F. Shanahan, M. Di Marco, J. Allan, W.F. Laurance, E.W. Sanderson, B. Mackey, and O. Venter. "Catastrophic declines in wilderness areas undermine global environment targets." *Current Biology* 26, 2016. doi:10.1016/j.cub.2016.08.049; 28 (Environmental Stresses), Halpern, B. S. et al. "Spatial and temporal changes in cumulative human impacts on the world's ocean." *Nature Communications* 6:7615. 2015. doi: 10.1038/ncomms8615; Millennium Ecosystem Assessment. *Ecosystems and Human Well-Being, Synthesis*; NASA's Goddard Space Flight Center; van Donkelaar, A., R.V. Martin, M. Brauer, R. Kahn, R. Levy, C. Verduzco, and P.J. Villeneuve. "Global estimates of exposure to fine particulate matter concentrations from satellite-based aerosol optical dept." *Environmental Health Perspective* 118(6), 2010. doi:10.1289/ehp.0901623; 30 (Number of Threatened Species, 2016), IUCN 2017. The IUCN Red List of Threatened Species. Version 2016-3. www.iucnredlist.org; 32 (Natural Disasters), USGS Earthquake Hazards Program and USGS National Earthquake Information Center (NEIC). earthquake.usgs.gov; Smithsonian Institution, Global Volcanism Program. volcano.si.edu; USGS and the International Association of Volcanology and Chemistry of the Earth's Interior. vulcan .wr.usgs.gov; National Geophysical Data Center/World Data Service (NGDC/WDS): Global Historical Tsunami Database. National Geophysical Data Center, NOAA; 36 (Population Density), Landscan 2014 Population Dataset created by UT-Battelle, LLC, the management and operating contractor of the Oak Ridge National Laboratory acting on behalf of the U.S. Department of Energy under Contract No. DE-AC05-00OR22725. Distributed by East View Geospatial: geospatial.com and East View Information Services: eastview .com/online/landscan; 36 (Urban Area Population), United Nations, Department of Economic and Social Affairs, Population Division (2016). *The World's Cities in 2016–Data Booklet*; 26 (Urban Population Growth, 1950–2015, and Population Graph), United Nations Department of Economic and Social Affairs Population Division. *World Urbanization Prospects: The 2014 Revision*; *World Population Prospects: The 2012 Revision*; and *Trends in International Migrant Stock: The 2013 Revision*; 38 (Projected Population Change (%), 2015–2050), CIA. *The World Factbook*. cia.gov; Population Reference Bureau. prb.org/DataFinder; 38 (Population Pyramids) U.S. Census Bureau; 40 (Major Language Families Today), Global Mapping International (GMI) and SIL International. World Language Mapping System, version 3.2.1; 42 (Dominant Religion), Johnson, Todd M., and Brian J. Grim, eds. World Religion Database. worldreligiondatabase.org. Leiden/Boston: Brill; 44 (Dominant Economic Sector), CIA. *The World Factbook*. cia.gov; 46 (World Economies), World Bank. data.worldbank.org; 46 (Single-Commodity-Dependent Economies), International Trade Centre. intracen.org; 47 (Major Regional Trade Agreements), APEC (apec.org); ASEAN (asean.org); COMESA (about.comesa.int); ECOWAS (comm.ecowas.int); EU (europa.eu); MERCOSUR (mercosur.int); NAFTA (ustr.gov); SAFTA (saarc-sec.org); 48 (Renewable Freshwater Resources per Capita), Food and Agriculture Organization. AQUASTAT data; 50 (Crop Allocation), Global Landscapes Initiative, Institute on the Environment, University of Minnesota. Hooke, Roger LeB., and José F. Martín-Duque. "Land Transformation by Humans: A Review." *GSA Today* (2012), Volume 22 (12): 4–10; 52 (Total Energy Consumption, Major Energy Deposit), EIA (U.S. Energy Information Administration); 137 (Changing the Land), UN Food and Agricultural Organization. www.fao.org/docrep/008/ y5744e/y5744e04.htm.

Illustrations Credits

Cover
(Empire State Building), Cedric Weber/Shutterstock; (Indian girl), Bartosz Hadyniak/E+/Getty Images; (red-eyed tree frog), Jeffrey Mcgraw/Dreamstime; (dolphin), tubuceo/ Shutterstock; back cover (Arches National Park), Lunamarina/Dreamstime; (Volga River), Iakov Filimonov/Shutterstock; back cover (tiger), estima/iStockphoto; (African girl), Blend Images/Getty Images

Front of Book
1, Premium Stock/Corbis; 2, Premium Stock/Corbis; 2 (FAR LE), Roy Toft/NG Creative; 2 (LE), Tom Murphy/NG Creative; 2 (RT), Cary Wolinsky/NG Creative; 2 (FAR RT), Richard Nowitz/NG Creative; 3 (FAR LE), Ron Kimball Stock; 3 (LE), Jose Fuste Raga/Corbis; 3 (RT), Barbara Schneider/scxh; 3 (FAR RT), Brand X; 4 (UP RT), Todd Gipstein/NG Creative; 4 (LO), Richard Nowitz/NG Creative; 4 (UP LE), Tomasz Tomaszewski/NG Creative; 5 (LO RT), Cary Wolinsky/NG Creative; 5 (UP LE), Frans Lanting/NG Creative; 5 (UP RT), Gordon Wiltsie/NG Creative; 5 (LO LE), Taylor S. Kennedy/NG Creative; 10, Mark Theissen & Becky Hale/NG Staff; 11, NASA-JPL/Caltech; 14-15, David Aguilar; 20 (FAR LE), Maria Stenzel/ NG Creative; 20 (LE), Bill Hatcher/NG Creative; 20 (RT), Carsten Peter/NG Creative; 20 (FAR RT), Carsten Peter/NG Creative; 21 (FAR LE), Gordon Wiltsie/NG Creative; 21 (LE), James P. Blair/NG Creative; 21 (RT), Thomas J. Abercrombie/NG Creative; 21 (FAR RT), Anne Keiser/NG Creative; 24-25, NG Creative; 25 (UP), Kevin Rivoli/Associated Press; 25 (LO BOTH), Weiss and Overpeck, The University of Arizona; 26 (FAR LE), Raymond Gehman/NG Creative; 26 (LE), George F. Mobley/NG Creative; 26 (RT), Paul Nicklen/NG Creative; 26 (FAR RT), Raymond Gehman/NG Creative; 27 (FAR LE), Annie Griffiths Belt/NG Creative; 27 (LE), Beverly Joubert/NG Creative; 27 (RT), Michael Melford/NG Creative; 27 (FAR RT), Maria Stenzel/NG Creative; 28, James P. Blair/NG Creative; 29 (LE), William Thompson/NG Creative; 29 (CTR), Steve Mccurry/NG Creative; 29 (RT), Seyllou/AFP/Getty Images; 31 (A), Nature Picture Library/Alamy Stock Photo; 31 (B), Martin Harvey/Photolibrary RM/Getty Images; 31 (C), Martin Willis/Minden Pictures; 31 (D), Mike Bowie, Lincoln University, NZ; 31 (E), Suzi Eszterhas/Minden Pictures; 31 (F), Christophe Courteau/Nature Picture Library; 31 (G), Danita Delimont/Getty Images; 31 (H), Zoonar GmbH/ Alamy Stock Photo; 32 (UP), Ron Gravelle/National Geographic My Shot; 32 (LO), Gemma Handy/AFP/Getty Images; 33 (UP), Pablo Hidalgo/Shutterstock; 33 (LO RT), Jiji Press/ AFP/Getty Images; 33 (LO LE), Pacific Press/Alamy Stock Photo; 37, Justin Guariglia/NG Creative; 40, Maria Stenzel/NG Creative; 41 (LE), Justin Guariglia/NG Creative; 41 (RT), Phillipe Lissac/Godong/Corbis; 42 (LE), Martin Gray/NG Creative; 42 (CTR), Randy Olson/NG Creative; 42 (RT), Amit Dave/Reuters/Corbis; 43 (LE), Reza/NG Creative; 43 (RT), Richard Nowitz/NG Creative; 44 (LE), Jon Parker Lee/Alamy; 44 (RT), Justin Guariglia/NG Creative; 45 (LE), Mike Goldwater/Alamy Stock Photo; 45 (RT), Phil Schermeister/NG Creative; 46, hxdyl/Shutterstock; 48, Jodi Cobb/NG Creative; 50, Monty Rakusen/Cultura RF/Getty Images; 51 (LE), James P. Blair/NG Creative; 51 (UP RT), Stephen St. John/NG Creative; 51 (CTR RT), Joel Sartore/NG Creative; 51 (LO RT), Michael Nichols/NG Creative; 53 (FAR LE), Walter Rawlings/Robert Harding World Imagery/Corbis; 53 (LE), Richard Nowitz/NG Creative; 53 (RT), Sarah Leen/NG Creative; 53 (FAR RT), Priit Vesilind/NG Creative

North America
58 (UP), Lonely Planet Images/Getty Images; 58 (LO LE), Tomasz Tomaszewski/NG Creative; 58 (LO RT), Rex Stucky/NG Creative; 59 (UP), Michael Melford/NG Creative; 59 (LO), Jeff Vanuga/Corbis; 60 (UP LE), Ira Block/NG Creative; 60 (UP RT), NG Creative; 60 (LO LE), George F. Mobley/NG Creative; 60 (LO RT), Martin Gray/NG Creative; 61 (UP), vilainecrevette/iStockphoto; 61 (LO RT), Brad Mitchell/Alamy; 61 (LO LE), Glen Allison/The Image Bank/Getty Images; 62 (LO), Richard Nowitz/NG Creative; 62 (UP), Alaska Stock/NG Creative; 63 (LO), Michael S. Yamashita/NG Creative; 63 (UP), Tim Laman/NG Creative; 64 (UP), Zeljko Radojko/Shutterstock; 64 (LO), Todd Gipstein/NG Creative; 64-65, Norbert Rosing/NG Creative; 65 (UP), Brooks Walker/NG Creative; 66 (UP), Chris Jenner/Shutterstock; 66 (LO), Kenneth Garrett/NG Creative; 67 (UP LE), Macduff Everton/NG Creative; 67 (UP RT), worldswildlifewonders/Shutterstock; 68 (UP), Pablo Corral Vega/Corbis; 68 (LO), Steve Raymer/NG Creative; 68-69, Bill Curtsinger/NG Creative; 69 (UP), Michael Melford/NG Creative; 69 (LO), Jose Fuste Raga/Corbis

South America

74 (UP), Tim Laman/NG Creative; 74 (LO), Pablo Corral Vega/NG Creative; 75 (UP), Stephanie Maze/NG Creative; 75 (LO LE), Anne Keiser/NG Creative; 75 (LO RT), Todd Gipstein/NG Creative; 76 (UP LE), Jimmy Chin/NG Creative; 76 (UP RT), Catarina Belova/Shutterstock; 76 (LO RT), Pablo Corral Vega/NG Creative; 76 (LO LE), Ed George/NG Creative; 77 (UP), Richard Nowitz/NG Creative; 77 (LO LE), Joel Sartore/NG Creative; 77 (LO RT), Melissa Farlow/NG Creative; 78 (UP), William Albert Allard/NG Creative; 78 (LO), Pablo Corral Vega/NG Creative; 78-79, Meredith Davenport/NG Creative; 79 (UP), O. Louis Mazzatenta/NG Creative; 80 (UP), Macduff Everton/NG Creative; 80 (LO), Priit Vesilind/NG Creative; 81 (UP), Joel Sartore/NG Creative; 81 (LO), James L. Amos/NG Creative; 82, O. Louis Mazzatenta/NG Creative; 82-83, Dmitry Saparov/Shutterstock; 83 (UP), Maria Stenzel/NG Creative; 83 (LO), Joel Sartore/NG Creative

Europe

88 (UP), Richard Nowitz/NG Creative; 88 (LO), Priit Vesilind/NG Creative; 88-87, Pavel Svoboda/Shutterstock; 89 (LE), Melissa Farlow/NG Creative; 89 (RT), Richard Nowitz/NG Creative; 90 (UP), Taylor S. Kennedy/NG Creative; 90 (LO LE), Steve Mccurry/NG Creative; 90 (LO RT), Sisse Brimberg/NG Creative; 90-91, Richard Nowitz/NG Creative; 91 (LO LE), Richard Nowitz/NG Creative; 91 (CTR), Nicole Duplaix/NG Creative; 91 (LO RT), James P. Blair/NG Creative; 92 (UP), Karen Kasmauski/NG Creative; 92 (LOLE), Priit Vesilind/NG Creative; 92 (LO RT), Gregory Davies/Alamy; 93, The Art Archive/Corbis; 94 (UP), Richard Nowitz/NG Creative; 94 (CTR), Skip Brown/NG Creative; 94 (LO), Jim Richardson/NG Creative; 95, Richard Nowitz/NG Creative; 96 (UP), Catherine Karnow/NG Creative; 96 (LO), Catherine Karnow/NG Creative; 97 (LE), Sissie Brimberg/NG Creative; 97 (RT), Sissie Brimberg/NG Creative; 98 (UP), James P. Blair/NG Creative; 98 (LO LE), Freesurf69/Dreamstime; 98 (LO RT), Richard I'Anson/Lonely Planet Images/Getty Images; 99, James L. Stanfield/NG Creative; 100 (UP), Steve Raymer/NG Creative; 100 (LO), Steve Raymer/NG Creative; 101, Richard Nowitz/NG Creative

Asia

106 (UP), Taylor S. Kennedy/NG Creative; 106 (LO), Steve Mccurry/NG Creative; 107 (UP), Steve Raymer/NG Creative; 107 (LO LE), Justin Guariglia/NG Creative; 107 (LO RT), David Edwards/NG Creative; 108 (UP), Fred de Noyelle/Godong/Corbis; 108 (LO LE), Jodi Cobb/NG Creative; 108 (LO RT), Justin Guariglia/NG Creative; 108-109, Todd Gipstein/NG Creative; 109 (LO LE), Michael Nichols/NG Creative; 109 (LO RT), Justin Guariglia/NG Creative; 110 (UP), Maria Stenzel/NG Creative; 110 (LO), Steve Winter/NG Creative; 111 (UP), Steve Raymer/NG Creative; 111 (LO), Alexander Zemlianichenko Jr./Bloomberg via Getty Images; 112 (UP), Medford Taylor/NG Creative; 112 (LO), Shamil Zhumatov/Reuters; 113 (UP), Wild Wonders of Europe/Shpilenok/Nature Picture Library; 113 (LO), Dean Conger/NG Creative; 114 (UP), H. Kim/NG Creative; 114 (LO), Justin Guariglia/NG Creative; 115 (UP), O. Louis Mazzatenta/NG Creative; 115 (LO), Roy Toft/NG Creative; 116 (UP), James L. Stanfield/NG Creative; 116 (LO), Alex Webb/NG Creative; 117 (UP), Martin Gray/NG Creative; 117 (LO), Priit Vesilind/NG Creative; 118 (UP LE), Morteza Nikoubazl/Reuters/Corbis; 118 (UP RT), Arthur Thèvenart/Corbis; 118 (LO), Robb Kendrick/NG Creative; 119, Bill Lyons/NG Creative; 120 (UP), Ed George/NG Creative; 120 (LO), James P. Blair/NG Creative; 121 (UP), iStockphoto; 121 (LO), Bobby Model/NG Creative; 122 (UP LE), Paul Chesley/NG Creative; 122 (UP RT), Macduff Everton/NG Creative; 122 (LO), deepblue-photographer/Shutterstock; 123 (UP), Jack Fields/Corbis; 123 (LO), Steve Raymer/NG Creative; 124 (UP), Reuters/Corbis; 124 (LO), Richard Nowitz/NG Creative; 125 (UP LE), Paul Chesley/NG Creative; 125 (UP RT), Tim Laman/NG Creative; 125 (LO), Tim Laman/NG Creative

Africa

130 (UP), George F. Mobley/NG Creative; 130 (LO LE), Michael Nichols/NG Creative; 130 (LO RT), Instinia/Shutterstock; 131 (UP), Skip Brown/NG Creative; 131 (LO LE), Bill Curtsinger/NG Creative; 131 (LO RT), Cary Wolinsky/NG Creative; 132 (UP), Georg Gerster/NG Creative; 132 (LO LE), Digital Vision/Getty Images; 132 (LO RT), Kenneth Garrett/NG Creative; 133 (UP), Cary Wolinskyng Creative; 133 (LO LE), Bill Curtsinger/NG Creative; 133 (LO RT), Michael Nichols/NG Creative; 134 (UP), Thomas J. Abercrombie/NG Creative; 134 (LO), Jose Fuste Raga/Corbis; 135 (UP), Kenneth Garrett/NG Creative; 135 (CTR), Richard Nowitz/NG Creative; 135 (LO), Christian Wilkinson/Alamy Stock Photo; 136 (UP), W. Robert Moore/NG Creative; 136 (CTR), NG Creative; 136 (LO), Adisa/Shutterstock; 137 (UP), James L. Stanfield/NG Creative; 138 (UP), Randy Olson/NG Creative; 138 (CTR), Michael Lewis/NG Creative; 138 (LO), Deanne Fitzmaurice/NG Creative; 139 (UP), Suzi Eszterhas/Minden Pictures; 139 (LO), Bobby Haas/NG Creative; 140 (UP), robertharding/Alamy Stock Photo; 140 (LO), AGF Srl/Alamy Stock Photo; 141 (UP), Werner Forman/Corbis; 141 (LO), Xinhua/Alamy Stock Photo; 142 (UP), George F. Mobley/NG Creative; 142 (LO), Tim Laman/NG Creative; 143 (UP), Kenneth Garrett/NG Creative; 143 (LO), Bob Krist/Corbis

Australia, New Zealand & Oceania

148 (UP), Nicole Duplaix/NG Creative; 148 (LO), Frans Lanting/NG Creative; 148-149, Tim Laman/NG Creative; 149 (UP), Art Wolfe/NG Creative; 149 (LO), Nicole Duplaix/NG Creative; 150 (UP), Medford Taylor/NG Creative; 150 (CTR), N.Minton/Shutterstock; 150 (LO), Danita Delimont Creative/Alamy; 150-151 (UP), Tim Laman/NG Creative; 150-151 (LO), travellight/Shutterstock; 151 (CTR), Paul Chesley/NG Creative; 151 (LO), Mark Cosslett/NG Creative; 152 (LE), Jim Agronick/Shutterstock; 152 (RT), Sam Abell/NG Creative; 153 (LE), Jason Edwards/NG Creative; 153 (RT), Paul Chesley/NG Creative; 154 (UP), bumihills/Shutterstock; 154 (LO), Carsten Peter/NG Creative; 155 (UP LE), Martin Gray/NG Creative; 155 (UP RT), Randy Olson/NG Creative; 155 (LO), Jodi Cobb/NG Creative

Antarctica

158, Steve Bloom Images/Alamy Stock Photo; 159 (UP), Vicki Beaver/Alamy Stock Photo; 159 (LO), Alex Huizinga/NiS/Minden Pictures; 160 (UP), Science Source/Getty Images; 160 (LO), Michael Nolan/Robert Harding World Imagery/Getty Images; 161 (UP), Paul Nicklen/NG Creative; 161 (LO), Norbert Wu/Minden Pictures

The Oceans

165 (UP), NOAA; 165 (LO LE), Scripps Institute of Oceanography; 165 (LO RT), NASA; 166 (UP), Wolcott Henry/NG Creative; 166 (LO), Karen Kasmauski/NG Creative; 168 (UP), Tom Murphy/NG Creative; 168 (LO LE), Emory Kristof/NG Creative; 168 (LO RT), John Eastcott and Yva Momatiuk/NG Creative; 170, Hans Fricke/NG Creative; 172 (UP), Nicole Duplaix/NG Creative; 172 (LO), Norbert Rosing/NG Creative

Since 1888, the National Geographic Society has funded more than 12,000 research,
exploration, and preservation projects around the world. The Society receives funds from
National Geographic Partners, LLC, funded in part by your purchase. A portion of the proceeds
from this book supports this vital work. To learn more, visit natgeo.com/info.

NATIONAL GEOGRAPHIC and Yellow Border Design are trademarks of the
National Geographic Society, used under license.

For more information, visit nationalgeographic.com, call 1-800-647-5463,
or write to the following address:

National Geographic Partners
1145 17th Street N.W.
Washington, D.C. 20036-4688 U.S.A.

Visit us online at nationalgeographic.com/books

For librarians and teachers: ngchildrensbooks.org

More for kids from National Geographic: natgeokids.com

For information about special discounts for bulk purchases, please contact
National Geographic Books Special Sales: specialsales@natgeo.com

For rights or permissions inquiries, please contact National Geographic Books Subsidiary Rights:
bookrights@natgeo.com

Designed by Rachel Kenny

The publisher would like to thank everyone who worked to make this book come together:
Martha Sharma, writer/researcher; Suzanne Patrick Fonda, project manager; Angela Modany,
associate editor; Kathryn Robbins, art director; Lori Epstein, photo director; Debbie Gibbons,
Mike McNey, and Jon Bowen, map production; Irene Berman-Vaporis, Theodore A. Sickley,
Rosemary P. Wardley, Ryan T. Williams, and Scott A. Zillmer, map research and edit; Stuart
Armstrong, illustrator; Sean Philpotts, production director; Sally Abbey, managing editor; Joan
Gossett, production editor; and Gus Tello and Anne LeongSon, design production assistants.

National Geographic supports K–12 educators with ELA Common Core Resources.
Visit natgeoed.org/commoncore for more information.

Trade paperback ISBN: 978-1-4263-3199-2
Hardcover ISBN: 978-1-4263-3247-0
Reinforced library binding ISBN: 978-1-4263-3200-5

Printed in Hong Kong
18/PPHK/1

Metric Conversion Tables

CONVERSION TO METRIC MEASURES

SYMBOL	WHEN YOU KNOW	MULTIPLY BY	TO FIND	SYMBOL
		LENGTH		
in	inches	2.54	centimeters	cm
ft	feet	0.30	meters	m
yd	yards	0.91	meters	m
mi	miles	1.61	kilometers	km
		AREA		
in^2	square inches	6.45	square centimeters	cm^2
ft^2	square feet	0.09	square meters	m^2
yd^2	square yards	0.84	square meters	m^2
mi^2	square miles	2.59	square kilometers	km^2
—	acres	0.40	hectares	ha
		MASS		
oz	ounces	28.35	grams	g
lb	pounds	0.45	kilograms	kg
—	short tons	0.91	metric tons	t
		VOLUME		
in^3	cubic inches	16.39	milliliters	mL
liq oz	liquid ounces	29.57	milliliters	mL
pt	pints	0.47	liters	L
qt	quarts	0.95	liters	L
gal	gallons	3.79	liters	L
ft^3	cubic feet	0.03	cubic meters	m^3
yd^3	cubic yards	0.76	cubic meters	m^3
		TEMPERATURE		
°F	degrees Fahrenheit	5/9 after subtracting 32	degrees Celsius (centigrade)	°C

CONVERSION FROM METRIC MEASURES

SYMBOL	WHEN YOU KNOW	MULTIPLY BY	TO FIND	SYMBOL
		LENGTH		
cm	centimeters	0.39	inches	in
m	meters	3.28	feet	ft
m	meters	1.09	yards	yd
km	kilometers	0.62	miles	mi
		AREA		
cm^2	square centimeters	0.16	square inches	in^2
m^2	square meters	10.76	square feet	ft^2
m^2	square meters	1.20	square yards	yd^2
km^2	square kilometers	0.39	square miles	mi^2
ha	hectares	2.47	acres	—
		MASS		
g	grams	0.04	ounces	oz
kg	kilograms	2.20	pounds	lb
t	metric tons	1.10	short tons	—
		VOLUME		
mL	milliliters	0.06	cubic inches	in^3
mL	milliliters	0.03	liquid ounces	liq oz
L	liters	2.11	pints	pt
L	liters	1.06	quarts	qt
L	liters	0.26	gallons	gal
m^3	cubic meters	35.31	cubic feet	ft^3
m^3	cubic meters	1.31	cubic yards	yd^3
		TEMPERATURE		
°C	degrees Celsius (centigrade)	9/5 then add 32	degrees Fahrenheit	°F